Intrusion Detection Systems

Advances in Information Security

Sushil Jajodia
Consulting Editor
Center for Secure Information Systems
George Mason University
Fairfax, VA 22030-4444
email: jajodia@gmu.edu

The goals of the Springer International Series on ADVANCES IN INFORMATION SECURITY are, one, to establish the state of the art of, and set the course for future research in information security and, two, to serve as a central reference source for advanced and timely topics in information security research and development. The scope of this series includes all aspects of computer and network security and related areas such as fault tolerance and software assurance.

ADVANCES IN INFORMATION SECURITY aims to publish thorough and cohesive overviews of specific topics in information security, as well as works that are larger in scope or that contain more detailed background information than can be accommodated in shorter survey articles. The series also serves as a forum for topics that may not have reached a level of maturity to warrant a comprehensive textbook treatment.

Researchers, as well as developers, are encouraged to contact Professor Sushil Jajodia with ideas for books under this series.

Additional titles in the series:

VULNERABILITY ANALYSIS AND DEFENSE FOR THE INTERNET edited by Abhishek Singh; ISBN: 978-0-387-74389-9
BOTNET DETECTION: Countering the Largest Security Threat edited by Wenke Lee, Cliff Wang and David Dagon; ISBN: 978-0-387-68766-7
PRIVACY-RESPECTING INTRUSION DETECTION by Ulrich Flegel; ISBN: 978-0-387-68254-9
SYNCHRONIZING INTERNET PROTOCOL SECURITY (SIPSec) by Charles A. Shoniregun; ISBN: 978-0-387-32724-2
SECURE DATA MANAGEMENT IN DECENTRALIZED SYSTEMS edited by Ting Yu and Sushil Jajodia; ISBN: 978-0-387-27694-6
NETWORK SECURITY POLICIES AND PROCEDURES by Douglas W. Frye; ISBN: 0-387-30937-3
DATA WAREHOUSING AND DATA MINING TECHNIQUES FOR CYBER SECURITY by Anoop Singhal; ISBN: 978-0-387-26409-7
SECURE LOCALIZATION AND TIME SYNCHRONIZATION FOR WIRELESS SENSOR AND AD HOC NETWORKS edited by Radha Poovendran, Cliff Wang, and Sumit Roy; ISBN: 0-387-32721-5
PRESERVING PRIVACY IN ON-LINE ANALYTICAL PROCESSING (OLAP) by Lingyu Wang, Sushil Jajodia and Duminda Wijesekera; ISBN: 978-0-387-46273-8
SECURITY FOR WIRELESS SENSOR NETWORKS by Donggang Liu and Peng Ning; ISBN: 978-0-387-32723-5
MALWARE DETECTION edited by Somesh Jha, Cliff Wang, Mihai Christodorescu, Dawn Song, and Douglas Maughan; ISBN: 978-0-387-32720-4
ELECTRONIC POSTAGE SYSTEMS: Technology, Security, Economics by Gerrit Bleumer; ISBN: 978-0-387-29313-2

Additional information about this series can be obtained from http://www.springer.com

Intrusion Detection Systems

Edited by

Roberto Di Pietro
Università di Roma Tre
Italy

and

Luigi V. Mancini
Università di Roma "La Sapienza"
Italy

Editors:
Roberto Di Pietro
Università di Roma Tre
Dip.to di Matematica
L.go S. Leonardo Murialdo, 1
00146 - Roma
Italy
dipietro@di.uniroma1.it

Luigi V. Mancini
Università di Roma "La Sapienza"
Dip.to di Informatica
Via Salaria, 113
00197 - Roma
Italy
lv.mancini@di.uniroma1.it

Series Editor:
Sushil Jajodia
George Mason University
Center for Secure Information Systems
4400 University Drive
Fairfax VA 22030-4444, USA
jajodia@gmu.edu

ISBN 978-1-4419-4585-3 e-ISBN: 978-0-387-77266-0

Softcover reprint of the hardcover 1st edition 2008

Printed on acid-free paper

9 8 7 6 5 4 3 2 1

springer.com

Foreword

In our world of ever-increasing Internet connectivity, there is an on-going threat of intrusion, denial of service attacks, or countless other abuses of computer and network resources. In particular, these threats continue to persist even on account of the flaws of current commercial Intrusion Detection Systems (IDS). These flaws are the result of the concurrence of several shortcomings such as excessive resource requirements, limited precision, lack of flexibility, and scope limitation. The aim of this book is to present the contributions made by both academia and industry to thwart those threats. In particular, this book includes a selection of the best research outcomes on intrusion detection of the Italian FIRB WEB-MINDS project (Wide scalE, Broadband MIddleware for Network Distributed Systems), plus several international contributions.

The goal of an Intrusion Detection System (IDS) is to monitor network assets in order to detect misuse or anomalous behavior. Several types of IDS have been proposed in the literature, and they can be divided into two broad classes, i.e., network based (NIDS) and host based (HIDS). The former tries to detect any attempt to subvert the normal behavior of the system by analyzing the network traffic, while the latter is intended to act as the last line of defense. The host based IDS strives to detect intrusions by analyzing the events on the local system where the IDS is being run. Host based IDSs are generally classified into two categories: *anomaly detection* and *misuse detection*. Misuse detection systems try to identify behavior patterns that are characteristic of intrusions, but this can be difficult if an attack exhibits *novel* behavior, as it may when attackers develop new strategies. On the other hand, anomaly detectors try to characterize the *normal* behavior of a system so that any deviation from that behavior can be labeled as a possible intrusion. Anomaly detection assumes that misuse or intrusions are strongly correlated to abnormal behavior exhibited by either the user or by the system itself. Anomaly detection approaches must first determine the normal behavior of the object being monitored, then use deviations from this baseline to detect possible intrusions.

Unlike the behavior of a human user or the behavior of network traffic, the behavior of a program ultimately stems from a series of machine instructions. Thus, intrusions can be detected as deviations from normal program behavior. The question, however, is how to characterize normal program behavior so as to minimize both false positives (false alarms caused by legitimate changes in program behavior) and false negatives (missed intrusions caused by attackers that mimic benign users).

As can be seen from the short description of the main issues in IDS, the area is far from being fully investigated. Furthermore, there is a need to develop new approaches that could bridge the gap between the flexibility and the precision required by IDS and current solutions. In particular, this book collects several contributions from the research units that are active in the area of Intrusion Detection. The objectives of this book are threefold: to provide an up-date on the state of the art of the research in this area; to indicate possible research directions, and to make practitioners and the industry aware of the most promising IDS technologies.

Contributions and roadmap

Chapter 1 deals with data showing that payload-based approaches are becoming the most effective methods to detect attacks. The chapter describes some approaches for Anomaly-based network detection systems (NIDSs) which focus on packet headers, payload, or a combination of both. The results of the proposed approaches are also discussed. This chapter paves the way for further studies into this segment of interest.

Chapter 2 proposes a methodology for the synthesis of the behavior of an application program in terms of the set of system calls invoked by the program. The methodology is completely automated except for the description of the high level specification of the application program which is demanded of the system analyst. The technology (VSP/CVS) employed for such synthesis minimizes the efforts required to code the specification of the application, thus making the proposal viable for industrial products as well.

Chapter 3 introduces a sophisticated mechanism that can be used to model profiles i.e., Hierarchical Hidden Markov Models. Consequently, abstract process behavior corresponds to probabilistic regular expressions. A learning algorithm built over this abstraction mechanism is proposed; such an algorithm can automatically infer a profile from a set of traces of the process behavior. This chapter pushes forward the application of sophisticated statistical tools and shows promising research directions.

Chapter 4 stems from the observation that the multiple, possibly complementary security devices that are used to defend against computer and network attacks, and that include intrusion detection systems (IDSs) and firewalls are widely deployed to monitor networks and hosts, may flag alerts when suspicious events are observed. Alert correlation focuses on discovering the existing relationships among individual alerts; this chapter gives an overview of current alert correlation techniques. Finally, it also introduces privacy issues in the IDS field.

Chapter 5 describes recent research on attack graphs that represent the known attack sequences which can be used by attackers to penetrate computer networks. This chapter will show how attack graphs can be used to compute actual sets of hardening measures for the safety of given critical resources. Note that the degree of safety that is provided within the approach proposed in this chapter is tunable and guaranteed.

Chapter 6 introduces a new mechanism for adapting the security policy of an information system according to the threat it receives, and hence its behavior and the services it offers. The proposed mechanism bridges the gap between preventive security technologies and intrusion detection, and builds upon existing technologies to facilitate formalization on one hand, and deployment on the other hand.

Lastly, Chapter 7 identifies the fundamental requirements that must be satisfied to protect hosts and routers from any form of Distributed DoS (DDoS). Then, a framework that satisfies most of the identified requirements is proposed. It appropriately combines Intrusion Detection and Reaction techniques, and comprises a number of components that actively co-operate to effectively react to a wide range of attacks.

Roma, January 2008

Roberto Di Pietro
Dipartimento di Matematica
Università di Roma Tre
L.go S. Leonardo Murialdo, 1
00146 Roma, Italy
ricerca.mat.uniroma3.it/users/dipietro
dipietro@mat.uniroma3.it

Luigi V. Mancini
Dipartimento di Informatica
Università di Roma "La Sapienza"
Via Salaria, 113
00198 Roma, Italy
www.di.uniroma1.it/mancini
lv.mancini@di.uniroma1.it

Contents

Approaches in Anomaly-based Network Intrusion Detection Systems

Damiano Bolzoni and Sandro Etalle

Abstract Anomaly-based network intrusion detection systems (NIDSs) can take into consideration packet headers, the payload, or a combination of both. We argue that payload-based approaches are becoming the most effective methods to detect attacks. Nowadays, attacks aim mainly to exploit vulnerabilities at application level: thus, the payload contains the most important information to differentiate normal traffic from anomalous activity. To support our thesis, we present a comparison between different anomaly-based NIDSs, focusing in particular on the data analyzed by the detection engine to discover possible malicious activities. Furthermore, we present a comparison of two payload and anomaly-based NIDSs: PAYL and POSEIDON.

1 Introduction

Network intrusion detection systems (NIDSs) are considered an effective second line of defense against network-based attacks directed at computer systems [1, 2], and – due to the increasing severity and likelihood of such attacks – are employed in almost all large-scale IT infrastructures [3].

There exist two main types of intrusion detection systems: signature-based (SBS) and anomaly-based (ABS). SBSs (e.g. Snort [4, 37]) rely on pattern-matching techniques: they contain a database of *signatures* of known attacks and try to match these signatures against the analyzed data. When a match is found, an alarm is raised. On the other hand, ABSs (e.g. PAYL [6]) first build a *statistical model* describing the normal network traffic, then flag any behaviour that significantly deviates from the model as an attack.

University of Twente,
P.O. Box 2100, 7500 AE Enschede, The Netherlands
e-mail: {damiano.bolzoni, sandro.etalle}@utwente.nl

Intuitively speaking, anomaly-based systems have the advantage that (unlike signature-based systems) they can detect zero-day attacks, since novel attacks can be detected as soon as they take place. On the other hand, ABSs (unlike SBSs) require a training phase and a careful setting of the detection threshold (more about this later), which makes their deployment more complex.

Contribution

In this paper, we discuss anomaly-based systems, focusing in particular on a specific kind of them: the ABSs *payload-based*. We argue that payload-based systems are particularly suitable to detect advanced attacks, and we describe in detail the most prominent and the most recent of them: respectively Wang and Stolfo's PAYL [6] and our POSEIDON [7].

2 Anomaly-Based Intrusion Detection Systems

In this section, we present the basic working of anomaly-based systems, and we explain the different kinds of ABSs existing. The thesis we try to substantiate here is that, because of the kind of attacks that are carried out nowadays, packed-based and payload-based systems are becoming the most interesting kind of ABS.

Anomaly-based NIDSs can be classified according to:

1. the underlying algorithm they use,
2. whether they analyze the features of each packet singularly or of the whole connection, and
3. the kind of data they analyze. In particular, whether they focus on the packet headers or on the payload.

Regarding the underlying algorithm, Debar et al. [8, 2] define four different possible approaches, but only two of them have successfully employed in the last decade: algorithms based on statistical models and those based on neural networks. The former is the most widely used: according to Debar et al. [8] more than 50% of existing ABSs is statistic-based. In these systems, the algorithm (during the so-called *training phase*) first builds a statistical model of the – legitimate, attack-free – network behaviour; later (in the *detection phase*), the input data is compared to the model using a distance function, and when the distance measured exceeds a given *threshold*, the input is considered *anomalous*, i.e., it is considered an attack. ABSs based on neural networks work in a similar way (they also have a training phase, a detection phase and a threshold), but instead of building a statistical model, they train a neural network which is then in charge of recognizing regular traffic from anomalous one. Good training is of crucial importance for the effectiveness of the system: in particular, the data used in the training phase should be (at least in principle) as *attack-free* as possible: training data must reflect as much as possible the normal system data flow, not including malicious activity. Furthermore, the training phase should be long enough to allow the system to build a faithful model: a too short training phase could lead to a (too) coarse data classification, which – in the detection phase – translates into flagging legitimate traffic too often as anomalous (false positives).

Concerning feature (b) the distinction one has to make is between *packet-oriented* and *connection-oriented* ABSs. A packet-oriented system uses a single packet as minimal information source, while a connection-oriented system considers features of the whole communication before establishing whether it is anomalous or not. Theoretically, a connection-oriented system could use as input the content (payload) of a whole communication (allowing – at least in principle – a more precise analysis), but this would require a long computational time, which would seriously limit the throughput of the system. In practice, connection-oriented systems typically take into account the number of sent/received bytes, the duration of the connection and layer-4 protocol used. According to Wang and Stolfo's benchmarks [6], payload-based ABSs do not show a sensible increase in performance when they also reconstruct the connection, instead of just considering the packets in isolation. In practice, most ABSs are packet-oriented (see also Table 1).

The last, more practically relevant distinction we can make is between *header-based* and *payload-based* system. Header-based systems consider only packet headers (layer-3 and, if present, layer 4 headers) to detect malicious activities; payload-based systems analyze the payload data carried by the layer-4 protocol; there are also hybrid systems which mix information gathered observing packet headers and (if present) layer-4 payload data. We are going to elaborate on this distinction in the rest of this section. Before we do so, we want to present a table reporting some of the most important ABSs: we select the systems which have been benchmarked with public data sets (either DARPA 1998 [9] or DARPA 1999 [10] data sets, which contain a full dump of the packets, or the KDD 99 [11] data set, which contains only connection meta data).

iSOM [12] uses a one-tier architecture, consisting of a Self-organizing Map [13], to detect two attacks in the 1999 DARPA data set: the first attack against the SMTP service and the other attack against the FTP service. Intel information from the connection meta data once it has been reassembled. PHAD [14] combines 34 different values extracted from the packet headers. MADAM ID [15] extracts information from audit traffic and builds classification models (specifically designed for certain types of intrusion) using data mining techniques. The system indicated by SSAD [16] (Service Specific Anomaly Detection) combines different information such as type, length and payload distribution (computing character frequencies and aggregating then them into six groups) of the request. PAYL [6] and POSEIDON [7] detect anomalies only looking at the full payload. Table 1 summarizes the properties of some ABSs.

System	Detection Engine	Semantic Level	Analyzed Data
iSOM	NN	PO + CO	Meta data
IntelligentIDS	NN	CO	Meta data
PHAD	S	PO	H
MADAM ID	S	CO	Meta data
SSAD	S	PO	H + P
PAYL	S	PO	P
POSEIDON	NN + S	PO	P

Table 1 Anomaly-based systems: NN stands for Neural Networks, S for Statistical model, PO is Packet-Oriented while CO is Connection-Oriented, H and P stand for Headers and Payload respectively

2.1 Payload-based vs header-based approaches

We now elaborate the differences in effectiveness between payload-based and header-based systems. We begin by showing some examples of attacks that can be detected by the systems of one kind, but not by the system of the other kind.

Attacks detectable by header-based systems

Example 0.1. The teardrop exploit [17] is a remote Denial of Service attack that exploits a flaw in the implementation of older TCP/IP stacks: some implementations of the IP fragmentation re-assembly code on these platforms do not properly handle overlapping IP fragments. Figure 1 shows how the attacks takes place: the attacker sends fragmented packets forged so that they overlap each other when the receiving host tries to reassemble them. If the host does not check the boundaries properly, it will try to allocate a memory block with a negative size, causing a kernel panic and crashing the OS.

IDSs can find this attack only by looking for two specially fragmented IP datagrams, analyzing the headers. This attack exploits a vulnerability at the network layer.

Example 0.2. The Land attack [17] is a remote Denial of Service attack that is effective against some older TCP/IP implementations: the attack involves sending a spoofed TCP SYN packet (connection initiation) with the same source and destination IP address (the target address) and the same (open) TCP port as source and destination.

Some implementations cannot handle this theoretically impossible condition, causing the operating system to go into a loop as it tries to resolve a repeated connections to itself. IDSs detect this attack by looking at packet headers, since TCP SYN segments do not carry any payload. This attack exploits a vulnerability at the transport layer.

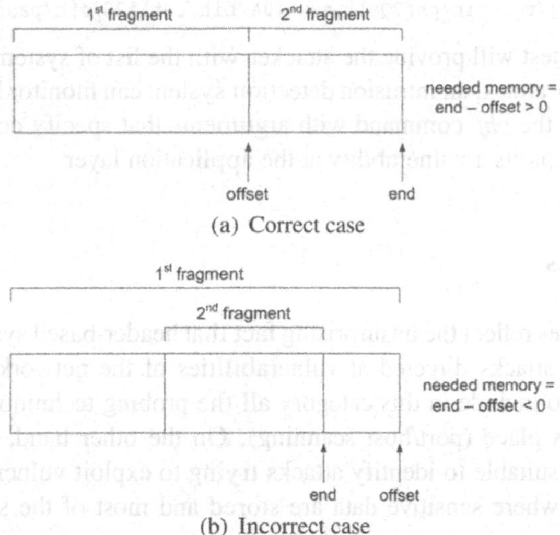

Fig. 1 A correct and incorrect case of fragment management by the network layer

Attacks detectable by payload-based systems

Example 0.3. SQL injection is a technique that exploits vulnerabilities of (web-based) applications which are interfaced to an SQL database: if the application does not sanitize potentially harmful characters first [18], an intruder can *inject* an SQL query in the database, and force the database to output sensitive data (e.g. user passwords and personal details) from database tables, without being authorized. SQL Injections are considered a serious threat and are constantly listed in the "Top Ten Most Critical Web Application Security Vulnerabilities" [19] by "The Open Web Application Security Project".

For instance, the following HTTP request is actually a well-known attack [20] against the Content Management System (CMS) PostNuke [21] that can be used to get hold of the user passwords:

```
http://[target]/[postnuke_dir]/modules.php?op=modload&
name=Messages&file=readpmsg&start=0%20UNION%20SELECT%20
pn_uname,null,pn_uname,pn_pass,pn_p
```

When such an attack is carried out successfully, the output (a database table) is significantly different from the HTML page usually rendered. This attack exploits a vulnerability at the application layer.

Example 0.4. The PHF attack [22] exploits a badly written CGI script to execute commands with the privilege level of the HTTP server user. Any CGI program which relies on the function *escape_shell_cmd()* may be vulnerable: this vulnerability is manifested by the *phf* program that is distributed with the example code for the Apache web server.

```
http://[target]/cgi-bin/phf?Qalias=x\%0A/bin/cat\%20/etc/passwd
```

The issued request will provide the attacker with the list of system users.

To detect a PHF attack, an intrusion detection system can monitor HTTP requests for invocations of the *phf* command with arguments that specify commands to be run. This attack exploits a vulnerability at the application layer.

Some Conclusions

The above examples reflect the unsurprising fact that header-based systems are more suitable to detect attacks directed at vulnerabilities of the network and transport layers; we can also include in this category all the probing techniques used before a real attack takes place (port/host scanning). On the other hand, payload-based systems are more suitable to identify attacks trying to exploit vulnerabilities at the application level, where sensitive data are stored and most of the systems can be subverted.

Here, we must take notice of the trend that shows that this second kind of attack is increasingly gaining importance: this is due both to the large success of web-based services, and to the fact that attacks at network and transport layers are becoming rare. Because of this, we believe that payload-based system will be increasingly useful in the future. We believe that this trend not only favors payload-based IDS wrt header-based ones, but also anomaly-based systems wrt signature-based ones (we are going to elaborate on this in the conclusions).

We should not forget, however, that payload-based NIDSs cannot function properly in combination with applications or application protocols (e.g. SSH and SSL) which apply data encryption, unless the encryption key is provided. A possible solution to this makes use of a host-based component to access data once they have been decrypted, but this causes an overhead on the monitored host. This problem is going to grow in importance when IPv6 will gradually replace IPv4: in fact, one of the main design issues of IPv6 is the authentication and confidentiality of data (through cryptography).

As we mentioned before, header-based approaches alone do not represent a valid solution to detect modern attacks. In this case, we believe that further research on approaches based on the analysis of connection meta data (connection duration, sent/received bytes, etc.), which are not affected by cryptographic content, should be conducted to verify their application in real environment, since they show to be quite effective in detecting malicious activity with standard data set such as DARPA 1999 and KDD 99.

3 Setting up an ABS

As we have seen, to determine whether a certain input is anomalous or not, an ABS compares it to the model it has: if the distance between some function of the input and the model exceeds a given *threshold*, the input is considered anomalous. This shows that the quality of the model and the value of the threshold have a direct influence on the effectiveness of the ABS. Both the model and the threshold are determined during the system setup (though the threshold could be refined successively). In the rest of this section we elaborate on these two crucial aspects.

Before we do so, we define that the effectiveness of a NIDS is determined by its *completeness* and its *accuracy*.

- $completeness = TP/(TP + FN)$
- $accuracy = TP/(TP + FP)$

Here, TP is the number of true positives, FN is the number of false negatives and FP is the number of false positives raised during a given time frame.

The number of false positives per hour determines the workload of IT personnel: with a hundred thousands input packets per hour (which is a reasonable figure for a web server), a false positive rate of 1% still determines a thousand false positive per hour, which is more than a typical company can afford to handle. When a system raises too many false positives, then system managers tend to ignore alerts raised. As a matter of fact, a high false positive rate is generally cited as one of the main disadvantages of ABSs.

3.1 Building the Model

The model an ABS refer to should reflect the behaviour of the system *in absence of attacks*, otherwise the ABS may fail to recognize an attack as such. Because of this, the ABS should be trained with a *clean* data set. However, obtaining such a data set is difficult in practice: a casual dump of network traffic is likely to be *noisy*, i.e., to contain attacks.

The standard way to deal with this is by cleaning the data set by manual inspection. This relies completely on the expertise of the IT personnel which must analyze a large amount of data. Clearly, this approach it is labour intensive, also because the model of the ABS needs to be updated regularly to adapt to environment changes. The manual inspection can be aided by an automatic inspection using a signature-based IDS, which can pre-process the training data and discover well-known attacks (e.g. web-scanners, old exploits, etc.). A signature-based IDS however will not detect all attacks in the data, leaving the training set with a certain amount of noise.

Nevertheless, we believe that it is possible to clean automatically the data set in such a way that the resulting model is a faithful representation of the legitimate network traffic. Intuitively, we apply an anomaly-based intrusion detection algorithm in which the threshold is set in such a way that we are sure of catching all attacks: this is possible because noise typically forms a small percentage of the total data [23], moreover, its content is typically very different from the content of regular data [24, 25]. The fact that we eliminate also a percentage of the legitimate data with them is – at this stage – not a serious concern.

In our experience clustering techniques from data mining can be quite useful to obtain a good training set. Clustering is the classification of similar objects into different groups, or more precisely, the partitioning of a data set into subsets (clusters), so that the data in each subset (ideally) shares some common trait, often according to a defined distance measure. Past research applies this concept to detect network attacks [26], but because of the intrinsic limitations of the classification algorithms, it does not achieve a high detection rate. There exists a large number of clustering algorithms which deal with different data types: in our case, we can use clustering algorithms to classify the training data and then disregard the data belonging to the clusters which are not dense enough to be considered significant for the training the model.

3.2 Setting the threshold

The value of the threshold has an obvious and direct impact on the accuracy and completeness: a low threshold yields a high number of alarms, and therefore a low false negative rate, but a high false positive rate. On the other hand, a high threshold yields a low number of alarms in general (therefore a high number of false negatives, but a low number of false positives). Therefore, setting the threshold requires skill: its "optimal" value depends on environment monitored and on the distribution of the training data.

In our ATLANTIDES system [27] we introduce a simple heuristics to set the threshold value when using a *noisy* data set: our experiments show that setting the threshold at $\frac{3t_{max}}{4}$, usually yields reasonably good results; here t_{max} is the maximum distance between the analyzed data and the model observed during the training phase.

4 PAYL and POSEIDON

In this section, we present PAYL and POSEIDON, the first is recognized as the most prominent payload-based anomaly-based NIDS, POSEIDON is the improvement on PAYL we have developed.

4.1 PAYL

PAYL (Wang and Stolfo [6]) is a system based on a 2-step algorithm. First, packets are classified according to the payload length, then an n-gram [28] analysis is applied to the payload. PAYL works as follows (see Appendix 6.1 for the pseudo-code).

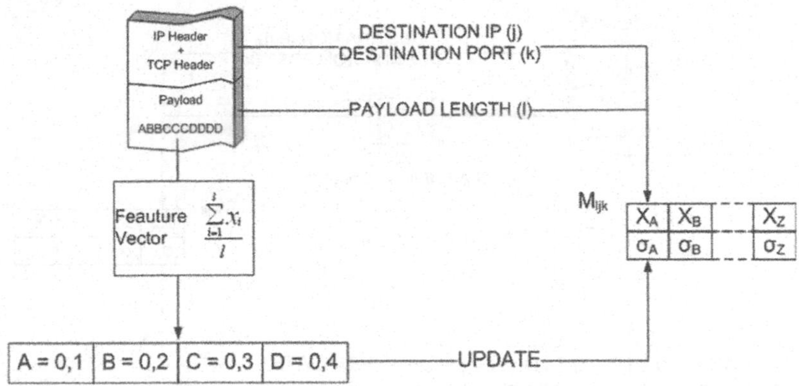

Fig. 2 PAYL architecture

During the *training phase*, the training set T is split into a number of disjoint subsets T_{ljk}, where each T_{ljk} contains the packets of length l, destination IP address j and TCP port k. Then PAYL creates statistical models M_{ljk} of each T_{ljk} by first carrying out n-gram analysis [28] of size 1 on each packet of T_{ljk}, and then incrementally storing in M_{ljk} a feature vector containing the average byte frequency distribution together with the variance value of each frequency.

During the *detection phase*, the same values are computed for incoming packets and then compared to model values: a significant difference from the norm produces an alert. To compare models, PAYL uses a simplified version of the Mahalanobis distance, which has the advantage of taking into account not only the average value but also its variance and the covariance of the variables measured.

The maximum amount of space required by PAYL is: $p*l*k$, where p is the total number of ports monitored (each host may have different ports), l is the length of the longest payload (payload length can vary between 0 and 1460 in a Local Area Network infrastructure based on Enthernet) and k is a constant representing the space required to keep the mean and the variance distribution values for each payload byte (PAYL uses a fixed value of 512). To reduce the otherwise large number of models to be computed, PAYL collapses similar models. After comparing two neighbouring models using the Manhattan distance, if the distance is smaller than a given threshold t, models are merged: the means and variances are updated to produce a new combined distribution. This process is repeated until no more models can be merged. Experiments with PAYL show [6] that a reduction in the number of model of up to a factor of 16 can be achieved.

4.2 POSEIDON

The Achille's heel of PAYL lies in the classification phase: a good classification algorithm should produce clusters with high intra-class similarity and high inter-

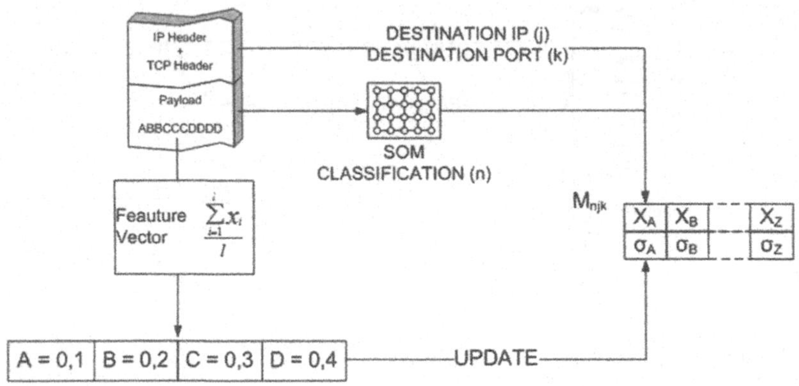

Fig. 3 POSEIDON architecture

class dissimilarity. Using the payload length information as primary method to divide packets into clusters, similar payloads could be classified in different clusters because they present a small difference in their length; on the other hand, dissimilar payloads could be classified in the same cluster because they present the same length. This can affect negatively the subsequent n-gram analysis.

To solve this problem, we designed POSEIDON. The design goal was to obtain a good – unsupervised – classification method for network packets (which are high-dimensional data). This is a typical clustering problem which can be tackled using neural networks in general and Self-Organizing Maps (SOM) [13] in particular. SOMs have been widely used in the past both to classify network data and to find anomalies. in POSEIDON, we use them for pre-processing.

The POSEIDON architecture combines a SOM with a modified PAYL algorithm and works as follows. The SOM is used to pre-process each packet, afterwards PAYL uses the classification value given by the SOM instead of the payload length. Instead of using model M_{ijk}, PAYL uses the model M_{njk} where j and k are the usual destination address and port and n is the classification derived from the neural network. Then, mean and variance values are computed as usual.

Having added a SOM to the system we must allow for both the SOM and PAYL to be trained separately. Regarding resource consumption, we have to revise the required amount of space to: $p * n * k$, where the new parameter n indicates the amount of SOM network nodes. Our experiments show that POSEIDON allows to reduce the number of models needed (wrt PAYL) by a factor of 3 while achieving a better accuracy and completeness.

How the SOM works

Self-organizing maps are topology-preserving single-layer maps. SOMs are suitable to analyze high-dimensional data and belong to the category of competitive learning networks [13]. Nodes are also called *neurons*, to remind us of the artificial intelligence nature of the algorithm. Each neuron n has a *vector of weights* w_n associated to it: the dimension of the weights arrays is equal to the length of longest input data. These arrays (also referred as *reference vectors*) determine the SOM behaviour. Appendix 6.2 reports the SOM pseudo-code.

To accomplish the classification, SOM goes through three phases: initialization, training and classification.

Initialization

First of all, some system parameters (number of nodes, learning rate and radius) are determined by e.g. the IDS technician. The number of nodes directly determines the classification given by the SOM: a small network will classify different data inputs in the same node while a large network will produce a too sparse classification. Afterwards, the array of node weights is initialized, usually with random values (in the same range of input values).

Training

The training phase consists of a number of iterations (also called *epochs*). At each iteration one input vector x is compared to all neuron weight arrays w_n with a distance function: the most similar node (also called *best matching unit*, BMU) is then identified. After the BMU has been found, the neighbouring neurons and the BMU itself are updated. The following update parameters are used: the neighbourhood is governed by the *radius* parameter (r) and the magnitude of the attraction is affected by the *learning rate* (α).

During this phase, the map tends to converge to a stationary distribution, which approximates the probability density function of the high-dimensional input data. As the learning proceeds and new input vectors are given to the map, the learning rate and radius values gradually decrease to zero.

Classification

During the classification phase, the first part of the training phase is repeated for each sample: the input data is compared to all the weight arrays and the most similar neuron determines the classification of the sample (but weights are not updated). The winning neuron is then returned.

Conclusions

Our approach to designing a payload-based ABS involves the combination of two different techniques: a self-organizing map and the PAYL architecture. We modify the original PAYL to take advantage of the unsupervised classification given by the SOM, which then functions as pre-processing stage.

We benchmark our system using the DARPA 1999 data set [10]: this standard data set is used as a reference by a number of researchers (e.g. [14, 12, 6]), and offers the possibility of comparing the performance of various IDSs. Experiments show that our approach achieves a better completeness and accuracy than the original PAYL algorithm: Table 2 reports the results for the four most representative protocols (FTP, Telnet, SMTP and HTTP) inside the data set. Moreover we observe a reduction of models used by PAYL by a factor of 3 when taking advantage of the SOM classification (payload length can vary between 0 and 1460 in a Local Area Network Ethernet-based, while the SOM neural network used in our experiments has less than one hundred nodes).

		PAYL	POSEIDON
Number of models used		4065	1622
HTTP	DR	89,00%	100,00%
	FP	0,17%	0,0016%
FTP	DR	95,50%	100,00%
	FP	1,23%	0,93%
Telnet	DR	54,17%	95,12%
	FP	4,71%	6,72%
SMTP	DR	78,57%	100,00%
	FP	3,08%	3,69%
Overall DR with FP < 1%		58,8% (57/97)	73,2% (71/97)

Table 2 Comparison between PAYL and POSEIDON; DR stands for detection rate (completeness), while FP is the false positive rate (accuracy)

5 Conclusions

This paper makes a reasoned case for anomaly payload-based network intrusion detection systems.

Header-Based vs Payload-Based

We have argued that header-based approaches are useful in detecting principally attacks at network level, and that of most modern remote attacks target vulnerabilities at the application layer: thus, we can no longer rely solely on header-based approaches. Moreover, firewalling systems can easily detect (and discard) well-known malicious packets as well. The fact that header-based approaches manage to achieve high detection rates when benchmarked using the DARPA 1999 data set is – as explained by Mahoney and Chan [29] – often due to the fact that it is possible to tune an IDS which uses some attributes – specifically: remote client address, TTL, TCP options and TCP window size (these present a small range in the DARPA simulation, but have a large and growing range in real traffic) – in such a way that it scores particularly well on this data set. Because most of the attacks to the application significantly differ in content from legitimate traffic (while they are similar when considering header attributes), a payload-based approach is necessary to detect malicious activities.

Signature-based vs Anomaly-Based

The fact that that modern attacks are usually directed to weaknesses of the application rather than weaknesses of the underlying system has another important consequence: as we mentioned in the introduction, next to anomaly-based intrusion detection systems, there exist also *signature-based* systems. These system rely on a set of pre-defined signatures (typically defined by the NIDS manufacturer and updated regularly via Internet). Because of the ad-hoc nature of attacks directed at applications, in which it is often possible to modify the syntax of an attack without changing its semantics, signature-based system are becoming easier to circumvent than anomaly-based systems. For instance, due to the high level of polymorphisms presented by SQL Injection attacks, it is impossible to produce few generic signatures to detect them, and most of these attacks will go unnoticed by a SBS.

We believe that the next generation IDS architectures will have to combine signature-based and anomaly-based approaches, as well as network-based with host-based systems: these architectures, supported by adequate correlation techniques, will combine the advantages offered by each approach, improving at the same time the overall completeness and accuracy.

6 Appendix

6.1 PAYL algorithm

DATA TYPE

```
feature vector = RECORD [
   mean = array [1..256] of Reals,
     /* average byte frequency */
   stdDev = array [1..256] of Reals
     /* standard deviation of each */
     /* byte frequency */
]

/* Defining M_ljk model */
model = RECORD [
   ip ∈ ℕ, /* destination host address */
   sp ∈ ℕ, /* destination service port */
   l ∈ ℕ, /* payload length */
   fv : feature vector
]

PAYLOAD = array [1..l] of [0..255]
```

DATA STRUCTURE

```
M = set of finite models
threshold ∈ ℝ
  /* numeric value used for anomaly */
  /* detection given by user */
```

TRAINING PHASE

```
INPUT:
  ip : IP address ∈ ℕ
  sp : service port ∈ ℕ
  l : payload length
  x : PAYLOAD

for each m ∈ M do
```

```
  if (m.ip = ip and m.sp = sp and
  m.l = l) then
    m.fv.update(x)
    /* update byte frequency */
    /* distributions */
  end if
done(for)

TESTING PHASE

INPUT:
  ip : IP address ∈ ℕ
  sp : service port ∈ ℕ
  l : payload length
  x : PAYLOAD

OUTPUT:
  isAnomalous : BOOLEAN
    /* is the packet anomalous ? */

dist := +∞
isAnomalous := FALSE

for each m ∈ M do
  if (m.ip = ip and m.sp = sp and
  m.l = l) then
    dist := m.fv.getDistance(x)
    /* get the distance between input */
    /* data and associated model */
  end if
done(for)

if (dist ≥ threshold) then
  isAnomalous := TRUE
end if

return isAnomalous
```

6.2 SOM algorithm

```
DATA TYPE

RR = [0.0..255.0]
  /* Reals (Double) between 0.0 and 255.0 */
l = length of the longest packet payload
PAYLOAD = array [1..l] of [0..255]

DATA STRUCTURE

N = non-empty finite set of neurons
for each n ∈ N let
  w_n := array [1..l] of RR
       /* array of weights associated */
       /* to each neuron n */
α_0 ∈ ℝ
       /* Initial learning rate */
α := α_0
       /* Current learning rate */
r_0 ∈ ℝ
       /* Initial radius */
r := r_0
       /* Current radius */
τ ∈ ℕ
       /* Number of training epochs */
k ∈ ℕ
       /* Smoothing factor */

INIT PHASE

for each n ∈ N
  for i := 1 to l
    w_n[i] := random(RR)
    /* Initialize with values in RR */

TRAINING PHASE

INPUT:
  x_t : PAYLOAD

for t := 1 to τ

  /* Find winning neuron */
  win_dist := +∞
  win_neuron := n_0

  for each n ∈ N do
    dist := manhattan_dist(x_t, w_n)
    if (dist ≤ win_dist) then
      win_dist := dist
      win_neuron := n
    end if
  done(for)

  /* Process neighbouring neurons */
  N_n = {n ∈ ℕ | trig_dist(n, win_neuron) ≤ r}

  for each n_n ∈ N_n
    for i := 1 to l
      w_{n_n}[i] := w_{n_n}[i] + α * (w_{n_n}[i] - x_t[i])

  α := α_0 * k/(k+t)
  r := r_0 * (τ-t)/τ

done(for)

CLASSIFICATION PHASE
```

```
INPUT:
  x : PAYLOAD
OUTPUT:
  win_neuron ∈ ℕ

win_dist := +∞
dist := win_dist
win_neuron := n0
for each n ∈ N do
  dist := manhattan_dist(x, w_n)
  if (dist ≤ win_dist) then
    win_dist := dist
    win_neuron := n
  end if
done(for)
return win_neuron
```

References

1. Bace, R.: Intrusion detection. Macmillan Publishing Co., Inc. (2000)
2. Debar, H., Dacier, M., Wespi, A.: A Revised Taxonomy of Intrusion-Detection Systems. Annales des Télécommunications **55**(7–8) (2000) 361–378
3. Allen, J., Christie, A., Fithen, W., McHugh, J., Pickel, J., Stoner, E.: State of the practice of intrusion detection technologies. Technical Report CMU/SEI-99TR-028, Carnegie-Mellon University - Software Engineering Institute (2000)
4. Roesch, M.: Snort - Lightweight Intrusion Detection for Networks. In: LISA '99: Proc. 13th USENIX Conference on System Administration, USENIX Association (1999) 229–238
5. Sourcefire: Snort Network Intrusion Detection System web site (1999) URL http://www.snort.org.
6. Wang, K., Stolfo, S.J.: Anomalous Payload-Based Network Intrusion Detection. In Jonsson, E., Valdes, A., Almgren, M., eds.: RAID '04: Proc. 7th Symposium on Recent Advances in Intrusion Detection. Volume 3224 of LNCS., Springer-Verlag (2004) 203–222
7. Bolzoni, D., Zambon, E., Etalle, S., Hartel, P.: POSEIDON: a 2-tier Anomaly-based Network Intrusion Detection System. In: IWIA '06: Proc. 4th IEEE International Workshop on Information Assurance, IEEE Computer Society Press (2006) 144–156
8. Debar, H., Dacier, M., Wespi, A.: Towards a Taxonomy of Intrusion-Detection Systems. Computer Networks **31**(8) (1999) 805–822
9. Lippmann, R.P., Cunningham, R.K., Fried, D.J., Garfinkel, S.L., Gorton, A.S., Graf, I., Kendall, K.R., McClung, D.J., Weber, D.J., Webster, S.E., D. Wyschogrod, M.A.Z.: The 1998 DARPA/AFRL off-line intrusion detection evaluation. In: RAID '98: Proc. 1st International Workshop on the Recent Advances in Intrusion Detection. (1998)
10. Lippmann, R., Haines, J.W., Fried, D.J., Korba, J., Das, K.: The 1999 DARPA off-line intrusion detection evaluation. Computer Networks: The International Journal of Computer and Telecommunications Networking **34**(4) (2000) 579–595
11. Bay, S.D., Kibler, D., Pazzani, M., Smyth, P.: The UCI KDD archive of large data sets for data mining research and experimentation. SIGKDD Exploration: Newsletter of SIGKDD and Data Mining **2**(2) (2000) 81–85
12. Nguyen, B.V.: Self organizing map (SOM) for Anomaly Detection. Technical report, Ohio University (2002)
13. Kohonen, T.: Self-Organizing Maps. Volume 30 of Springer Series in Information Sciences. Springer (1995) (Second Extended Edition 1997).
14. Mahoney, M.V., Chan, P.K.: Learning nonstationary models of normal network traffic for detecting novel attacks. In: KDD '02: Proc. 8th ACM SIGKDD International Conference on Knowledge Discovery and Data mining, ACM Press (2002) 376–385
15. Lee, W., Stolfo, S.J.: A Framework for Constructing Features and Models for Intrusion Detection Systems. ACM Transactions on Information and System Security **3**(4) (2000) 227–261

16. Kruegel, C., Toth, T., Kirda, E.: Service specific anomaly detection for network intrusion detection. In: SAC '02: Proc. 2002 ACM Symposium on Applied Computing, ACM Press (2002) 201–208
17. CERT: Ip Denial of Service Attacks. Technical report, CERT Coordination Center (1997) http://www.cert.org/advisories/CA-1997-28.html.
18. Web Application Security Consortium: Web Security Threat Classification (2005) URL http://www.webappsec.org/projects/threat/.
19. The Open Web Application Security Project: OWASP Top Ten Most Critical Web Application Security Vulnerabilities (2006) URL http://www.owasp.org/documentation/topten.html.
20. Security Reason: PostNuke Input Validation Error (2005) URL http://securitytracker.com/alerts/2005/May/1014066.html.
21. PostNuke: PostNuke Content Managament System (2006) URL http://www.postnuke.com/.
22. CERT: Vulnerability in NCSA/Apache CGI example code. Technical report, CERT Coordination Center (1996) URL http://www.cert.org/advisories/CA-1996-06.html.
23. Portnoy, L., Eskin, E., Stolfo, S.J.: Intrusion detection with unlabeled data using clustering. In: DMSA '01: Proc. of ACM CCS Workshop on Data Mining for Security Applications, 8th ACM Conference on Computer Security (CCS' 01), ACM Press (2002) xx–yy
24. Denning, D.E.: An Intrusion-Detection Model. IEEE Transactions on Software Engineering **SE-13**(2) (1987) 222–232
25. Javitz, H.S., Valdes, A.: The NIDES Statistical Component Description and Justification. Technical Report A010, SRI (1994)
26. Lee, W., Stolfo, S.: Data mining approaches for intrusion detection. In: Proc. 7th USENIX Security Symposium, USENIX Association (1998) 79–94
27. Bolzoni, D., Crispo, B., Etalle, S.: ATLANTIDES: An architecture for alert verification in network intrusion detection systems. In: LISA '07: Proc. 21st Large Installation System Administration Conference, USENIX Association (2007)
28. Damashek, M.: Gauging similarity with n-grams: Language-independent categorization of text. Science **267**(5199) (1995) 843–848
29. Mahoney, M.V., Chan, P.K.: An Analysis of the 1999 DARPA/Lincoln Laboratory Evaluation Data for Network Anomaly Detection. In Vigna, G., Kruegel, C., Jonsson, E., eds.: RAID '03: Proc. 6th Symposium on Recent Advances in Intrusion Detection. Volume 2820 of LNCS., Springer-Verlag (2003) 220–237

Formal Specification for Fast Automatic Profiling of Program Behavior

Roberto Di Pietro, Antonio Durante, and Luigi.V. Mancini

Abstract This paper illustrates a methodology for the synthesis of the behavior of an application program in terms of the set of system calls invoked by the program. The methodology is completely automated, with the exception of the description of the high level specification of the application program which is demanded to the system analyst. The technology employed (VSP/CVS) for such synthesis minimizes the efforts required to code the specification of the application. The methodology we propose has been applied to several daemons; as a case study, we discuss it in details to the Post Office Protocol, the ipop3d daemon. Though the methodology is independent from the intrusion detection tool adopted, the results have been employed to configure the REMUS intrusion detection system and are shown in this paper.

1 Introduction

Nowadays computer systems work in highly dynamic and distributed environments and require the protection mechanisms to prevent intentional or unintentional violation to the security policies. Often the attackers are able to circumvent the access control mechanisms exploiting the applications flaws. As an example, in many cases the attackers tend to hijack the control of privileged processes, such as the daemon processes. A well-known family of this kind of attack is called *buffer overflow* attack [2].

Our proposed methodology is aimed at mapping the normal behavior of an application program onto its allowed system calls, thus enabling the detection of attacks

---

Roberto Di Pietro
Università di Roma Tre, Dipartimento di Matematica, L.go S. leonardo Murialdo n. 1, 00146 - Roma, Italy, e-mail: dipietro@mat.uniroma3.it

Antonio Durante · Luigi V. Mancini
Dipartimento di Informatica, Università di Roma "La Sapienza", Via Salaria 113, 00198 - Roma, Italy e-mail: {mancini,durante}@di.uniroma1.it

that attempt to hijack the execution of privileged processes the application is possibly composed of.

The methodology we describe starts from a high level description of the daemon, such as an IETF RFC [12] and derives the set of the system calls that can be invoked by the daemon, during its normal execution. Note that the generated system calls are specific for the particular implementation of the daemon the proposed methodology is applied to. For instance, consider an FTP daemon that receives USER/PASS requests; while processing these requests, the daemon could execute different kinds of system calls depending on its implementation. To perform authentication, the FTP daemon may need to read a security-sensitive file (using regular I/O system calls), or it may access the same sensitive file via memory mapping (using the `mmap` system call), or it may access the sensitive file via NIS (using socket connects, reads, and writes), etc. Note that the particular set of system calls to perform the FTP authentication is chosen by the programmer while implementing the daemon. Hence, we do not try to synthesize the allowed system calls of all the possible implementations for a given specification, but we consider a specific implementation of the daemon that will run on the specific system under consideration.

In this paper, we assume that the specific implementation of the daemon to which the proposed methodology is applied to does not contain malicious code, though it should not be necessarily trusted. In other word, the daemon could contain potential bugs in the implementation of the high level specification (e.g. bugs that could be exploited by a buffer overflow attack), but should not contain arbitrary malicious operations (e.g. a malicious programmer adds a trojan code which creates a root account in the password file even if such operation is not strictly required by the high level specification of the particular daemon).

The main novelty of our methodology is that it represents a first attempt for the automatic definition of the daemon normal behavior profile starting from its interface definition. To derive a daemon normal profile in terms of system calls, we *specify* the daemon interface using a technology that has been successfully applied to protocol design and analysis [3, 4]. The specification produced can be used for every version of daemon having the same interface, also if it runs on different a OS.

The main contributions of this paper are: a methodology to speed-up the synthesis of the normal behavior of an application program. This methodology differs from that based on the source code analysis, since our approach synthesizes the program behavior starting from both a high-level specification document, such as an IETF RFC, and a specific implementation. An implicit advantage of not relying on source code, is that our approach is applicable even if the source code is not available for analysis. Moreover, the process is automated, with the only exception of the specification phase, which is a high level human-activity. Further, to show the effectiveness of such a methodology, we used it to configure a particular anomaly based IDS prototype: REMUS [1].

The paper is organized as follows: next section summarizes the related works in the field. Section 3 illustrates the proposed methodology. Section 4 offers a case study, applied to the *ipop3d* daemon, while Section 5 presents a description of how the methodology can be used to configure the REMUS prototype. In Section 6 some concluding remarks and further research directions are exposed. Finally, the appendix reports the system calls intercepted as a result of the work developed in Section 5, and the VSP specification of the Postgres daemon. This paper is a revised and extended version of the work previously reported in [5].

2 Related works

There are several IDS proposed in literature that can be divided into two broad classes: network based and host based IDS. The former tries to detect the attempts to subvert the normal behavior of the system, analyzing the traffic of the network. The latter is intended to perform as last line of defense.

The host based IDS strives to detect intrusions analyzing the behavior of the system on which the IDS is run. The host based IDS can be further distinguished into three categories: (1) anomaly detection, (2) misuse detection, (3) specification-based. In particular, the main characterization of the three methods can be summarized as follows: (1) the anomaly detection method is based on revealing the behavior of the system that differs from a profile that depicts the normal behavior of the system that is automatically updated; (2) the misuse detection tries to classify all the possible known attacks to the system creating an association between each attack and a sort of signature. Recognizing such a signature on the system, raises an alarm; (3) the specification based approach tries to specify the intended behavior of the monitored program. Even slight variation from this behavior, raises an alarm.

The performance of these approaches is measured in terms of: (1) false positive, e.g. an alarm raised in correspondence to a regular situation; (2) false negative, e.g. the IDS did not raise an alarm while an intrusion occurred. The fundamental characteristic of the proposed approaches consist in defining the system behavior in terms of the sequences of the system calls invoked by the monitored application [10]. However, the approaches differ since the system behavior can be modeled in different way, e.g. formal specification [21], neural networks [9], sequences of pattern [14]. The strength and the weaknesses of each of the approach can be classified as follow:(1) the strength of the anomaly detection approaches is based on the capacity of the algorithm to generalize the model of the normal behavior of the monitored program. The higher the ability of generalization of the algorithm, the higher the probability to individuate new typology of attack. The drawback of such an approach is that when the IDS experiences for the first time a new behavior, it raises an alarm, which may be a false positive; (2) using the misuse detection approach, it is difficult to individuate new kinds of attack since this approach detects only the old ones, so false negative can occur. However, when an alarm is raised, this is because a signature has been detected, and therefore a false positive cannot occur. Note that the set of signatures could include ambiguous patterns that can be generated by an attacker as well as a legitimate user; (3) the specification techniques try to overcome the deficiencies of the anomaly detection and misuse detection approaches, defining the intended behavior of the controlled program. Any behavior that differs from the expected one is marked as illegal and an alarm is raised.

The specification-based technique should have the precision of the misuse detection technique and also the ability of detecting new kinds of attack as the anomaly detection technique. However, on one hand, specification based techniques require a good level of technical competence: indeed, a good knowledge of the operation performed by the application program is needed because such a knowledge must be translated in a specification of the expected behavior in a format comprehensible to the IDS. On the other hand, the IDS based on anomaly and misuse detection technique are respectively self-calibrating or just calibrated. Indeed, automatic techniques that lead the learning of the IDS have been proposed [20, 26, 10]. A more feasible specification based approach is that proposed in [7]. Using this approach it is possible to implement several kinds of security mechanisms. Moreover, the described approach gives the possibility of combining in different ways various IDS mechanism.

The network intrusion-detection systems (NIDSs), i.e. [24], often report a massive number of simple alerts of low-level security-related events. Many of these alerts are logically involved in a single multi-stage intrusion incident and a security officer often wants to analyze the complete incident instead of each individual simple alert.

[15] proposes a well-structured model that abstracts the logical relation between the alerts in order to support automatic correlation of those alerts involved in the same intrusion. The basic building block of the model is a logical formula called a capability. We use capability to abstract consistently and precisely all levels of accesses obtained by the attacker in each step of a multistage intrusion. We then derive inference rules to define logical relations between different capabilities. Based on the model and the inference rules, we have developed several novel alert correlation algorithms and implemented a prototype alert correlator.

Another network based intrusion detection is proposed in [22]. The network base intrusion detection consists in a distributed multiagent intrusion detection system (IDS) architecture, which attempts to provide an accurate and lightweight solution to network intrusion detection by tackling issues associated with the design of a distributed multiagent system, such as poor system scalability and the requirements of excessive processing power and memory storage. The proposed IDS architecture consists of (i) the Host layer with lightweight host agents that perform anomaly detection in network connections to their respective hosts, and (ii) the Classification layer whose main functions are to perform misuse detection for the host agents, detect distributed attacks, and disseminate network security status information to the whole network.

Among other approaches that cannot be classified in the exposed taxonomy, it is worth noting [19, 28], which try to implement a Mandatory Access Control policy. If the security policy defined is too restrictive, the process has less privilege than the minimal ones needed to execute its functionality and then the system cannot work properly, requiring the intervention of the system administrator. However, such an approach detects all the attempts to bypass the assigned privileges.

Attackers often try to evade an intrusion detection system (IDS) when launching their attacks. There have been several published studies in evasion attacks i.e. [29], some with available tools, in the research community as well as the hackers community. Some payload-based network anomaly detection systems can be evaded by a polymorphic blending attack (PBA). The main idea of a PBA is to create each polymorphic instance in such a way that the statistics of attack packet(s) match the normal traffic profile. [25], present a formal framework for the open problem: given an anomaly detection system and an attack, can one automatically generate its PBA instances? The framework not only expose how the IDS can be exploited by a PBA but also suggest how the IDS can be improved to prevent the PBA.

We now focus on the REMUS prototype [1]. Its design is based on the analysis of critical system calls. In particular, the overhead introduced by REMUS with respect to others IDS is negligible. The system calls have been partitioned in level of threat: the system calls of level 1 are those utilized from the hacker to gain complete control of the system. REMUS checks the system call of level 1, if the invoking process is a root daemon or if it is setuid to root; indeed, only in this case the attacker can gain access to the system as a privileged user. System calls belonging to other levels of threat are discarded by the IDS since they cannot lead to a subversion of a privileged process. REMUS allows a goods security level while intercepting only the 10% of the total number of system calls performed during execution.

3 Methodology

The methodology we propose takes in input a formal specification of daemon *A*, and returns as output a subset of the system calls that a specific program implementation of *A* is allowed to invoke.

Throughout this paper, we apply our methodology to the RFC1939 (*ipop3d*) [12], as an example. Note that any other specification of a daemon, with the level of detail of an RFC, could have been adopted as the starting point of our methodology. However, we have based our discussion on RFC since we intend to address the implementation of any secure Internet servers, which are mainly based on the execution of standard daemons, whose expected behavior is described through RFCs. In the following, we detail the steps of the methodology and subsequently develop a simple example.

The **first step** of the methodology consists in modeling the daemon behavior as a that can recognize any session of commands execution of the daemon *A*, triggered by a client. This step requires a human intervention to express the RFC specification of the daemon *A* with state transition semantic (an automaton). The states of the FSM are derived from the RFC, and the transitions between states are the possible commands that the daemon can be requested to execute.

The **second step** consists in formalizing the FSM using the VSP language [3]. This step must be carried out by the system analyst too.

In the **third step**, the VSP specification is compiled using the CVS compiler [3], detailed in Section 4.4. In particular, the result of the compilation produces a Security Process Algebra (SPA) [6] that we call FSM1.

The **fourth step** of the methodology consists in exploring the FSM1 to obtain the finite set of command sequences that may be invoked by an execution of the daemon. A commands execution set accepted by FSM can be equivalently represented as a subset of the command sequences produced by FSM1. Thus, executing the set of command sequences accepted by the FSM1 will invoke the same set of system calls invoked by the daemon when executing the command sequences recognized by the FSM. We assume that any command implementation invokes the same set of system calls regardless of the value and of the size on input parameters.

In the **fifth step,** the sequences of commands produced by CVS are translated, by a simple parsing algorithm, in the sequences of commands executable by a tool called ILSC (Invocation of Legal Sequences of Commands). The ILSC executes such command sequences on a specific implementation of the daemon. During this step the module REMUS is loaded in configuration mode to intercept and log all the system calls invoked by the daemon. Then, the logged system calls are used to update the ACL.

Note that the first and second steps above are carried out by the system analyst, while the others are automated. In the following, we illustrate the whole sequence of steps in the case study.

4 Case Study

4.1 POP3 commands

When the *ipop3d* daemon service is started, it listens on TCP port 110 [12]. When a client host wishes to make use of the service, it establishes a TCP connection with the server host. When the connection is established, the *ipop3d* server sends a greeting. The client and the *ipop3d* server daemon then exchange commands and responses until the connection is closed or aborted.

The commands of the *post office protocol* consist of a keyword followed by one or zero arguments. The response of the *ipop3d* daemon consists of a success indicator possibly followed by additional information. There are currently two indicators: positive ("+OK") and negative ("-ERR"). A post office protocol session progresses through a number of states during its lifetime. Once the TCP connection has been opened and the *ipop3d* server has sent the greeting command, the session enters the AUTHORIZATION state. In this state, the client must identify itself to the *ipop3d* server. Once the client has been successfully identified, the server acquires the resources associated with the client's maildrop, and the session enters the TRANS-

ACTION state. In this state, the client requests actions to the *ipop3d* server. When the client has finished its transactions, the session enters the UPDATE state.

In this state, the *ipop3d* server releases any resource acquired during the TRANSACTION state and says goodbye. The TCP connection is then closed. For a complete description of the post office protocol see RFC1939 [12].

4.2 The FSM (step 1)

To model the interactions between a client and the *ipop3d* we use a Finite State Machine, FSM.

We define the FSM, where the transitions represent the commands invoked by a client and the states are those reached by the daemon as a consequence of such an interaction. Figure 1 shows the FSM derived from the RFC for the *ipop3d* daemon. In each state an error can occur due to a bad input command, that is BAD_INP. The errors can be divided in two kinds, as reported in Table 1.

Table 1 Possible errors recognized by the ipop3d daemon

Error	**Description**
command error	the name of the command does not coincide with anyone of those specified in the RFC, given the current state of execution of the daemon.
parameter error	the parameter is omitted if required or it is wrong: out of range, mismatch.

Each time the *ipop3d* daemon receives a bad input command (BAD_INP), the software send back to the client as output an error message err-"error message". When the client sends a "well formed" command (a command and its parameters are well formed if they respect the RFC specification) the daemon returns as output an OK+ "message". The daemon terminates its execution when it reaches one of the two possible final states: UPDATE (U) or LOGOUT (L).

In Figure 1, the label TRANS_INP represents a set S={STAT, NOOP, LAST, RSET, LIST, DELE, RETR} of *post office protocol* commands that a client can independently invoke while *ipop3d* runs in the TRANSACTION state (T in the Figure 1).

We call *trace* a finite sequence of commands accepted by the FSM. If we consider the set of all the traces recognized by the FSM, they correspond to the set of all possible different sequences of commands invoked by a client and executed by the *ipop3d* daemon. Note that there is a correspondence between each command invocation and a set (possibly empty) of system calls executed at kernel level.

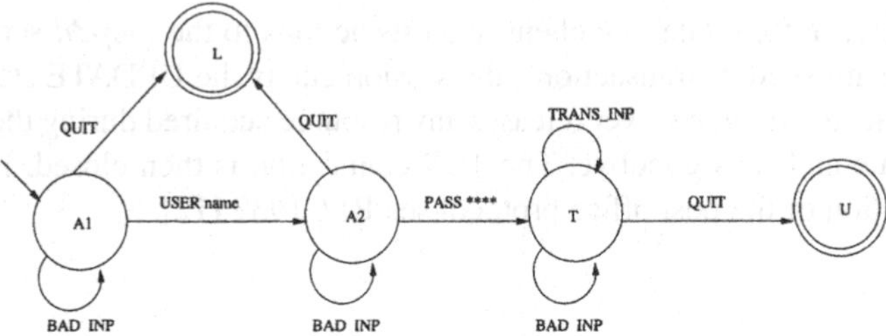

Fig. 1 The FSM of the `ipop3d` daemon.

4.3 VSP specification for ipop3d (step 2)

To obtain the FSM1, the system analyst has to specify the daemon using the VSP language. VSP is a value-passing language like CCS value passing [18] that allows protocol specification. A VSP specification is translated in a Security Process Algebra (SPA) [6] specification using the CVS compiler. The process of describing an Internet daemon through VSP is an extension of the use for which the VSP was initially intended for, that is VSP was developed to describe protocols [3, 4]. In general, a protocol consists of a set of *messages* (that contain a set of values) exchanged by two or more entities to reach a common goal (e.g. authentication). Indeed, a daemon is specified in VSP *via* a set of messages exchange. A daemon can accept a *command* and give as output: (1) an `error` message if the command is not well formed; (2) an `ok` message if the command is well formed. Therefore, describing a daemon through messages is a task that can be achieved if we employ messages that contain as parameters: the name of the *command* that the daemon has to execute and the parameters of the invoked command.

Given the idea of how it is possible to employ the VSP to describe the behavior of a daemon, we detail below the four steps of the procedure that leads the system analyst to the specification in VSP of the FSM:

- *definition of the commands and the values of the commands parameters*; in this step the system analyst has to synthesize the set of commands that a daemon can accept and the values that the command's parameter can assume during a daemon normal session. Table 2 describes the first step of the VSP specification.
- *definition of the messages accepted by the daemon*; as above expressed, the messages accepted by the daemon contains the name of the command that the daemon has to execute and the values of its parameters;
- *declaration and definition of the body of the daemon process*; this part specifies the "body" of the daemon server. The body of a process consists of a sequence of messages. There are two kind of messages: (1) the input messages that correspond to a command invocation; (2) the output messages, which correspond to the output of the *ipop3d* daemon. An output message can assume two values: (a) OK; (b)err¬ according to the fact that the received command is well formed or not. In Table 4.3 the messages of the *ipop3d* daemon. It is not necessary to

VSP	Description
#Names	* VSP section name
	* POP3 server: commands grouped according * to the state of execution and parameters number.
CmdA:USER,PASS,WC;	* commands executable in the Authorization State
CmdT1:STAT,NOOP,LAST,RSET,WC;	* commands executable in the Transaction state * with 0 parameter
CmdT2:LIST,WC;	* commands executable in the Transaction State * with 1 optional parameter
CmdT3:DELE,RETR,WC;	* commands executable in Transaction State * with 1 parameter
CmdU:QUIT,WC;	* commands executable in the Update State
	* WC = wrong command in a state
	* Set of parameter values of the POP3 commands.
Agent:Sam,Null;	* user name
Pass:bianco,Null;	* Passwords
Msg:1,2,3,4,Null;	* message ids
	* NULL : null parameter value

Table 2 Command and parameters definition

VSP	Description
#ActionDec	* action containing the command type and the parameter type * that the POP3 server executes
cmd_1 (CmdA,Agent)	* action for the execution of a command of type CmdA * and parameter type Agent
cmd_2 (CmdA,Pass)	* action for the execution of a command of type CmdA * and parameter type Pass
cmd_31 (CmdT1)	* action for the execution of a command of type CmdT1
cmd_32 (CmdT2,Msg)	* action for the execution of a command of type CmdT2 * and parameter type Msg
cmd_33 (CmdT3,Msg)	* action for the execution of a command of type CmdT3 * and parameter type Msg
cmd_4 (CmdU)	* action for the execution of a command of type CmdU
OK+()	* action that communicates the good result of a command execution
err-()	* action that communicates the bad result of a command execution
Sayonara()	* action that communicates the session ending

Table 3 POP3 messages

specify the body of the client process, as usually required by the VSP specification, because the specification of the behavior of the daemon is comprehensive of all possible interactions that the daemon itself can perform with any client. Table 4 reports the VSP specification of the *ipop3d* daemon.

- *definition of a generic session*; it is sufficient to consider a single instance of the daemon VSP process because the VSP coding of the daemon process generates all the sequences of the messages that could be executed during a session with a generic client. Table 5 reports the VSP invocation of a POP3 session performed by the daemon **ipop3d**.

Table 4 The VSP specification of POP3

```
#ProcessesDef POP3ser(u:Agent)
Var
Agent:name;
CmdA:c1,c2;
CmdT1:c31;
CmdT2:c32;
CmdT3:c33;
CmdU:c4;
Pass: p;
Msg:m,m1,m2;
Begin
   cmd_1(c1,name).
   if ((c1=USER) & (name=Sam))
      'OK+().
     cmd_2(c2,p).
     if ((c2=PASS) & (p=bianco))
        'OK+().
        cmd_31(c31).
        if (c31!WC)
          'OK+().
          cmd_32(c32,m1).
          if (c32!WC)
            'OK+().
            cmd_33(c33,m2).
            if ((c33!WC)& (m2!Null))
               'OK+().
               cmd_4(c4).
               if (c4=QUIT)
                  'Sayonara().
               else
                  'err-().
               endif
            else
               'err-().
            endif
          else
            'err-().
          endif
        else
          'err-().
        endif
     else
        'err-().
     endif
   else
     'err-().
   endif
End
```

#Session *invocation
POP3ser(sam)
#RestrictionOn
channel(cmd_1,cmd_2,cmd_3,cmd_31,cmd_4)

Table 5 the session invocation for VSP daemon

4.4 Compiling VSP (step 3)

The CVS compiler takes in input the VSP specification of the daemon and generates the FSM1. The body of the VSP process is made up of a linearly ordered sequence of input and output messages. The FSM1 obtained using the CVS compiler can be modeled as a tree. The corresponding tree model for the generation of the FSM1 can be obtained according to the rules in Figure 2.

```
TreeGeneration (node *m, CartesianP *P)
Begin
If (m==root) {
GenerateSPA(m);
m=m->next;
  } else If (m==InputMessage) {
  If (checkInBound (m)) {
    GenerateSPA(m);
    m=m->next;
    TreeGeneration(m,P);
  } else {
    while (P!=Null) {
      P = GenerateCartesianP(m);
      TreeGeneration(m,P);
    }
} else if (m==OutMessage) {
  if (checkInBound (m)) {
    GenerateSPA(m);
    m=m->next;
    TreeGeneration(m,P);
  } else {
    print(err);
    exit
  }
} else if (m==Null)
  exit;
End
```

Fig. 2 The SPA generation code.

In the routine for the generation of the FSM1 code we call m the message that we want to translate in SPA code. P is a possible instance of the message m. Each time the routine generates a FSM1 message, the routine moves to the next message via the statement m=m → next. When a message is translated from the VSP to the FSM1, we say that a VSP message is *expanded* in a FSM1 messages. The routine in Figure 2 works as follows:

1. the root of the tree is the FSM1 name of the process;
2. if the next examined message m is an input message, this message must consist of a set of parameters, say par1,par2,..,parK usually not instanced. The routine checks out if the current message has parameters that can assume only one possible value with the function checkInBound. If this is not the case, the CVS compiler, starting from this message, generates the Cartesian product of the value of the command parameters. Each element of the Cartesian product constitutes a different son of the root if the expanded message is the first. Otherwise, the generated messages are the sons of the previous *expanded* message;
3. if the examined message m is an output message, then its parameters are usually instanced. If the parameters are bounded, that is they assume just a value, the compiler generates a son of the previous *expanded* message. Such a node is labeled with the output message and the actual values of the parameters. If the parameters are not instanced, that is they assume more than one value, an exception is raised and the routine is stopped;
4. the routine terminates when there are no more messages to expand.

Note that the representation of FSM1 is indeed a tree, since it does not contain neither links to other nodes at the same level, nor links to the ancestor. Moreover, each node has one parent only. Finally, there cannot be isolated messages, since the compiler always links a generated node to one and exactly one of the previously generated nodes. Therefore, we are assured that the generated FSM1 graph is a tree.

4.5 Visiting the FSM1 (step 4)

Producing all the traces of the FSM1 consists of a depth first search in the process algebra tree produced by the CVS compiler. We use the algorithm `GetTraces` which takes as input: the first line of the SPA code firstline; the root node, e.g. the name of the SPA process firstnode; and an emptybuffer that will contain the execution traces, e.g. the command sequences. Note that the algorithm `GetTraces` follows a classical depth-first visit, getting all the paths root-leaf of the FSM1.

4.6 Executing Traces (step 5)

The traces produced by the `GetTraces` algorithm are translated in command sequences that can be invoked by the ILSC module. The ILSC executes such command sequences on a specific implementation of the daemon (that we want to profile) when the IDS is loaded in the OS kernel.

5 Using the Methodology to Configure REMUS

To exemplify the application of our methodology to an IDS based on the analysis of the system calls invoked by a program, we have used the methodology to configure REMUS. In REMUS, the system calls that are considered critical for the security of the system, (see Table 6), are intercepted by a LINUX kernel module specifically designed for this purpose. This module operates as reference monitor that denies or allows the execution of a particular system call invoked by a daemon or by a setuid software program. The decision of the reference monitor is based on a kernel data structure, the ACL, that maintains the set of authorized system calls and their relative parameters. The content of such a data structure can be seen as a classification of the behavior of a program.

Table 6 Critical system calls

system calls	dangerous parameter
`chmod, fchmod`	a system file or a directory
`chown, fchown, lchown`	a system file or a directory
`execve`	an executable file
`mount`	on a system directory
`rename, open, mknod`	a system file
`link, symlink, unlink`	a system file
`setuid, setresuid, setfsuid, setreuid`	UID set to zero
`setgroups, setgid, setfsgid, setresgid, setregid`	GID set to zero
`init_module`	modules not in `/lib/modules`

During the execution of the ILSC, the module REMUS stores the system calls invoked by the daemon in a file with the following format: system call name –parameters –invoking program. The first field consists of the name of the system call that the application program can invoke; the second field consists of the argument values of the system call; the third field is the name of the monitored application program. The content of this file is subsequently used to update the ACL. A schema of the methodology applied to the REMUS IDS is showed in Figure 3.

The first two steps in Figure 3 are carried out by the system analyst while the others are automatic. During the fifth step the module REMUS is loaded in configuration mode to intercept and log all the system calls invoked by the ILSC. Then, the logged system calls are used to update the ACL. After the fifth step completes, the system is ready to provide its intended services. During this production mode, REMUS allows a system call execution if and only if the invoking process and the value of the arguments comply with the contents of the ACL previously build in the configuration mode. We could have both false positive and false negative. As

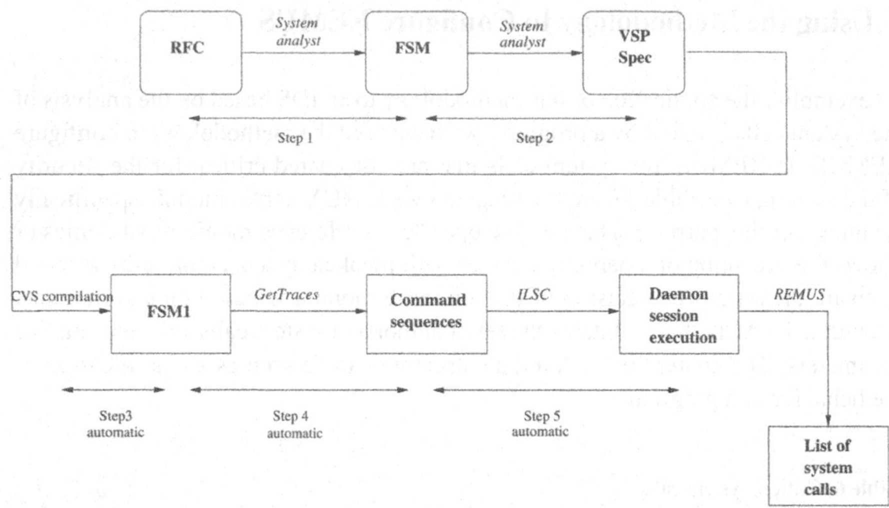

Fig. 3 The manual and automated steps of the methodology.

for false positive: the set of system calls intercepted by REMUS can be an underestimated approximation of the normal behavior of the analyzed daemon, because there could be sequence of command not specified in the VSP (due to system analyst error). As for false negative, REMUS does not take in account the order whom the system calls has to be invoked, for instance a mimicry attack could have success [27].

However, the majority of penetration techniques that allows an attacker to hijack the control of a privileged process will be blocked by the IDS configured in this way (buffer overflow technique is among the blocked ones).

5.1 Results

The described methodology has been applied to a set of daemons. We report the results in Table 7. From the above table, it is remarkable that: (a) only a limited number of daemons requires the execution of critical system calls; (b) the number of critical system calls intercepted, for those daemons that invoke them, is quite low. These findings can be explained with the growing attention that has been paid to security. Indeed, a basic step to minimize the possibility of system subversion is to reduce the number of critical system calls invoked by daemons in privileged mode.

It is worth noting that the objective of the REMUS prototype is to prevent the subversion of the system. Henceforth, if a non-super user application is compromised, this is not detected by REMUS. This point is clearly stated by the REMUS developers [1] and leveraged throughout this paper. However, this assumption may

Table 7 Methodology results

OS	Daemon	FSM1 sessions	Number of Critical Sys Calls
red hat 7.2	Qmail 1.03 (smtp service)	5922	0
mandrake 9.0	wu-sftpd 2.62	6014	0
mandrake 9.0	vs-ftpd 1.1.3	4890	0
mandrake 9.0	Postgres	77272	0
mandrake 9.0	sendmail 8.11.6	5348	5
mandrake 9.0	postfix	4920	21
redhat 7.3	pop3d	5230	3

raise some objection in adopting REMUS together with the proposed methodology; for instance, the subversion of the Postgres daemon, run by a non-privileged user, could possibly compromise a sensitive Database while not compromising the entire system. This point can be addressed intercepting the critical system calls the Postgres daemon invokes when run with normal user privileges. The normal behavior profile obtained can thus be used to prevent the daemon subversion also when it is run as a non-privileged process. Note that this operation allows a complete re-use of the VSP daemon specification.

In Appendix 7 we report: (1) the name of the system calls intercepted and the appropriate commands to be added to the ACL; (2) the VSP specification of the Postgres daemon. In particular, note that the specification of the Postgres daemon is compact and almost self-explanatory. To specify the daemon behavior according to the VSP language took one day only. This should testify the feasibility of the proposed methodology.

6 Concluding remarks

In this paper, we have drawn a methodology to derive, starting from a high level specification of an application program, the set of the system calls an application can invoke. Our methodology does not need to access the source code, thus, it can be adopted even in those environment in which only the executable is available. Moreover, the methodology is completely independent from the IDS tool adopted. Note that when a new release of a daemon implementation becomes available, it is necessary only to execute the ILSC to upgrade the ACL (step 5), while preserving the efforts spent in the steps 1-4 of the methodology. Finally, except for the first two step of the methodology described in Section 3, which are at a high level of design, the process is completely automatic.

The adoption of a specific technology (VSP/CVS), which is internally based on automaton representation, allows us to obtain a good profile of the normal behavior of the application program.

We tested the proposed methodology to derive the normal behavior profile of a set of daemons critical for the deployment of a secure WEB server. The results we obtain encourage us to explore the program normal behavior space using the specification driven methodology we propose. As a future work we plan to extend the methodology in order to deal with the so called evasion attacks [29].

7 Appendix

In the following we report two test cases. The first is related to the pop3d, sendmail and postfix daemon; the second is related to the Postgres daemon. The first test case shows the effectiveness of the proposed approach used with the REMUS IDS. The second test case is intended to apply our methodology to a more complex daemon.

7.1 The critical system calls

Table 8 reports the critical system calls intercepted by REMUS, set in DEBUG mode, when the sessions produced by the CVS compiler are executed, for the pop3d the sendmail and postfix daemon.

The second column reports as first field the system call name, then the system call parameters, and finally the name of the program that could invoke that system call.

7.2 Postgres VSP Specification

Table 9 reports the VSP specification of the *Postgres* daemon version 7.2. Once compiled CVS produce a *.trc* file, which comprises 77272 *Postgres* sessions. The sessions executed, with REMUS set in DEBUG mode, did not produce any critical system calls. Hence, the Postgres daemon either does not execute critical system calls or when it execute them, it runs without privileged rights.

References

1. M. Bernaschi, E. Gabrielli, and L. V. Mancini. Remus: a security-enhanced operating system. *ACM Transactions on Information and System Security (TISSEC)*, 5(1):36–61, 2002.
2. C. Cowan, P. Wagle, C. Pu, S. Beattie, and J. Walpole. Buffer overflows: attacks and defences for the vulnerability of the decade. In *Proceedings IEEE DARPA Information Survivability Conference and Expo*, Jan. 2000.
3. A. Durante, R. Focardi, and R. Gorrieri. A compiler for analyzing cryptographic protocols using noninterference. *ACM Transactions on Software Engineering and Methodology (TOSEM)*, 9(4):488–528, 2000.

Table 8 The critical system calls

OS & Version	Critical System calls in the ACL

Mandrake 9.0 Gnu-pop3d 0.9.8	`unlink /var/spool/mail/root.lock gnu-pop3d`
	`open /var/spool/mail/root.lock gnu-pop3d`
	`open /var/spool/mail/root gnu-pop3d`

Mandrake 9.0 Sendmail 8.12.5	`exec /usr/bin/procmail/ sendmail`
	`open /var/spool/mqueue/ sendmail`
	`link /var/spool/mqueue/ sendmail`
	`unlink /var/spool/mqueue/ sendmail`
	`rename /var/spool/mqueue/ sendmail`

Mandrake 9.0 Postfix	`open /var/spool/postfix/pid/master.pid master`
	`open /var/spool/postfix/pid/unix.local local`
	`open /var/spool/postfix/pid/unix.showq showq`
	`open /var/spool/postfix/pid/unix.flush flush`
	`exec /usr/lib/postfix/cleanup master`
	`fchmod /var/spool/postfix/maildrop/ postdrop`
	`open /var/spool/postfix/maildrop/ postdrop`
	`exec /usr/lib/postfix/bounce master`
	`exec /usr/lib/postfix/smtpd master`
	`exec /usr/lib/postfix/trivial-rewrite master`
	`open /var/spool/postfix/pid/unix.cleanup cleanup`
	`exec /usr/lib/postfix/nqmgr master`
	`exec /usr/lib/postfix/smtp master`
	`exec /usr/lib/postfix/pickup master`
	`exec /usr/lib/postfix/local master`
	`open /var/spool/postfix/public/pickup postdrop`
	`exec /usr/lib/postfix/showq master`
	`open /var/spool/postfix/pid/unix.rewrite trivial-rewrite`
	`open /var/spool/postfix/pid/unix.defer bounce`
	`exec /usr/lib/postfix/flush master`
	`open /var/spool/postfix/pid/unix.bounce bounce`

4. A. Durante, R. Focardi, and R. Gorrieri. CVS at work: A report on new failures upon some cryptographic protocols. In *Lecture Notes in Computer Science*, 2052:287–299, 2001.
5. A. Durante, R. Di Pietro, and L. V. Mancini. Formal specification for fast automatic IDS training. In *Lecture Notes in Computer Science* 2629, 2003.
6. R. Focardi and R. Gorrieri. The compositional security checker: A tool for the verification of information flow security properties. *Software Engineering*, 23(9):550–571, 1997.
7. T. Fraser, L. Badger, and M. Feldman. Hardening COTS software with generic software wrappers. In *IEEE Symposium on Security and Privacy*, pages 2–16, 1999.
8. D. P. Ghormley, D. Petrou, S. H. Rodrigues, and T. E. Anderson. SLIC: An extensibility system for commodity operating systems. In *Proceedings of the USENIX 1998 Annual Technical Conference*, pages 39–52, Berkeley, USA, June 15–19 1998.
9. A. K. Ghosh, C. C. Michael. Simple, state-based approaches to program-based anomaly detection. In *ACM Transactions on Information and System Security (TISSEC)*, Volume 5, Issue 3 (August 2002).
10. S. A. Hofmeyr, S. Forrest, and A. Somayaji. Intrusion detection using sequences of system calls. *Journal of Computer Security*, 6(3):151–180, 1998.
11. IETF repository retrieval, http://www.ietf.org/rfc.html.
12. The Post Office Protocol - Version 3, http://www.faqs.org/rfcs/rfc1939.html

Table 9 Postgres VSP specification: declarations

```
#Names
Agent: A,B;
CmdDB: CREATEDB;
CmdTB1: CREATETABLE;
CmdTB2: INSERT;
CmdTB3: SELECT;
CmdU: QUIT;
Namedb: DataBase;
Nametb: Table;
Field: ID, surname, Born;
Options: PrimaryKey, NotNull, NULL;
OptionsBy: Group,Order, NULL;
ValuesID: 1, 2, NULL;
ValuesSurn: Alice, Bob, NULL;
ValuesDN: 1975, 1976, NULL;
Parameter: Star, surname, NULL;
Condition: Condition1, Condition2, NULL;

#ActionDec
cmd_1 (CmdDB, Namedb)
cmd_21 (CmdTB1, Nametb, Field, Options, Field, Options, Field, Options)
cmd_22 (CmdTB2, Nametb, ValuesID, ValuesSurn, ValuesDN)
cmd_23 (CmdTB3, Parameter, Nametb, Condition, OptionsBy)
cmd_3 (CmdU)
OK+()
err-()

#RolesDec
first
second

#ProcessesDef
```


13. K. Ilgun, R.A. Kemmerer, and P.A. Porras. State Transition Analysis: A Rule-Based Intrusion Detection System. *IEEE Transactions on Software Engineering*, 21(3):181–199, March 1995.
14. S. Jajodia J. L. Lin, X. S. Wang. Abstraction-based misuse detection: High-level specifications and adaptable strategies. In *PCSFW: Proceedings of The 11th Computer Security Foundations Workshop*, pages 190–201. IEEE Computer Society Press, 1998.
15. Jingmin Zhou, Mark Heckman, Brennen Reynolds, Brennen Reynolds, Adam Carlson, Matt Bishop. Modeling network intrusion detection alerts for correlation. *ACM Transactions on Information and System Security* (TISSEC) Volume 10 , ISSN:1094-9224, Issue 1, February 2007.
16. R. P. Lippmann. Evaluating intrusion detection systems: The 1998 darpa off-line intrusion detection evaluation. In *Proceedings DARPA Information Survivability Conference and Expo–sition (DISCEX)*. IEEE Computer Society Press, Los Alamitos, CA, 2000.
17. Mei-Ling Shyu, Thiago Quirino, Zongxing Xie, Shu-Ching Chen, Liwu Chang. Network intrusion detection through Adaptive Sub-Eigenspace Modeling in multiagent systems. *ACM Transactions on Autonomous and Adaptive Systems* (TAAS), Volume 2, Issue 3 (September 2007).
18. R. Milner. Communication and concurrency. In *Prentice Hall, New York*, 1989.
19. Security Enhanced Linux, http://www.nsa.gov/selinux.

20. R. Sekar, M. Bendre, D. Dhurjati, and P. Bollineni. A fast automation-based method for detecting anomalous program behavior. In *IEEE Symposium on Security and Privacy*, pages 144–155, Oackland CA, May 2001.
21. R. Sekar and P. Uppuluri. Synthesizing fast intrusion prevention/detection systems from high-level specifications. In *Proceedings of the 8th USENIX Security Symposium*, pages 63–78, Washington DC, USA, August 1999.
22. Mei-Ling Shyu, Thiago Quirino, Zongxing Xie, Shu-Ching Chen, and Liwu Chang. Network intrusion detection through adaptive sub-eigenspace modeling in multiagent systems. *ACM Trans. Auton. Adapt. Syst.*, 2(3):9, 2007.
23. C. Szyperski, D. Gruntz, and S. Murer. Component software: Beyond object-oriented programming. In *Addison-Wesley / ACM Press*, 2002.
24. L. Portnoy, E. Eskin, and S. Stolfo. Intrusion Detection with Unlabeled Data Using Clustering. In *Proceedings of the ACM CSS Workshop on Data Mining for Security Applications*, November 8, 2001.
25. Prahlad Fogla, Wenke Lee. Evading network anomaly detection systems: formal reasoning and practical techniques *Proceedings of the 13th ACM conference on Computer and communications security*, ISBN:1-59593-518-5, Pages: 59 - 68, 2006.
26. D. Wagner and D. Dean. Intrusion detection via static analysis. In *IEEE Symposium on Security and Privacy*, pages 156–169, Oackland CA, 2001.
27. D. Wagner and P. Soto. Mimicry Attacks on Host-Based Intrusion Detection Systems. In *Ninth ACM Conference on Computer and Communications Security*, Washington, DC, USA, 18-22 November 2002.
28. K. M. Walker, D. F. Sterne, M. L. Badger, M. J. Petkac, D. L. Shermann, and K. Oostendorp. Confining root programs with domain and type enforcement (DTE). In *Proceeding of the 6th USENIX UNIX Security Symposium*, San Jose, California, USA, july 1996.
29. Kymie M. C. Tan, John McHugh, Kevin S. Killourhy Hiding Intrusions: From the Abnormal to the Normal and Beyond. In *Proceeding of the 5th Information Hiding International Workshop*, pages 1-17 , IH 2002, Noordwijkerhout, The Netherlands, October 7-9, 2002

Table 10 Postgres VSP specification: first agent

```
first(s1:Agent)
Var
CmdDB: c1_a;
CmdTB1: c21_a;
CmdTB2: c22_a;
CmdTB3: c23_a;
CmdU: c3_a;
Namedb: DBase;
Nametb: tab_1a;
Field: cp1_a, cp2_a, cp3_a;
Options: opz1_a, opz2_a, opz3_a;
OptionsBy: opzby_1a;
ValuesID: v_1a;
ValuesSurn: surn_1a;
ValuesDN: DN_1a;
Parameter: p_1a;
Condition: cond_1a;
  cmd_1(c1_a,DBase).
  if ((c1_a=CREATEDB) & (DBase=DataBase))
    'OK+().
    cmd_21(c21_a, tab_1a, cp1_a, opz1_a, cp2_a, opz2_a, cp3_a, opz3_a).
    if ((c21_a= CREATETABLE) & (tab_1a=Table) & (cp1_a!cp2_a) & (cp2_a!cp3_a) & (cp1_a!cp3_a))
      'OK+().
      cmd_22(c22_a, tab_1a, v_1a, surn_1a, DN_1a).
      if ((c22_a=INSERT) & (tab_1a=Table) & (v_1a!NULL) & (surn_1a!NULL) & (DN_1a!NULL))
        'OK+().
        cmd_23(c23_a, p_1a, tab_1a, cond_1a, opzby_1a).
        if ((c23_a=SELECT) & (tab_1a=Table) & (p_1a!NULL))
          'OK+().
          cmd_3(c3_a).
          if (c3_a=QUIT)
            'OK+().
          else
            'err-().
          endif
        else
          'err-().
        endif
      else
        'err-().
      endif
    else
      'err-().
    endif
  else
    'err-().
  endif
End
```

Table 11 Postgres VSP specification: second agent and session invockation

```
second(s2:Agent)
Var
CmdDB: c1_b;
CmdTB1: c21_b;
CmdTB2: c22_b;
CmdTB3: c23_b;
CmdU: c3_b;
Nametb: tab_2b;
Field: cp1_b, cp2_b, cp3_b;
Options: opz1_b, opz2_b, opz3_b;
OptionsBy: opby_2b;
ValuesID: v_2b;
ValuesSurn: surn_2b;
ValuesDN: DN_2b;
Parameter: p_2b;
Condition: cond_2b;
Begin
  cmd_21(c21_b, tab_2b, cp1_b, opz1_b, cp2_b, opz2_b, cp3_b, opz3_b).
  if ((c21_b=CREATETABLE) & (tab_2b=Table) & (cp1_b!cp2_b) & (cp2_b!cp3_b) & (cp1_b!cp3_b))
    OK+().
    cmd_22(c22_b, tab_2b, v_2b, surn_2b, DN_2b).
    if ((c22_b=INSERT) & (tab_2b=Table) & (v_2b!NULL) & (surn_2b!NULL) & (DN_2b!NULL))
      'OK+().
      cmd_23(c23_b, p_2b, tab_2b, cond_2b, opby_2b).
      if ((c23_b=SELECT) & (tab_2b=Table) & (p_2b!NULL))
        'OK+().
        cmd_3(c3_b).
        if (c3_b=QUIT)
          'OK+().
        else
          'err-().
        endif
      else
        'err-().
      endif
    else
      'err-().
    endif
  else
    'err-().
  endif
End
#Session *invocation
first(A)
second(B)
#RestrictionOn
channel(Cmd_1,Cmd_21,Cmd_22,Cmd_23,Cmd_3)
```

Learning Behavior Profiles from Noisy Sequences

Ugo Galassi

Abstract This paper proposes a new approach for building process profiles, which capture the abstract pattern of the temporal evolution of a process. Profiles are modeled as finite state stochastic automata, more specifically, by means of Hierarchical Hidden Markov Models. Consequently, abstract process behavior correspond to probabilistic regular expressions.

A learning algorithm based on an abstraction mechanism is proposed, which can automatically infer a profile from a set of traces of the process behavior. The induction algorithm proceeds bottom-up, progressively coarsening the sequence granularity, letting correlations between subsequences, possibly separated by long gaps, naturally emerge. Two abstraction operators are defined. The first one detects, and abstracts into non-terminal symbols, regular expressions not containing iterative constructs. The second one detects and abstracts iterated subsequences. By interleaving the two operators, regular expressions in general form may be inferred. Both operators are based on string alignment algorithms taken from bio-informatics. A restricted form of the algorithm has already been outlined in previous papers, where the emphasis was on applications. Here, the algorithm, in an extended version, is described and analyzed into details. An extensive experimentation, made using both artificial and real traces, concludes the paper.

1 Introduction

Many Intrusion Detection Systems (IDS's), in computer networks [18, 28] and Fraud Detection Systems (FDS's), in networks and telephony [8, 28], make an extensive use of agent profiling [23], being an agent a computer process or a human user. An agent profile is an abstract characterization of the agent activity which can

Ugo Galassi
Università Amedeo Avogadro, Dipartimento di Informatica, Via Bellini 25G, 15100 - Alessandria, Italy, e-mail: ugo.galassi@unipmn.it

be used both to check for *normal* behavior or to detect known *anomalous* behaviors. Therefore, an IDS (FDS) is as much effective as better the profile captures the aspects of the agent behavior which are relevant to the task. Nevertheless, the methods for building profiles are still quite primitive and, in many cases, reduce to measure the frequency of selected classes of actions (e.g system call) executed by an agent in a temporal window. This paper presents a new method, where more complex profiles, accounting for typical sequences of actions and for typical state transitions, are learned by induction from *logs* of the agent behavior.

The basic assumption is that the behavior of an agent periodically exhibits short sequences of actions, typical of the task it executes, interleaved with phases where the activity cannot be modeled, because it is non-repetitive. For analogy with the DNA sequences in molecular biology, we will call *motifs* such a kind of characteristic sequences of actions. In fact, under the previous assumptions, the problem of agent profiling presents strong analogy to the problem of discovering and characterizing coding subsequences in a DNA chromosome.

Here, probabilistic regular expressions, extended with attributes [12], are proposed to describe the abstract structure of profiles. Attributes are used to set constraints on atomic events. Therefore, the problem of discovering the structure of a profile is turned into the problem of learning probabilistic regular expressions from sequences containing gaps and noise.

The problem of inferring regular grammars from data has been previously investigated by many authors with approaches ranging from computational learning theory [1, 24, 21, 22, 5] to neural networks [7], syntactic pattern recognition [13, 25], and probabilistic automata [11]. Nevertheless, the problem considered here does not match immediately any one of the problems solved by the mentioned approaches. In fact, the task is more complex, because the sentences of the language to learn are hidden inside sequences containing a possibly large amount of irrelevant knowledge, which must be discarded.

By exploiting properties inherent to regular expressions, an abstraction mechanism has been defined: it allows a process behavior to be seen at different levels of granularity depending on the needs. Such a mechanism is exploited by the learning algorithm, which automatically infers the behavior description from a database of sequences. An important novelty, with respect to previous works, is a method for detecting and learning recurrent structures inside an event, in presence of noise.

The paper concludes with an extensive evaluation of the learning algorithm. A first set of tests is made using artificial traces generated in order to challenge the algorithm to discover known pattern hidden in a database of sequences. By carefully designing the model of the generative process, it has been possible to handcraft, quite difficult learning problem, where both the capabilities and the limitations of the algorithm emerge. Finally, a real agent profiling task has been designed, where the challenge is to characterize the behavior of a user typing on a keyboard. Also in this case, the algorithm was successful in discovering profiles, which clearly identify an user from another.

2 Learning by Abstraction

The main difficulty in discovering and modeling profiles hidden inside long sequences is due to the presence of long gaps, filled by irrelevant facts, between episodes belonging to a profile. On the one hand, statistical correlations among distant episodes are difficult to detect. On the other hand, the complexity of the *mining* algorithm increases with the length of the portion of sequence to be searched to detect such kind of correlations. The strategy proposed here to cope with such kind of problems is based on an abstraction mechanism.

In AI, abstraction has been proposed by several authors with different acceptions (see [27] for an introduction). The acception, adopted here, relays on the property of regular expressions of being closed under substitution [16]: by replacing a subexpression with a new symbol, an abstract expression is obtained. As previously mentioned, profiles are described by means of regular expressions extended with attributes. By applying the substitution property, a profile can be abstracted, or de-abstracted.

The idea will be further clarified describing the scheme of the algorithm used for discovering profiles hidden in a set, $\mathcal{LS}$, of learning sequences. The algorithm starts bottom-up to construct an abstraction hierarchy, layer after layer. The basic activity at each step consists in identifying episodes occurring with a relevant frequency in $\mathcal{LS}$: every episode is characterized by a regular expression $\mathcal{R}$. Then, the detected episodes are *named* by associating a new symbol to each one of them, and episode names become the alphabet for describing $\mathcal{LS}$ at the next abstraction level. Afterwards, every sequence in $\mathcal{LS}$ is abstracted (rewritten) by replacing every episode instance occurring in it with the corresponding episode name. Subsequences of consecutive atomic events, which have not been included in any episode, are replaced with a symbol denoting a *gap*. As it will be described in the next sections, gaps between episodes are considered as a special kind of episode.

In the new sequences obtained from the abstraction step, episodes, previously separated by subsequences of irrelevant facts, may become consecutive, only separated by one gap symbol. Then, at the next abstraction step, correlations at a wider range can be detected by repeating the same procedure described so far, while the complexity of the algorithm remains affordable.

Important aspects to consider, in order to correctly detect statistical correlations between consecutive atomic events, are the event duration and the distance from one another, which could be required to satisfy specific constraints. As an example, one may be willing to accept a correlation between two events A and B, when B frequently occurs few days after A, but one may want to reject a correlation if the distance of B from A randomly ranges from one day to one year.

The attributes extending regular expressions have principally the function of preserving the information about duration and distance between events through the abstraction process. Every atomic event E is denoted by a name (symbol) and by an attribute l_E reporting the length (duration) of E on the unabstracted sequence. When an episode is abstracted into a new atomic event at the higher level, the length of this last is set to the length of the episode. In the same way, gaps are denoted by a symbol, and have a length set to the distance between the two neighbouring episodes. As it will be described in the following, the event description language allows constraints on duration of an event to be specified. Therefore, to set constraints on the distance between two events is sufficient to set constraints on the gap in between.

This solution, of using gap symbols to fill spaces between non adjacent atomic events, allows for any discrete sequence to be transformed into a *string* of symbols. The important benefit is that a large set of string processing algorithms can be immediately exploited.

3 Regular Expressions

The standard formalism for regular expressions [16] is adopted for describing episodes and profiles. Regular language syntax contains meta-symbols for denoting disjunction and iteration. Disjunction is denoted by the symbol "|". For instance, the construct $a(c|d)a$ denotes a sequence of three symbols, where the first and the third are "a", and the second may be "c" or "d". Parentheses are used to enclose subexpressions. The special symbol ε denotes the null event and is used to model omission. For instance, expression $a(c|d|\varepsilon)a$ entails that also the sentence aa, is a possible event instance. Repetition is denoted by a superscript on a symbol, or on a subexpression, which indicates how many consecutive times it occurs. As an example, expression a^3b^2 is a compact form for denoting the sequence "aaabb".

In principle, regular expressions can also describe infinite sentences. The classical notation for handling infinity consists in using symbol "$\star$" as a superscript to expressions. Here, infinity is not allowed. Instead, the regular language notation is slightly extended to allow for nondeterminate iterations, where the number of repetitions may range inside a bounded interval. For instance, expression $ab^{3,9}$ denotes a sequence whose first element is "a" followed by a number of "b" ranging between 3 to 9.

Constraints on the event/gap length may be set by annotating symbols in regular expressions. Annotation must be included inside square brackets, following the symbol denoting an atomic event. For instance $a[n]$ means that the length l_a of a must be n ($l_a = n$), whereas $a[n,m]$ means that the length of a must range between n and m ($n \leq l_a \leq m$). A legal example of annotation can be as in the following:

$$a[3,5]^3 b[4,8]^2 \tag{1}$$

Informally, expression (1) specifies that the duration of any event of type a must be in the interval $[3,5]$ and the duration of any event of type b must be in the interval $[4,8]$. Gaps are named and annotated as atomic events. However, given the semantics of gaps, iteration has no meaning for them; then, gap names cannot have an exponent.

4 String Alignment and Flexible Matching

A key role in the abstraction process is played by the *approximate matching* of strings and of regular expressions, which, in turn, is based on *string alignment*. String alignment has been deeply investigated in Bio-informatics and a wide collection of effective algorithms are available for doing it[6, 15]. Here some basic concepts, necessary to make the paper self-consistent, will be recalled; the interested reader can find in[6, 15] an exhaustive introduction to the topic.

Definition 0.1. Given two strings s_1 and s_2, let s_1' and s_2' be two strings obtained from s_1 and s_2, respectively, by inserting an arbitrary number of spaces such that the atomic events in the two strings can be put in a one-to-one correspondence. The pair $A(s_1, s_2) = \langle s_1', s_2' \rangle$, is said a global alignment between s_1 and s_2.

From global alignment, local alignment and multi-alignment can be defined.

Definition 0.2. Any global alignment between a pair of substrings r_1 and r_2 extracted from two strings s_1 and s_2, respectively, is said a local alignment $LA(s_1, s_2)$, between s_1 and s_2.

Definition 0.3. Given a set S of strings, a multi-alignment $MA(S)$ on S is a set S' of strings, where every string $s \in S$ generates a corresponding string $s' \in S'$ by inserting a proper number of spaces, and every pair of strings $\langle s_1', s_2' \rangle$ is a global alignment $A(s_1, s_2)$ of the corresponding strings s_1, s_2 in set the S.

It is immediate to verify that, for a pair of strings s_1 and s_2, many alignments exist [1]. However, the interest is for alignments maximizing (or minimizing) an assigned scoring function[2]. A typical scoring function is string similarity [15], which can be stated in the following general form:

$$\int(s_1, s_2) = \sum_{i=1}^{n} \int(s_1'(i), s_2'(i)) \tag{2}$$

being n the length of the alignment $\langle s_1', s_2' \rangle$, and $\int(.,.)$ a scoring function, which depends upon the symbol pairs, which have been aligned.

An alternative to (2) for aligning strings and estimating similarity is based on a special kind of Hidden Markov Model (HMM) called *profile HMM* (see [6] for an introduction). The fundamental difference between profile HMM and (2) is that for the former the scoring function is stated in terms of a mixture model defining a probability distribution. Then the similarity between two strings s_1 and s_2, or between a string and a template, is defined as the probability that s_2 be obtained from s_1

[1] If no restriction is set on the possible number of inserted spaces, the number of possible alignments is infinite.

[2] As *approximate/flexible matching* between two strings, or between a string and a regular expression, is intended the problem of finding the optimal alignment with respect to an assigned scoring function

as the result of a stochastic sequence of insertions, deletions and substitutions. The structure of a profile HMM is described in Figure 1. It contains three types of states: *match states* where the emission corresponds to the expected nominal symbol, *null emission states* modeling deletion errors, and *insertion states* modeling insertion errors, where the emission is chosen among a set of possible symbols. Such a structure can be obtained by compilation from a string, as well as from a regular expression. In the case of Figure 1 the HMM has been obtained from the string "PARIS".

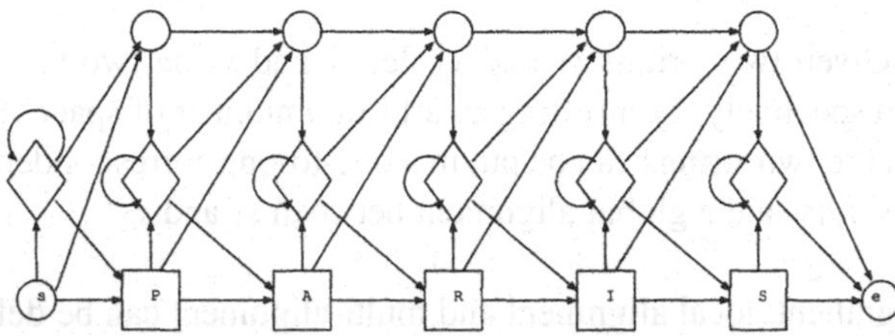

Fig. 1 Profile HMM obtained from the string "PARIS". Square nodes represent *match states*, circles represent *null emission states* and diamonds represents *insertion states*. Transitions, from one state to another, and emissions are governed by probability distributions not shown in the figure. States labeled by *s* and *e* are the initial and final state, respectively.

In the framework of Dynamic Programming, the problem of finding an alignment maximizing a similarity function is solvable with complexity of $O(nm)$ being n and m the length of s_1 and s_2, respectively. Nevertheless, approximate solutions can be found in linear time[15]. On the contrary, the problem of finding an optimal multi-alignment is exponential in the cardinality $|S|$ of set S. Therefore, only approximate solutions can be used when S is large.

The concept of similarity and alignment between strings is easy to extend to the concept of alignment between a string and a regular expression. A regular expression $\mathscr{R}$ is equivalent to a set of strings that can be derived from it. Therefore the optimal alignment between $\mathscr{R}$ and a string s, with respect to an assigned similarity function, is the best alignment among all possible alignments between s and anyone of the strings derivable from $\mathscr{R}$. In the general case, the complexity for finding such an alignment is $O(nm)$ being m the length of $\mathscr{R}$ and n the length of s [20].

A similar extension holds in the HMM framework, where regular expressions can be translated into HMMs. However, such translation requires the target HMM to be augmented in two ways: (a) in order to deal with the presence of insertion and deletion errors, extra states must be explicitly added; (b) in order to model specific probability distributions, cycles in regular expressions need to be unrolled into a feed-forward graph, where only self-loops are allowed. A description of the problem and of the related methodologies can be found in [6, 3, 14].

A last point to discuss is how constraints, set in regular expressions on event lengths, intervene in the matching procedure. Dealing with such kind of constraints requires only minor changes in the algorithms searching for an optimal alignment: symbols in the input string not matching the constraints will be considered as insertion errors that do not match any symbols. Consequently, the impact on the final alignment will depend upon the specific scoring function. In a similar way, considering iterated subexpressions, iterations in excess (defect), with respect to the bounds set in the exponent, will be considered as insertion (deletion) errors.

5 The Learning Algorithm

The main learning algorithm includes a basic cycle, activated bottom-up, in which a new abstraction layer is constructed, and a refinement cycle, which can be called top-down one or more times in order to refine the episode descriptions (see Figure 2). Both cycles are based on two abstraction operators, ω_S and ω_I, which are used to infer the structure of regular expressions. Operator ω_S constructs regular expressions non containing iterative constructs, whereas ω_I explicitly aims at discovering and abstracting iterative constructs. By interleaving the two operators, an abstraction hierarchy is obtained, from which regular expressions in general form are obtained.

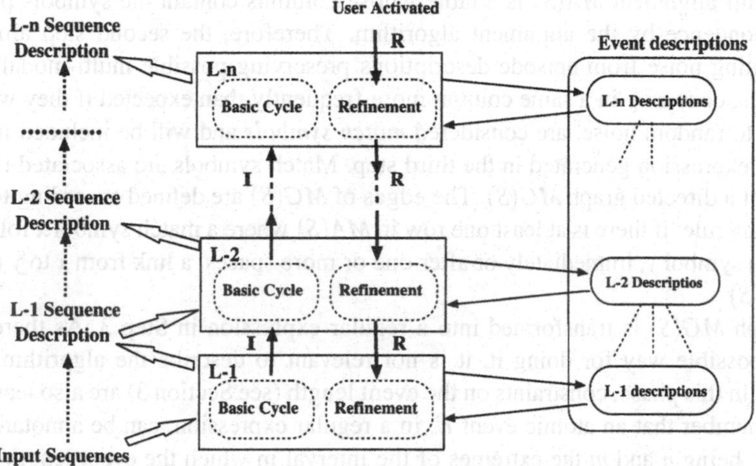

Fig. 2 The main learning algorithm structure. Every layer produces a more abstract description of the input sequences.

5.1 ω_S Operator

The ω_S operator takes in input a set S of similar substrings, detected using a local alignment algorithm, and constructs an abstract atomic event defined as a pair $\langle \mathscr{R}, E \rangle$ being $\mathscr{R}$ a regular expression generalizing the episode instances contained in S, and E is the abstract event associated to $\mathscr{R}$. The restriction is that items in $\mathscr{R}$ may be only symbols, or disjunction of symbols. Therefore, no iterative constructs are considered.

The core of ω_S is the construction of the multi-alignment of all strings in the set S; the similarity measure and the alignment procedure are parameters, which can be assigned according to the needs. The semantics of ω_S consists in the following three step algorithm:

Algorithm ω_S

1. Construct the multi-alignment $MA(S)$ for strings in S.
2. Construct the match graph $MG(S)$.
3. Transform $MG(S)$ into an equivalent regular expression.

The multi-alignment $MA(S)$ is a table whose columns contain the symbols put in correspondence by the alignment algorithm. Therefore, the second step aims at eliminating noise from episode descriptions preserving possible multi-modalities. Symbols, occurring in a same column more frequently than expected if they would be due to random noise, are considered *match symbols* and will be included in the regular expression generated in the third step. Match symbols are associated to the nodes of a directed graph $MG(S)$. The edges of $MG(S)$ are defined according to the following rule: if there is at least one row in $MA(S)$ where a match symbol x follows a match symbol y, immediately or after one or more spaces, a link from x to y is set in $MG(S)$.

Graph $MG(S)$ is transformed into a regular expression in Step 3. As there are many possible way for doing it, it is not relevant to describe the algorithm into details. In this phase, constraints on the event length (see Section 3) are also learned. We remember that an atomic event E, in a regular expression, can be annotated as $E[n,m]$, being n and m the extremes of the interval in which the event length l_E is accepted. The values for n and m are estimated from the lengths of the instances of E aligned in a same column in $MA(S)$. In this phase, constraints, given a-priori as background knowledge, can also be taken into account.

The algorithm is illustrated through an example in Figure 3, where a regular expression describing a dimorphic occurrence of the word *london*[3] in the Italian language is extracted from a set of words affected by typos.

[3] Names of foreign towns may occur in an Italian text both in their original orthographic form, or in Italian translation. In this case London is translated into "Londra".

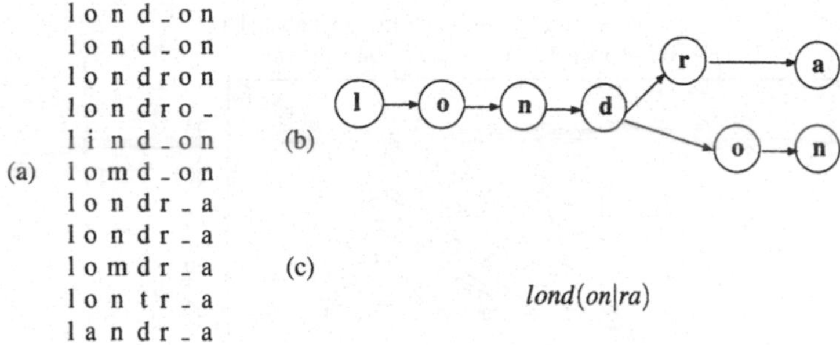

Fig. 3 Example of non-iterative expression obtained from the string set {london, londra, lomdra, lontra, londro, londron, rondon, lindon, london, lomdon, landra, londra, londla}. (a) Corresponding multi-alignment. (b) Retained alternatives. (c) Final regular expression.

5.2 ω_I Operator

Operator ω_I is complementary to ω_S, and explicitly searches for contiguous repetitions of a same substring inside a given string s. This is done by computing the self-correlation of the string similarity function. In fact, repeated substring instances are expected to be very similar each other (identical in absence of noise). Then, periods in self-similarity function locate where repetitions of a same substring occur. Let W_i and w_j denote a reference window and a sliding window (of equal size) on s beginning in position i and j, respectively. Let n be the length of s minus the length of W_i. Let, moreover, SC be a triangular matrix of size $n^2/2$; the notation $SC(i,j)$ will indicate the i, j element of SC. The basic self-correlation algorithm is the following:

Similarity self-correlation

1. Set i = 1
2. For j ranging from i to n evaluate $SC(i,j) = \int(W_i, w_j)$ between the substrings selected by W_i and w_j, respectively.
3. Set i = i+1
4. If i is smaller than n goto step 2, otherwise continue.
5. Detect chains of maxima on SC, where the maximum value is close to the maximum possible similarity value between two substrings W_i, w_j. A substring r of s, laying in between two consecutive maxima, is an iterated substring.
6. For every different iterated substring r construct a new hypothesis for an iterated episode.

The complexity of the algorithm is $O(n^2/2)$. However, it is easy to make the algorithm more efficient: when string similarity is close to zero, the windows can slide much faster than one position at-a-time.

The contour plot of the SC matrix of two different strings is reported in Figure 4 (for the sake of clarity, the entire square matrix has been computed).

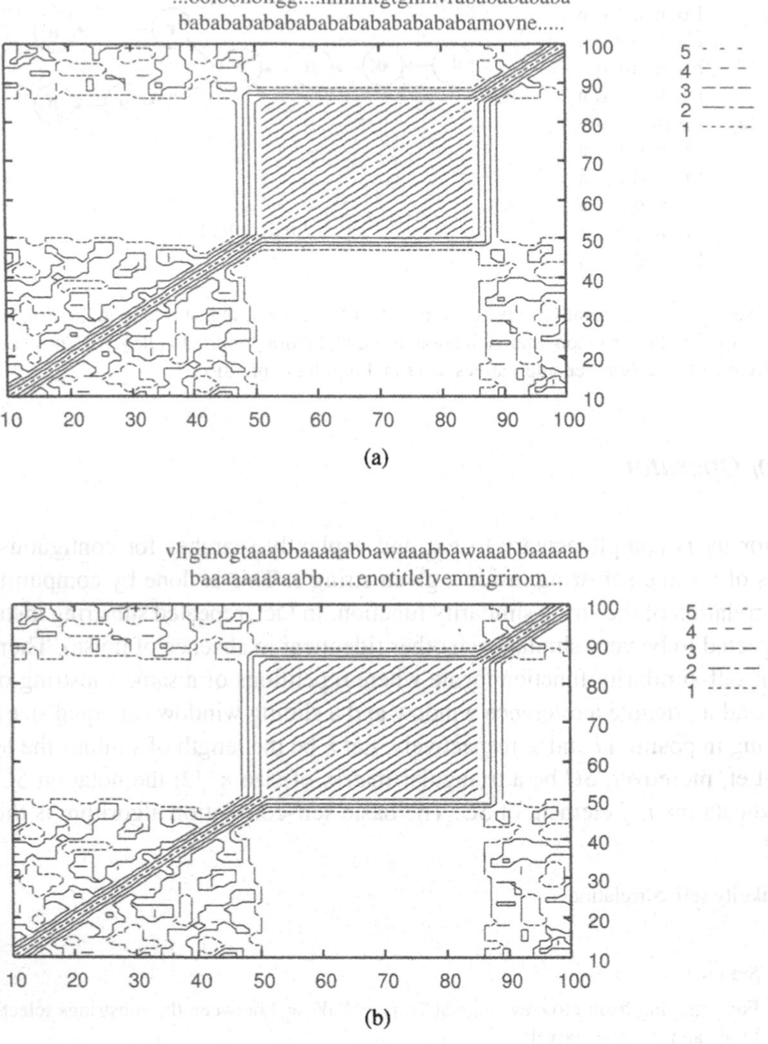

Fig. 4 Examples of similarity self-correlation patterns. (a) The repeated subsequence is "ab". (b) The repeated subsequence is "aaaaabb". In both sequences noise has been added. The rectangular patterns clearly indicate the region where the iterated subsequences are located.

5.3 *Basic learning cycle*

The basic learning cycle consists of four major steps:

1. Non-iterative episode detection. Episodes consisting of non-iterated substrings are detected and abstracted by applying operator ω_S.
2. Iterative episode detection. Episodes consisting of an iterated substring are detected and abstracted by applying operator ω_I.

3. Model construction. When necessary, an HMM is constructed for every abstracted episode.
4. Sequence abstraction. The input sequences are rewritten using as new alphabet the names of the abstract episodes.

Non-iterative episode detection. The core mechanism is represented by the abstraction operators ω_S. However, some preprocessing is required before applying the operator. In fact, ω_S takes in input a set S of strings that is constructed by applying a local alignment algorithm *LA* (see Section 4) followed by a clustering algorithm. More specifically, *LA* is repeatedly applied to a set of sequence pairs randomly sampled from the learning set $\mathcal{LS}$ and produces in output pairs of subsequences that exhibit strong similarity. It is expected that a frequent episode occurs in many pairs of sequences with minor differences from one instance to another. Then, episodes deriving from a same regular expression are easy to detect by using a clustering algorithm, which groups together most similar subsequences. The specific algorithm used for this step is not very much critical, because the refinement cycle allows possible errors to be recovered, as it will be explained later on. The currently used algorithm is an incremental variant of classical k-Means.

Finally, ω_S is applied to every cluster S obtained in this way, constructing a corresponding abstract event.

Iterative episode detection. In principle, the procedure described above is able to discover an iterated episode when the number of iterations is very similar in all sequences where the episode occurs. On the contrary, it does not work properly when the number of iterations is significantly different from one sequence to another, because the multi-alignment step fails. This problem is solved by operator ω_I, which is applied to a set of sequences sampled from $\mathcal{LS}$. All iterated episodes found in this way are collected into a set I. Afterwards, episodes characterized by an identical (or very similar) iterated substring are generalized to a unique abstract episode description: a common iterated subsequence is chosen, and the iteration limits are set in order to include all found instances. The abstract events constructed in this way are then added to the ones generated by operator ω_S.

Model Construction. This step is accomplished when an approximate matching based on HMM has been required and consists in constructing an HMM for every abstract event E characterized in the previous steps. Every expression $\mathcal{R}_E$ is converted into a HMM λ_E, and the sets of substrings, used to learn the regular expression describing the abstract events, are used to estimated the parameters of λ_E. The details of the algorithm can be found in [3, 14].

Sequence abstraction. Every sequence s in $\mathcal{LS}$ is rewritten into an abstracted sequence s' according to the following algorithm: s is scanned left-to-right searching for instances of episodes detected and abstracted in the previous steps. The presence of an episode E is decided by matching the corresponding regular expression $\mathcal{R}_E$ to s. Every time an instance is found, the *name* of E is appended to s'. However, conflicting interpretations of a same subsequence may exist. Conflict resolution is delayed to a second swept and, initially, a lattice is generated, containing all plausible hypotheses for episode instances. Afterward, lattices are processed extracting from each one the maximum scoring sequence, which includes the best scored hypotheses compatible with the given constraints. The default constraint is that hypotheses must not overlap. In the case a string similarity function of type (2) is used to match regular expressions, the score assigned to episode hypotheses is the value computed by the similarity function. Otherwise, if a matching based on HMM is used, the score of an event E is the probability assigned by the model λ_E. Portions of the string s not abstracted by any episode are abstracted as gaps and represented by a gap symbol.

The major steps of the basic cycle are illustrated through an example in Figure 5.

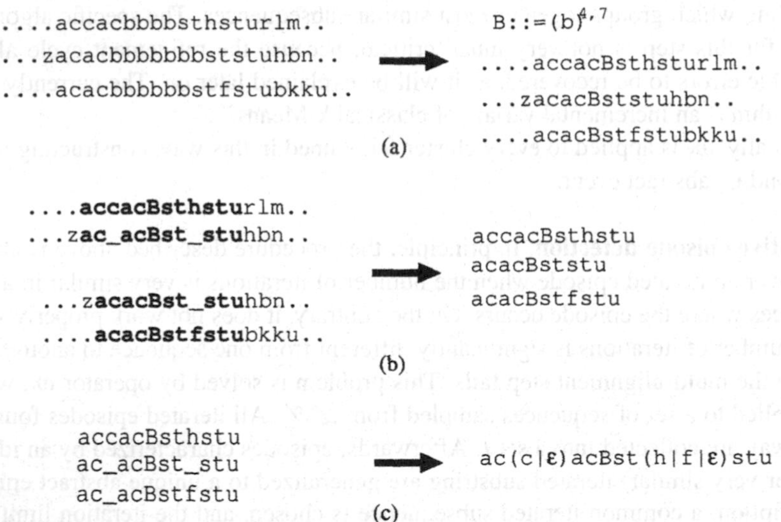

Fig. 5 Basic learning cycle example. (a) Iterated symbols are detected and replaced with the name of the corresponding regular expression. (b) Local alignments are detected and similar substrings are clustered together. (c) From the multiple alignment of elements in a same cluster a regular expression is obtained.

5.4 Refinement cycle

The refinement cycle may be activated at the abstraction layer L_i every time new episodes are detected and modeled at a level higher than i. The reason for doing it is illustrated in Figure 6. When an episode E is hypothesized and characterized at an abstraction level L_i, the context, i.e, the presence of other episodes before or after E, is not considered. Nevertheless, the context is considered later on when the episodes of layer L_i are linked together into an episode at level L_{i+1}. This means that some instances of E may be not included in any higher level episode and will be considered spurious. Nevertheless, such instances were included in the cluster

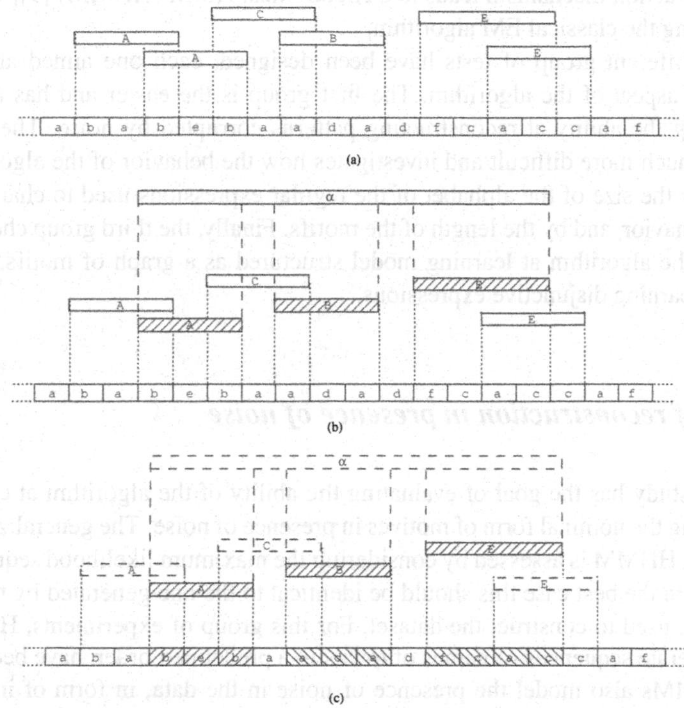

Fig. 6 The refinement step. (a) Episode lattice. (b) Some hypothesized events in (a) are not considered for a new episode. (c) Only the retained instances are used to re-train the episode model.

used to build up the regular expression describing E. In the refinement step, the regular expression describing E are re-learned using only the instances that have been retained.

As episode instances are detected using one of the approximate matching algorithms described in in Section 4, the outcome of the refining cycle heavily depends on it. Therefore, using a similarity function or an HMM can produce quite different results.

6 Evaluation on Artificial Traces

This section provides an extensive evaluation of the learning algorithm using artificial traces. More specifically, the algorithm has been validated using artificial sequence sets, where known patterns have been hidden. The challenge for the algorithm was to reconstruct the original model from the data.

It is worth noticing that, according with section 5 we use string similarity in the basic learning cycle, whereas, in the refinement cycle, regular expressions are translated into HMMs. More specifically, the cascade of regular expressions generated by the abstraction mechanism leads to a Hierarchical HMM (HHMM) [9], which is trained using the classical EM algorithm.

Three different group of tests have been designed, each one aimed at testing a different aspect of the algorithm. The first group is the easier and has the goal of checking the ability at reconstructing patterns corrupted by noise. The second group, is much more difficult and investigates how the behavior of the algorithm is affected by the size of the alphabet of the regular expressions used to characterize process behavior, and by the length of the motifs. Finally, the third group checks the ability of the algorithm at learning model structured as a graph of motifs, i.e. the ability at learning disjunctive expressions.

6.1 Motif reconstruction in presence of noise

This case study has the goal of evaluating the ability of the algorithm at correctly generalizing the nominal form of motives in presence of noise. The generalization of the learned HHMM is assessed by considering the maximum likelihood sequence, it generates. In the best case this should be identical to the one generated by the original model, used to construct the dataset. For this group of experiments, HHMMs, which generate sequences of names of towns in a predefined order, have been used. Such HHMMs also model the presence of noise in the data, in form of insertion, deletion and substitution errors. The gaps between the names are filled by symbols randomly chosen in the alphabet defined by the union of the letters contained in the names. Moreover, random subsequences, up to 15 characters long, have been added at the beginning and the end of each sequence. The global length of the sequences ranges from 60 to 120 characters. The difficulty of the task has been controlled by varying the degree of noise.

One set of experiments has been designed in this framework. More specifically, a sequence of problems has been generated varying the number of words ($5 \leq w \leq 8$), the word length ($5 \leq L \leq 8$) and the noise level ($N \in \{0\%, 5\%, 10\%, 15\%\}$. For every triple $< w, L, N >$, 10 different datasets has been generated for a total of 640 learning problems.

The most important results are summarized in Table 6.1. The error rate is evaluated as the edit distance (i.e. the minimum number of corrections) between the maximum likelihood sequence (maximum consensus) generated by the Viterbi algorithm [10] from the original HHMM and the one generated from the learned HHMM. When, an entire word is missed, the corresponding error is set equal to the its length. Experiments in table 6.1, reporting an error rate much higher than the others, have missed words. In all cases, the learning cycle has been iterated twice,

		Error rate after learning cycle				Error rate after refinement			
		Noise Level				Noise Level			
w	L	0%	5%	10 %	15%	0%	5%	10 %	15%
5	5	0.03	0.06	0.06	0.08	0.04	0.04	0.04	0.04
5	6	0.06	0.12	0.12	0.09	0.03	0.03	0.03	0.03
5	7	0.00	0.02	0.03	0.05	0.00	0.00	0.02	0.00
5	8	0.02	0.04	0.02	0.04	0.00	0.00	0.00	0.00
6	5	0.06	0.11	0.04	0.04	0.10	0.06	0.00	0.03
6	6	0.06	0.10	0.06	0.19	0.05	0.00	0.00	0.00
6	7	0.03	0.03	0.02	0.05	0.02	0.00	0.00	0.00
6	8	0.01	0.04	0.05	0.05	0.00	0.00	0.04	0.00
7	5	0.02	0.05	0.11	0.17	0.02	0.05	0.01	0.10
7	6	0.01	0.10	0.05	0.14	0.04	0.02	0.05	0.04
7	7	0.00	0.06	0.02	0.05	0.00	0.00	0.02	0.05
7	8	0.01	0.06	0.09	0.11	0.01	0.00	0.09	0.09
8	5	0.00	0.00	0.01	0.00	0.00	0.00	0.01	0.00
8	6	0.03	0.08	0.10	0.14	0.03	0.06	0.06	0.14
8	7	0.00	0.01	0.01	0.08	0.00	0.00	0.00	0.00
8	8	0.01	0.03	0.08	0.09	0.01	0.00	0.00	0.0

Table 1 Performances obtained with *town names* dataset. The sequence length ranges from 60 to 140 characters. The CPU time, for solving a problem, ranges from 42 to 83 seconds on a Pentium IV 2.4Ghz.

as explained in Section 5. It appears that the average error rate after the refinement cycle decreases of about 50% with respect to the basic learning cycle.

From Table 6.1, it appears that the model extracted from the data without noise is almost error free. Moreover, the method seems to be little sensitive with respect to the sequence length while the error rate roughly increases proportionally to the noise in the original model (the 15% of noise corresponds to an average error rate of about 19%).

6.2 Assessing the influence of alphabet size and motif length

Two sets of target HHMMs have been constructed and used to generate a large number of sequence datasets. The HHMMs in the first set contain three motifs separated by two gaps, plus an initial and a final random gap. The HHMMs in the second group have a similar, but more complex, structure. They encode a sequence of six motifs separated by 5 gaps.

Using a semi-automated procedure, 768 models (384 for each group) have been constructed; they differ in the nominal length of the motifs (5, 8, 11, 15 symbols), in the cardinality of the alphabet (4, 7, 14, 25 symbols) and in the probability distribution controlling transitions from state to state and symbol emission inside states. More specifically, four classes of normal distributions (N0, N1, N2, N3) of increasing variance have been considered. For every setting of the above parameters three different models have been generated. They differ one from another for a small perturbation in the center locations of the probability distributions. Finally, for every model, a learning set and a test set, each containing 100 sequences, have been generated.

The sequence length ranges from 600 to 2000. It is worth noticing that, considering the quite short motif length, the coding part is much smaller than the non coding part appearing in the gaps.

The perturbation effect on the sequences, due to the increase of the standard deviation in the probability distribution, has been evaluated as the average edit distance δ_E between the motif instances occurring in a dataset and the maximum likelihood instance, computed from the generative model by the Viterbi algorithm. The following average values have been obtained for the four distributions:

Class:	N0	N1	N2	N3
δ_E:	0.0	0.11	0.19	0.28

Notice that also the gap length spread is strongly affected by the increase in the distribution spread, even if it is not accounted for in the measures reported above.

In order to evaluate the accuracy of the algorithm, let λ_D be the model learned by the algorithm, and λ_T the target model, used to generate the data. Let moreover (λ_D) denote the test set tagged with λ_D and (λ_T) the one tagged with λ_T. The error $Err(\lambda_D)$ of λ_D on is measured as the average edit distance between the motif instances in (λ_D) and the motifs instances in (λ_T), divided by the length of the motif instances in (λ_T).

The performances obtained on the two groups of datasets are similar, even though the ones on the first group are slightly better. The results are reported in Figures 7 and 8.

In presence of noise, it appear that $Err(\lambda_D)$ increases when the alphabet cardinality and the motif length decrease, as well as when the standard deviation of the target model increases, as it is reasonable to expect. In fact, when the alphabet is small, it is more difficult to distinguish real motifs from apparent regularities due to randomness. For the same reason, short motifs are more difficult to detect. Then, the performance degradation is due, in general, to the failure of the algorithm, which searches for new motifs without finding the correct ones. However, it is surprising that in some cases the accuracy decreases again when motifs become longer than 11 symbols. A possible explanation is the following: when the average length of a motif instances increases in presence of noise, the number of alternative sequences, among which the correct instances of the motif are to be identified, increases, smoothing thus the similarity among strings and increasing confusion.

The decrease in the similarity between the target model and the discovered model, when the probability distributions have long tails, is also in agreement with what one expects. Nevertheless, it is interesting that the error rate remains comparable to the level of noise of the dataset. It is also worth noticing that the performances evaluated on the test sets and on the learning sets are almost identical, as their differences are not statistically significant.

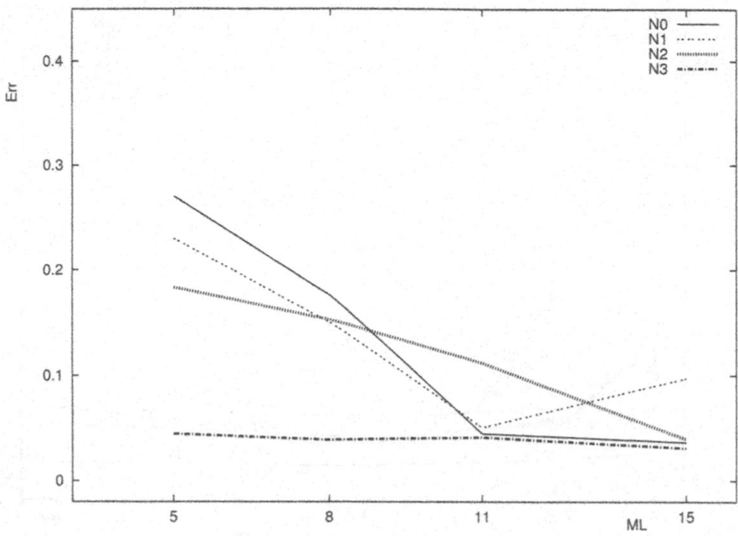

(Group 1)

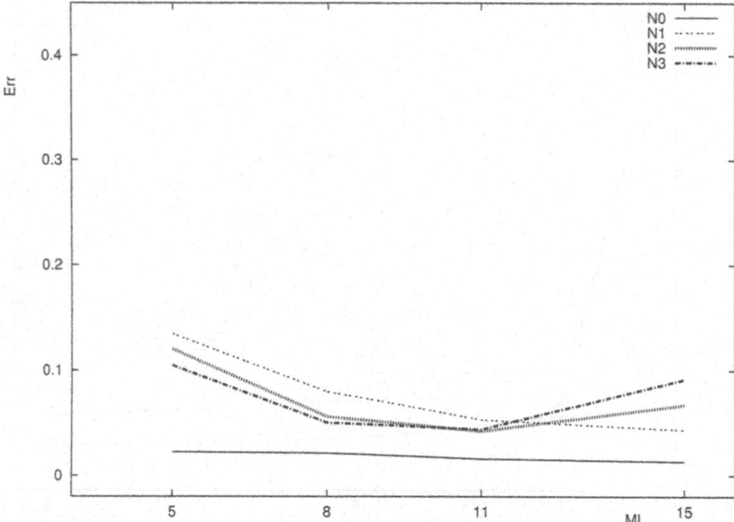

(Group 2)

Fig. 7 Algorithms performances on the sequences generated by models in Group 1 (3 motifs) and in Group 2 (6 motifs). The plot reports the error $Err = Err(\lambda_D)$ on the test set versus the motif length ML $\in (5, 8, 11, 15)$.

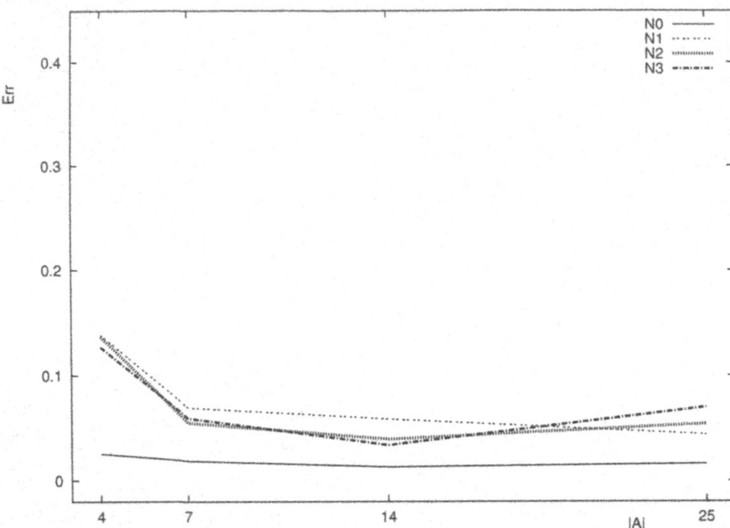

(Group 1)

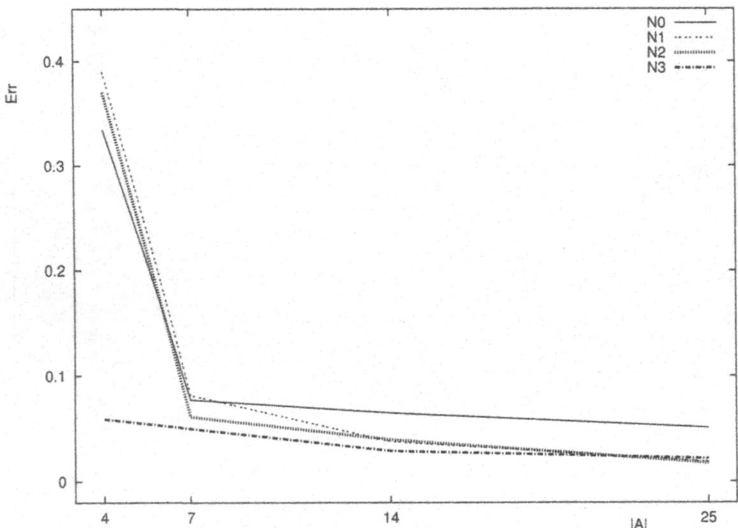

(Group 2)

Fig. 8 Algorithm performances on the sequences generated by models in Group 1 (3 motifs) and in Group 2 (6 motifs). The plot reports the error $Err = Err(\lambda_D)$ on the test set versus the alphabet cardinality $|\mathbf{A}| \in (5,7,14,25)$.

Finally, the system always converged to a stable model in a number of steps ranging from 11 to 35. The computational complexity for learning a model corresponding to a problem of the second group corresponds to a cpu time ranging from 30 to 40 minutes on a Opteron.

6.3 Discovering graph structured patterns

Aims of this case study is to check the ability of the algorithm at reconstructing patterns described by disjunctive expressions.

The testing procedure is similar to the one used in the previous case study. The difference is that, in this case target HHMMs have a a graph like structure at the abstract level, instead of a sequential one. Moreover, spurious motifs have been added to all sequences filling the gaps between consecutive motives, in order to make the task more difficult.

Three target HHMMs, each one constructed according to a two level hierarchy have been used to generate a set of 72 learning tasks (24 for every model). Every learning task consists of a set of 330 traces. The 90% of the sequences contain an instance of a target HHMM that should be discovered by the learning program, whereas the 10% contain sequences of spurious motives non generated by the target HHMM. The sequence length ranges from 80 to 120 elementary events.

The structure for the high level of the three models is shown in Figure 9. Every state at the high level emits a string (motif) generated by an HMM at the low level, indicated with a capital letter (A,B,C,D,E). A different HMM (F) has been used to generate spurious motives. The gaps between motives have been filled with subsequences containing random noise.

In this case, the evaluation of the results has been done on the base of the *bayes classification error* between two (or more HHMMs). Formally, given two HHMMs, λ_1 and λ_2, and the set L of all possible traces, which can be generated by λ_1 or λ_2, the Bayes classification error $C(\lambda_1,\lambda_2)$ is defined as:

$$C(\lambda_1,\lambda_2) = \sum_{x \in L} [min(p(\lambda_1|x), p(\lambda_2|x)]p(x) \tag{3}$$

being $p(\lambda_1|x)$ and $p(\lambda_2|x)$ the probability that, given a trace x, it has been generated by λ_1 or λ_2, respectively, and $p(x)$ the a priori probability of x. We notice that the upper-bound for $C(\lambda_1,\lambda_2)$is 0.5, when λ_1 and λ_2 are identical. In general, for N models, the upper-bound is given by the expression $1-1/N$.

In general, expression (3) cannot be computed because L is too large. Therefore, we adopted an approximate evaluation made using a subset of L stochastically sampled.

The bayes classification error 3 intervenes in the evaluation procedure in two different ways. A first way is to measure the quality of the learned models. A perfect learner should learn a model identical to the one used to generate the traces. There-

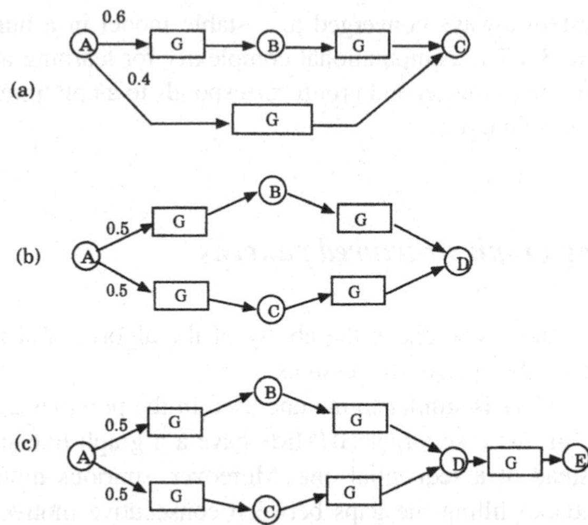

Fig. 9 HHMM used for evaluation on artificial data

fore, a learned model has to be considered as much accurate as much close to 0.5 the classification error, between it and the original model, is.

The second way is to estimate the difficulty of the learning task. It is reasonable to assume that the difficulty of identifying a model hidden in a set of traces grows along with the similarity among the motives belonging to the model and the spurious motives. Moreover, the difficulty grows also when the motives belonging to a same model become similar each other, because it becomes more difficult to discover the correspondence between a motif and the hidden state it has been emitted from. Therefore, the experimentation has been run using different versions of models A, B, C, D, E, F with different bayes classification error among them.

The results obtained under three different conditions of difficulty are summarized in Table 6.3. The similarity between the six kinds of motives has been varied from 0.2 to 0.55. For every setting, the experiment has been repeated 8 times for each one of the three models. The reported results are the average over the 8 runs. In all cases, the bayes classification error has been estimated using a set of traces obtained by collecting 500 sequences generated from each one of the models involved in the specific comparison.

Motives	0.2	0.4	0.55
Model (a)	0.48	0.46	0.45
Model (b)	0.47	0.42	0.42
Model (c)	0.43	0.42	0.41

Table 2 Bayes classification error between the target model and the learned model, versus the confusion among the basic motives (reported in the first line).

It appears that the performances suffer very little from the similarity among the motif models, and in all cases, the similarity between the original model and the learned model is very high ($C(\lambda_1, \lambda_2)$, is close to 0.5).

7 User Profiling

User profiling is widely used to detect intrusions in computer or in telephony networks. The possibility of automatically building a profile for *users* or for *network services* reflecting their temporal behavior would offer a significant help to the deployment of adaptive Intrusion Detection Systems (IDSs) [19].

The experiments described in the following investigate the possibility of automatically constructing a user profile from the logs of her/his activity. The task that has been selected consists in learning to identify a user from his/her typing style on a keyboard. The basic assumption is that every user has a different way of typing, which becomes particularly evident when he/she types words which are specifically important for him/her, such as his/her own name, or words referring to his/her job. This application has not been selected with the goal of challenging the results previously obtained [17, 2, 4], but because it is highly representative of the class of tasks we tackle, and the data are easy to acquire. In other words, if the methodology described so far succeeds in building up a HHMM for this kind of user profiling, it is likely that it will succeed in other cases as well. Two experiments, described in the following subsections, have been performed.

7.1 Key Phrase Typing Model

In the first experiment, the goal was to construct a model for a user typing a key phrase, discriminant enough to recognize the user among others. A selected sentence of 22 syllables has been typed many times on the same keyboard, while a transparent program recorded, for every typed key, the duration of each stroke and the delay between two consecutive strokes. Then, every repetition of the sentence generated a sequence, where every key stroke corresponded to an atomic event; the delay between two strokes was represented as a gap, whose length was set to the corresponding duration. Four volunteers provided 140 sequences each, and, for every one of them, a model has been built up using 100 traces (for each user) as learning set. The four learned models have been tested against the remaining 160 traces. For each model λ and for each trace s, the probability of λ generating s has been computed using the forward-backward algorithm [26]. Then, s has been assigned to the model with the highest probability. The results reported only one commission error and two rejection errors (no decision taken), when a trace was not recognized by any one of the models. The models were organized on two levels. The first one contained from 10 to 12 episodes separated by gaps. Even if the recognition rate is high, it does not seem realistic to use the acquired models to build up a deployable authentication system. In fact, a user profile based on a key phrase only is too restricted. The positive result is that a Markov model of a user typing on a keyboard seems to be appropriate.

7.2 Text Typing Model

The second experiment addressed the more general problem of modeling a user during a text editing activity. A corpus of several paragraphs, selected from newspapers and books, has been collected. The total number of words was 2280, and the number of typed keys 14273. Again, four users typed the entire corpus in several different sessions, without any constraint, in order not to modify their natural typing style.

In this kind of application, a user model should be centered not on the specific words he/she types, but on the user typing style, which, in turns, depends on the position of the keys on the keyboard. Therefore, a standard keyboard subdivision into regions, used in dactylography, has been considered, and, on this basis, keys have been grouped into 10 classes. In this way, transition from one region of the keyboard to another should be emphasized. Afterwards, the sequences generated during a typing session have been rewritten by replacing every character with the name of the class it has been assigned to. Moreover, only the gap duration between strokes has been considered, disregarding the length of the key strokes themselves. Finally, long sequences deriving from an editing session have been segmented into shorter sequences, setting the breakpoint in correspondence of long gaps. The idea is that typical delays due to the user typing style cannot go beyond a given limit. Longer delays are imputable to different reasons, such as thinking or change of the focus of attention. In this way a set of about 1350 subsequences has been obtained. For every user, a subset of 220 subsequences has been extracted in order to learn the corresponding model. The remaining ones have been used for testing. As in the previous case, the probability of generating each one of the sequences in the test set has been computed for every model.

The results are summarized in Figure 10, where the distribution of the scoring rate on the test sequences is reported for every model. The scoring rate is measured in *log odds*[4]. The continuous line, labelled "Pos", represents the distribution of the scores assigned to the correct model (user), whereas the other one, labelled "Neg", represents the distribution of the scores assigned to all other models (users), considered together . The sequences on the extreme left have been rejected. It is evident from the figure that sequences belonging to the model are well separated from the other ones. Referring to the data in the test set, a monitoring system using the simple rule that, in a set of three consecutive sequences generated by a user at least two must have a score higher than '0', would give a perfect discrimination of the legal user without rising false alarms.

[4] The logarithm of the ratio between the probability that the observed sequence is generated by the model and the probability that it is generated by a random process.

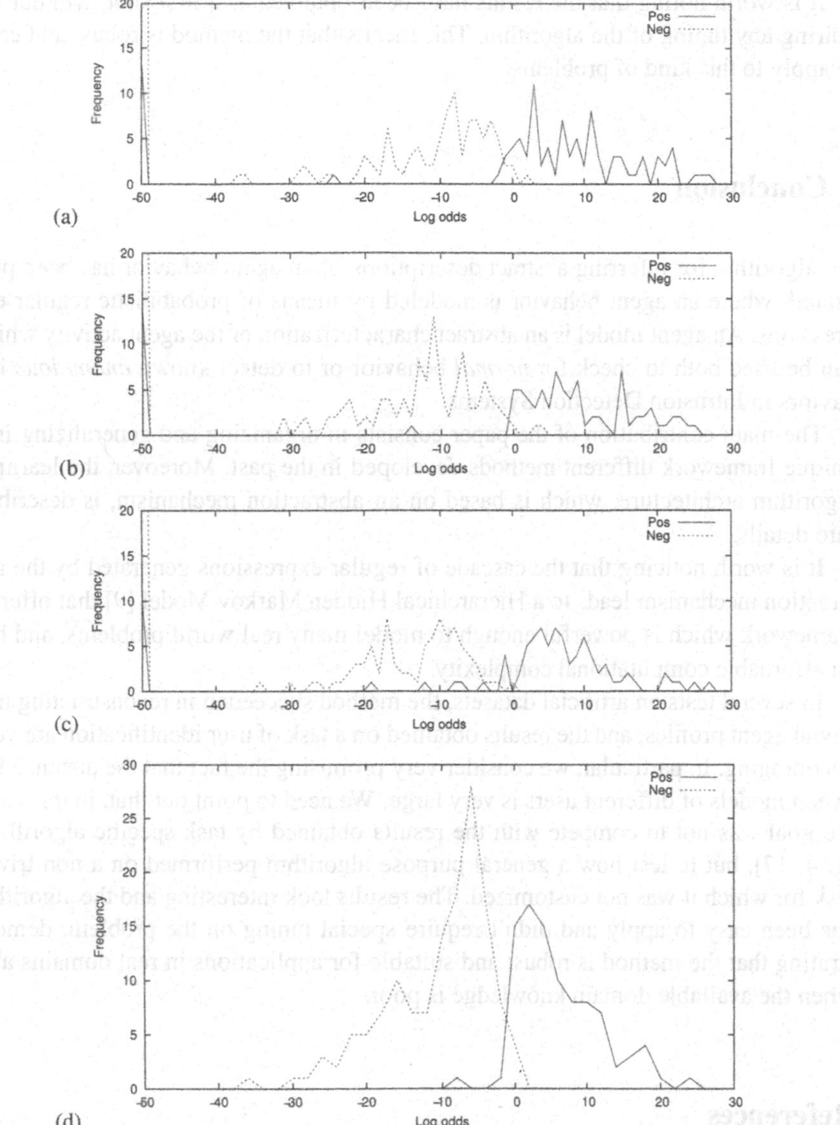

Fig. 10 User profiling statistics. Graphs (a), (b), (c) and (d) refer each one to a different user profile. The continuous line "Pos" reports the scoring, measured in log odds, for the the sequences belonging to the profile. The dotted line "Neg" refers to the sequences not belonging to the profile.

It is worth noting that the results have been obtained as a first shot, without requiring any tuning of the algorithm. This means that the method is robust and easy to apply to this kind of problems.

8 Conclusion

An algorithm for inferring abstract descriptions of an agent behavior has been presented, where an agent behavior is modeled by means of probabilistic regular expressions. An agent model is an abstract characterization of the agent activity which can be used both to check for *normal* behavior or to detect known *anomalous* behaviors in Intrusion Detection Systems.

The main contribution of the paper consists in organizing and generalizing in a unique framework different methods developed in the past. Moreover, the learning algorithm architecture, which is based on an abstraction mechanism, is described into details.

It is worth noticing that the cascade of regular expressions generated by the abstraction mechanism leads to a Hierarchical Hidden Markov Model [9] that offers a framework which is powerful enough to model many real world problems, and has an affordable computational complexity.

In several tests on artificial datasets, the method succeeded in reconstructing non trivial agent profiles, and the results obtained on a task of user identification are very encouraging. In particular, we consider very promising the fact that the distance between models of different users is very large. We need to point out that, in this case, the goal was not to compete with the results obtained by task specific algorithms [2, 4, 17], but to test how a general purpose algorithm performed on a non trivial task for which it was not customized. The results look interesting and the algorithm has been easy to apply and didn't require special tuning on the problem, demonstrating that the method is robust and suitable for applications in real domains also when the available domain knowledge is poor.

References

1. D. Angluin. Queries and concept learning. *Machine Learning*, 2(4):319342, 1988.
2. S. Bleha, C. Slivinsky, and B. Hussein. Computer-access security systems using keystroke dynamics. *IEEE Transactions on Pattern Analysis and Machine Intelligence*, PAMI-12(12):1217–1222, 1990.
3. M. Botta, U. Galassi, and A.Giordana. Learning complex and sparse events in long sequences. In *Proceedings of the European Conference on Artificial Intelligence, ECAI-04*, Valencia, Spain, August 2004.
4. M. Brown and S.J. Rogers. User identification via keystroke characteristics of typed names using neural networks. *International Journal of Man-Machine Studies*, 39:999–1014, 1993.
5. F. Denis. Learning regular languages from simple positive examples. *Machine Learning*, 44(1/2):37–66, 2001.

6. R. Durbin, S. Eddy, A. Krogh, and G. Mitchison. *Biological sequence analysis*. Cambridge University Press, 1998.
7. J. L. Elman. Distributed representations, simple recurrent networks, and grammatical structure. *Machine Learning*, 7:195–225, 1991.
8. T. Fawcett and F. Provost. Adaptive fraud detection. *Data Mining and Knowledge Discovery Journal*, 1:291–316, 1997.
9. S. Fine, Y Singer, and N. Tishby. The hierarchical hidden markov model: Analysis and applications. *Machine Learning*, 32:41–62, 1998.
10. G. D. Forney. The viterbi algorithm. *Proceedings of IEEE*, 61:268–278, 1973.
11. P. Frasconi and Y. Bengio. An em approach to grammatical inference: iputo/output hmms. In *Proceedings of International Conference on Pattern Recognition, ICPR-94*, 1994.
12. K. S. Fu. *Syntactic pattern recognition and applications*. Prentice Hall, 1982.
13. K.S. FU and T.L. Booth. Grammatical inference: Introduction and survey (part 1). *IEEE Transaction on System, Men and Cybernetics*, 5:85–111, 1975.
14. U. Galassi, A. Giordana, and D. Mendola. Learning user profiles from traces. *Technical report TR-INF-2005-04-02-UNIPMN*, 2005.
15. D. Gussfield. *Algorithms on Strings, Trees, and Sequences*. Cambridge University Press, 1997.
16. J.E. Hopcroft and J.D. Ullman. *Formal languages and their relation to automata*. Addison-Wesley, 1969.
17. R. Joyce and G. Gupta. User authorization based on keystroke latencies. *Communications of the ACM*, 33(2):168–176, 1990.
18. W. Lee and S.J Stolfo. Data mining approaches for intrusion detection. In *Proceedings of the Seventh USENIX Security Symposium (SECURITY '98)*, San Antonio, TX, 1998.
19. W. Lee, w. Fan, M. Miller, S.J. Stolfo, and E. Zadok. Toward cost-sensitive modeling for intrusion detection and response. *Journal of Computer Security*, 10:5 – 22, 2002.
20. E.W. Myers and W. Miller. Approximate matching of regular expressions. *Bulletin of Mathematical Biology*, 51(2):5 – 37, 1989.
21. R. G. Parekh and V. G. Honavar. Learning DFA from simple examples. In *Proceedings of the 8th International Workshop on Algorithmic Learning Theory (ALT'97), Lecture Notes in Artificial Intelligence*, volume 1316, pages 116 –131, Sendai, Japan, 1997. Springer.
22. Rajesh Parekh, Codrin Nichitiu, and Vasant Honavar. A polynomial time incremental algorithm for learning DFA. *Lecture Notes in Computer Science*, 1433:37–50, 1998.
23. M. Pazzani and D. Billsus. Learning and revising user profiles: The identification of interesting web sites. *Machine Learning*, 27:313331, 1997.
24. S. Porat and J. Feldman. Learning automata from ordered examples. *Machine Learning*, 7:109–138, 1991.
25. P.Garca and E.Vidal. Inference of k-testable languages in the strict sense and applications to syntactic pattern recognition. *IEEE Transactions on Pattern Analysis and Machine Intelligence*, 12(9):920–925, 1990.
26. L.R. Rabiner. A tutorial on hidden markov models and selected applications in speech recognition. *Proceedings of IEEE*, 77(2):257–286, 1989.
27. L. Saitta, editor. *The abstraction paths, Special issue of the Philosophical Transactions of Royal Society, Series B*. 2003.
28. S.j. Stolfo, W. Fan, W. Lee, A. Prodromidis, and P. Chan. Cost-based modeling for fraud and intrusion detection: Results from the jam project. In *Proceedings of the 2000 DARPA Information Survivability Conference and Exposition (DISCEX '00)*, 2000.

Correlation Analysis of Intrusion Alerts

Dingbang Xu and Peng Ning

Abstract To defend against computer and network attacks, multiple, possibly complementary security devices such as intrusion detection systems (IDSs) and firewalls are widely deployed to monitor networks and hosts, and may flag alerts when suspicious events are observed. However, at present, security systems such as IDSs still suffer from several limitations. First, IDSs may flag a large volume of alerts everyday, overwhelming security administrators. Second, among the alerts reported by the IDSs, a possibly large proportion of false alerts (i.e., false positives) are mixed with true ones, and it is usually difficult for human users to differentiate between them. Third, there are certain attacks that may not be detected by IDSs. That is, IDSs may miss attacks. To address these challenges and learn the network security threats, it is necessary to perform alert correlation.

Alert correlation focuses on discovering various relationships between individual alerts. This chapter gives an overview of current alert correlation techniques. Existing alert correlation techniques can be roughly divided into four categories: (1) The approaches based on similarity between alert attributes, which group alerts through computing attribute similarity values; (2) the techniques based on predefined attack scenarios, which construct attack scenarios through matching alerts to predefined scenario templates; (3) the methods based on prerequisites (i.e., pre-conditions) and consequences (i.e., post-conditions) of attacks, which build attack scenarios through matching the consequences of earlier attacks with the prerequisites of later attacks; and (4) the approaches based on multiple information sources, which integrate different types of information and may further perform reasoning based on IDS alerts and other information. In each category, representative approaches and systems are discussed. In addition, this chapter also addresses privacy issues in alert correlation.

Peng Ning
North Carolina State University, Department of Computer Science, Raleigh, NC 27695-8206 e-mail: pning@ncsu.edu

Dingbang Xu
Governors State University, 1 University Parkway, University Park, Illinois 60466-0975 e-mail: d-xu@govst.edu

1 Introduction

Intrusion detection has been an active research field for more than 25 years since Anderson published his seminal work on *Computer Security Threat Monitoring and Surveillance* [2]. Intrusion detection techniques can be roughly classified into two categories: *misuse detection* and *anomaly detection*. To perform misuse detection, a repository of all known attack patterns is necessary. Misuse detection systems examine security events to see whether they match these attack patterns. If they are, the corresponding security events are flagged as attacks. To perform anomaly detection, a repository of normal behaviors for each entity (e.g., each user) is usually necessary. Anomaly detection systems monitor each entity's activity, and once they find an entity's behavior significantly deviates from the corresponding normal profile, an alert is generated.

Since Anderson's report, many intrusion detection systems (IDSs) have been designed, implemented and deployed into networks. They are a line of defense to protect digital assets. Though many novel designs and improvements have been proposed, at present, intrusion detection systems still suffer from a few drawbacks:

- Intrusion detections systems may flag thousands of alerts everyday, thus overwhelming security officers. For example, our own experience shows that 325,968 alerts were reported when a Snort box was deployed for 6 days in a subnet hosting a teaching lab on a campus network.
- Among all the alerts reported by IDSs, false alerts (i.e., false positives) are mixed with true alerts. In addition, it is very possible that a large percentage of alerts are false alerts. For example, Julish [18, 19] and other researchers pointed out that up to 99% of alerts could be false positives. This may make the alert investigation very challenging.
- At present, IDSs cannot guarantee the detection of all attacks. In other words, they may miss some attacks, which could be critical for security officers to understand the current security threats.

These limitations of IDSs make security investigation not only time-consuming, but also error-prone. It is very challenging for security officers to fully learn the security threats in their networks as well as over the Internet.

To address these challenges, various alert correlation analysis techniques have been proposed in recent years. For example, to reduce the number of alerts reported to security officers, Valdes and Skinner [34] propose probabilistic alert correlation, and Debar and Wespi [11] propose techniques to identify *duplicates* and perform aggregation based on different *situations*. To address the false positive issue, Porras, Fong, and Valdes [30] propose mission-impact-based approach, where alerts are examined through checking vulnerability and host configuration information, and Zhai et al. [39] propose to use Bayesian networks to perform reasoning on complementary security evidence, and thus to potentially reduce false alert rates. To mitigate the missed attacks problem, Ning and Xu [27] propose to integrate complementary correlation methods, and perform hypothesizing, reasoning and filtering to look for potentially missed attacks, and Cuppens and Miège [7] propose to apply *abductive correlation*.

To help us better understand these alert correlation methods, we roughly classify these methods into four categories. (1) The approaches based on similarity between alert attributes. These approaches can group alerts through computing attribute similarity values. An example method in this category is [34]. (2) The techniques based on predefined attack scenarios. These techniques construct attack scenarios through matching alerts to predefined scenario templates. An example method in this category is [23]. (3) The methods based on prerequisites (i.e., pre-conditions) and consequences (i.e., post-conditions) of attacks. These methods build attack scenarios through matching the consequences of earlier attacks with the prerequisites of later attacks. Example methods in this category are [25, 7]. (4)The approaches based on multiple information sources. These approaches provide frameworks to model different types of information and may further perform reasoning based on IDS alerts and other information. Example methods in this category are [30, 24].

The reminder of this chapter is organized as follows. In Section 2, we discuss the similarity based correlation approaches. In Section 3, we present predefined attack scenarios based approaches. In Section 4, we survey the prerequisites and consequences based methods, and in Section 5, we discuss the multiple information sources based approaches. In each of these four sections, the typical approaches in the corresponding category are also presented. Furthermore, we notice that the privacy issues have gained a lot of interests in the field of alert correlation, so in Section 6, we discuss the privacy issues. And finally, in Section 7, we conclude this chapter.

2 Approaches Based on Similarity between Alert Attributes

IDSs may flag alerts when suspicious events are observed. Each alert usually has several attributes associated with it. For example, network based IDSs report the suspicious event's source IP address, source port number, destination IP address, destination port number, and timestamps information. Based on these attribute values, some similarity based alert correlation approaches first compute how similar two or more alerts are, and then group alerts together based on these computed similarity values. These methods are closely related to data clustering techniques in data mining [15, 20]. Approaches in this category can potentially reduce the number of alerts reported to the security officers, because a group of similar alerts may correspond to the same attack or attack trend.

To help us understand this idea, let us take a look at an example. Assume there are two network based IDSs: Snort [3] and RealSecure network sensor [17]. Further assume that there is an FTP attack in the network, and this attack is detected by both Snort and RealSecure network sensor. For the alerts reported by Snort and RealSecure, it is very likely that they have the same source IP addresses, the same destination IP addresses, identical destination port numbers, identical or very close timestamps, etc. Through identifying these similar attribute values, security officers may realize that these alerts correspond to the same attack. Notice that in these correlation approaches, how to define similarity measures usually is one of the major focuses. There are several different similarity measures being proposed. For example, Julisch [18] defines similarity/dissimilarity measures based on generalization hierarchies. In the following, we discuss some typical approaches in this category.

2.1 Probabilistic Alert Correlation

In 2001, Valdes and Skinner [34] proposed a probabilistic approach to performing alert correlation. One of the main focuses in their approach is to compute the similarity values among alerts. In their approach, heterogeneous sensors such as network based IDSs as well as host based IDSs are considered. Each alert reported by IDSs is assumed to have several features, for example, target hosts and ports, and timestamps. Since IDS sensors are heterogeneous, it is not necessary that alerts reported by different sensors have the same list of features. Thus to compute the similarity among different alerts, Valdes and Skinner propose to first identify the common (overlapping) features. Next, this approach specifies *expectation of similarity* and *minimum similarity* for the features. In addition, for each feature, a similarity function is defined, which will be used to calculate the similarity value for the same feature among different alerts. Notice that feature similarity functions may be defined through various criteria. For example, the similarity between IP addresses may consider if they are identical or from the same subnet; if a feature has a list of values (e.g., all open ports reported by a scanning attack), the overlapping values among multiple lists can be considered when calculating similarity. The similarity value is between 0 to 1.

For two alerts with several common features, their overall similarity is a function related to similarity values for individual features, the expectation of similarity for each feature, and the minimum similarity for each feature. Specifically, for each feature, if their similarity value is less than the corresponding predefined minimum similarity, then the overall similarity is 0; if the minimum similarity is satisfied, then the overall similarity is the weighted average of similarity values for those common features, where the weights are the expected similarity values for the corresponding features. The formula for overall similarity computation [34] is defined as

$$SIM(A,B) = \frac{\sum_{i=1}^{n} SIM(A_i,B_i) \times E_i}{\sum_{i=1}^{n} E_i},$$

where A and B are two alerts have n features in common, A_i and B_i are values for the common feature i in A and B, respectively, $SIM(A_i,B_i)$ is the similarity between A_i and B_i, and E_i is the expected similarity value for feature i.

In order to evaluate this approach, Valdes and Skinner performed experiments in a live environment as well as a simulated network. As an example to show the effectiveness of the proposed approach, in the live environment experiment, IDS sensors reported 4439 alerts, and their approach correlated them into only 604.

2.2 Statistical Anomaly Analysis to Detect Stealthy Portscans

In 2002, Staniford, Hoagland and McAlerney [32] proposed an approach to automatically detecting stealthy portscans. Although their approach focuses on port scanning detection, it can be extended to correlate other security events.

In this approach, network packets are the primary information to be dealt with. To detect port scanning, feature data such as source IP addresses, destination IP addresses, and destination ports are extracted from network packets. The combination of these features are also called events. The detection of port scanning can be performed into two steps: anomalous event identification and portscan correlation. In the first step, based on the distribution of network traffic, an *anomaly score A(x)* is computed [32] as

$$A(x) = -\log(P(x)),$$

where x is an event (e.g., a network packet in terms of feature data), and $P(x)$ is x's probability value based on network traffic distribution. When the anomaly scores of events (network packets) are greater than certain thresholds, these events are passed to the second step.

The general idea of the second step is to correlate (group) certain events together, and the groups of events may be identified as portscans. To group events, Staniford, Hoagland and McAlerney propose to compute the strength of connections between events using the evaluation function. Given two events e_1 and e_2, the evaluation function [32] is defined as

$$f(e_1,e_2) = c_1h_1(e_1,e_2) + c_2h_2(e_1,e_2) + \cdots + c_jh_j(e_1,e_2),$$

where c_1, c_2, $\cdots$, c_j are some constants, and $h_1(e_1,e_2), h_2(e_1,e_2), \cdots, h_j(e_1,e_2)$ are some heuristic evaluation functions. These heuristics may be *feature equality heuristics, feature proximity heuristics, feature separation heuristics, feature co-variance heuristics*, and so forth. As an example, a feature equality heuristics may check to see if two destination IP addresses are the same, if two destination ports are the same, etc. After computing the strengths of connections, a set of events may be grouped if the strengths of connections between events are greater than a certain threshold. In addition, the anomaly score of each group is the summation of the anomaly scores of all events in the group. If the anomaly score of a group is greater than a threshold, a port scanning alert is reported to a security officer.

In order to evaluate the proposed approach, a system called SPADE (Statistical Packet Anomaly Detection Engine) was implemented, and experimental results were collected. As an example of experimental results, in a 3-week data set, SPADE flagged 28 horizontal scans (horizontal scan means attackers scan all IP addresses in a range of network addresses for some specific network services) as well as 4 nmap network scans. SPADE was implemented as a Snort preprocessor plugin and was publicly released.

2.3 Root Cause Analysis

In 2003, Julisch [18] proposed an alert clustering approach to performing root cause analysis, where the root cause is the reason why the alerts are triggered. As illustrated by Julisch, the root cause *an HTTP server with a broken TCP/IP stack* may trigger many *fragmented IP* alerts. The rationale of this approach is based on the observation that although IDSs flag thousand of alerts everyday, it is not uncommon that a few dominant root causes may trigger 90% of all alerts. Thus if security officers can identify these root causes (with the corresponding alerts), and remove these root causes, they can dramatically reduce the number of potential alerts in the future.

To perform root cause analysis for an alert log (a set of alerts), the general idea is to identify clusters of alerts so that the alerts in the same cluster are *similar* and correspond to the same root cause. Here *similarity* or *dissimilarity* measures are critical for this clustering analysis. To help define these measures, Julisch first introduce generalization hierarchies for alert attribute values. Alert attribute values, for example, IP addresses and timestamps, can be generalized to higher level concepts, which usually denote a subset of attribute domain. For example, individual IP addresses can be generalized to network addresses. Attribute values can be generalized into different levels of concepts and a generalization hierarchy is then formed. Julisch [18] defines a sequence of dissimilarity measures, which are all related to generalization hierarchies.

- Given an attribute A, a generalization hierarchy G for A, and two attribute values x_1 and x_2 in A's domain, the dissimilarity measure $d(x_1,x_2)$ computes the length of the shortest path between x_1 and x_2 such that x_1 and x_2 have a common parent node in the hierarchy G.
- The dissimilarity between two alerts is the summation of the dissimilarity between the corresponding attribute pairs.
- The average dissimilarity $\bar{d}(g,C)$ between a generalized alert g and an alert cluster C is defined as

$$\bar{d}(g,C) = \frac{\text{the summation of the dissimilarity between } g \text{ and each alert in } C}{|C|},$$

  where $|C|$ is the number of alerts in the cluster C.
- The heterogeneity $H(C)$ of an alert cluster C is the minimal value of the average dissimilarity values between any generalized alert and the cluster C.

In addition, Julisch [18] formally defines alert clustering problem. Given an alert log L, a set of generalization hierarchies for all attributes in alerts, and an integer *min_size*, the alert clustering is to find a cluster C, which is a subset of L, such that the heterogeneity $H(C)$ is minimal and $|C| \geq min\_size$. Since this alert clustering problem is an *NP*-complete problem, Julisch propose a heuristic algorithm to perform alert clustering. The basic idea of this heuristic is to select some attributes in the alerts, and then replace attribute values with their parent node values in the generalization hierarchies. This procedure continues until certain conditions are satisfied. This heuristic can guarantee that the cluster size $|C|$ is no less than *min_size*, but the heterogeneity value $H(C)$ may not be minimal.

To illustrate the effectiveness of this approach, Julisch analyzed an alert log with 156,380 alerts. He observed that the top 13 alert clusters account for 95% of all alerts. Through analyzing related data sets, the author also expected to reduce 82% of the future alert load.

2.4 Statistical Causality Analysis Based Approach

In 2003, Qin and Lee [31] proposed an alert correlation approach to performing statistical causality analysis. The focus of this approach is to conduct time series and statistical analysis to get attack scenarios, though Qin and Lee also propose clustering techniques to aggregate certain lower level alerts to a *hyper alert* (i.e., a group of alerts ordered by timestamps) thus potentially reduce the alert volume, and perform alert prioritization to identify important alerts. Generally speaking, the alert processing in this paper can be roughly divided into three steps.

In the first step, the major work is alert aggregation and clustering. Considering that each alert has several attributes such as source IP addresses, destination IP addresses, and timestamps. The proposed technique examines these attribute values, and put those alerts into the same cluster if their attribute values (except timestamps) match and the timestamps fall within a pre-defined time window. A cluster of the alerts ordered by timestamps is also represented as a hyper alert.

The second step is alert prioritization. The goal of this step is to rank the alert priority (importance). The priority computation and ranking is based on the alerts and the related network or host configurations. Qin and Lee adapt the techniques proposed by Porras, Fong and Valdes [30], and propose to use Bayesian networks to perform priority computation. Specifically, assume that a Bayesian network is a directed acyclic graph, and the root node denotes the priority with certain hypothesis states. In addition, let H_i be the ith hypothesis of the root node, e^k be the kth leaf node, and suppose each H_i is independent. Thus the belief in hypothesis is computed [31] as

$$P(H_i|e^1,\cdots,e^n) = \gamma P(H_i)\prod_{k=1}^{n} P(e^k|H_i).$$

In this formula, $\gamma = 1/P(e^1,\cdots,e^n)$, and $\sum_i P(H_i|e^1,\cdots,e^n) = 1$. The computed priority score falls within the range of $[0,1]$, where the higher value denotes the higher priority.

The third step is the main focus of this paper, where statistical Granger Causality Test is performed and attack scenarios are constructed accordingly. Given two time series variables *x* and *y*, Granger Causality Test is used to see if the lagged information in *x* can provide statistically significant information in y (please refer to [31, 14] for the details of Granger Causality Test). Given a hyper alert, a univariate time series can be generated through partitioning the time range into equal intervals, and then counting the number of alerts in the corresponding time intervals. To perform causality analysis for a target hyper alert *Y*, any other hyper alert, for example, hyper alert *X*, is chosen and the two corresponding univariate time series are tested through Granger Causality Test. Based on the results of Granger Causality Test, the candidate causal hyper alerts are ranked according to Granger Causality Index values. Next, the top *m* candidates in the ranked list are chosen and may possibly be used to build attack scenarios. In addition, realizing that removing background alerts is important for alert correlation, Qin and Lee also propose to use Ljung-Box test to achieve this goal.

To evaluate the effectiveness of the proposed approach, Qin and Lee conducted several experiments through the data sets from DARPA cyber panel program grand challenge problem [10] as well as DEF CON 9 Capture The Flag [12]. For example, in Scenario I data set from DARPA cyber panel program grand challenge problem, 25,000 low level alerts are aggregated into about 2,300 hyper alerts, and the causal relationships discovered in the data set are also desirable (In a network enclave, the experimental results demonstrate that the true causality rate is more than 95% and the false causality rate is less than 13%.).

2.5 Alert Clustering and Merging in MIRADOR Project

In 2001, Cuppens [6] proposed an approach to managing alerts in an environment with multiple IDSs. This work is related to MIRADOR project, which was funded by the French DGA/CASSI. In an environment with multiple IDSs, it is very possible that different IDSs may flag different alerts, even for the same attack. Alert clustering tries to put the alerts into the same cluster if they correspond to the same attack. Roughly speaking, alert processing in this paper is divided into three steps (functions): alert (base) management, alert clustering, and alert merging.

Usually, the alerts reported by different IDSs may have distinct data formats. For example, some IDSs report alerts into text files, some IDSs put alerts into databases, and these alerts may use different attribute names to denote attack information. To deal with this situation, Cuppens assumes that alerts should satisfy the requirement from Intrusion Detection Message Exchange Format (IDMEF) [9].

The first step of alert processing is alert (base) management. In this step, alerts reported by different IDSs are transformed into tuples (records) and then saved into relational databases. To perform this transformation, Cuppens first generate database schema based on DTD and XML alert messages (IDMEF alerts are represented in XML format). Multiple relations may be created to accommodate all entities, attributes, and elements. Next, each IDMEF alert message is analyzed and values are extracted to fill into database tables. It is possible that one alert corresponds to multiple tuples in a database.

The second step is alert clustering. In this step, alerts reported by different IDSs are grouped into clusters so that the alerts in one cluster correspond to one attack. The critical part in this step is to identify *similarity* between alerts. Cuppens propose to use an *expert system* to define similarity requirement. Similarity relations are specified for attributes, for various entities such as *Classification*, *Source*, *Target*, and *Detecttime*, for database tuples, for relationships, as well as for alerts. Next, domain specific *similarity expert rules* are further defined. Cuppens specifies rules for four entities: *classification*, *source*, *target*, and *time*.

- *Classification similarity*: assume that for each IDS, the classification reported has both *generated name* and *standard attack name*, where generated name is specific to this IDS, and standard attack name is from some common naming systems such as Common Vulnerability Enumeration (CVE). Two entities of *classification* are similar if their corresponding standard attack names have a common name.
- *Source similarity* and *target similarity*: two sources or targets are similar if their related information such as nodes, services, and/or processes are similar. Notices that it would be helpful to identify the similarity if the mapping between host names, IP addresses, service names, port numbers, and so on, is available.
- *Time similarity*: two attributes of *Detecttime* are considered similar if their difference is within certain predefined threshold.

The third step of alert processing is alert merging, where the alerts in each cluster are merged, and a global (representative) alert is created with merged data. One of the critical points here is how to merge different attributes such as *classification*, *source*, *target*, and *time* information.

- *Classification*: to merge attack classification for a cluster, a union of all classification values in this cluster is generated.
- *Source* and *Target*: when two or more sources/targets are similar, these sources/-targets are merged so that a unique (common) source/target is created for the global alert; when two or more sources/targets are different, all these different values will be included in the global alert.
- *Time*: usually, a time range [earliest_time, latest_time] will be generated based on timestamps information such as *Detecttime* in the alert cluster.

To evaluate the effectiveness of the proposed approach, Cuppens also did two experiments. As an example, in his first experiment, two IDSs Snort and e-Trust were deployed, and 87 attacks were tested. Among them, Snort detected 68 attacks with 264 alerts, and e-Trust detected 42 attacks with 61 alerts. Clustering analysis produced 101 clusters and hence 101 global alerts were generated after merging.

3 Approaches Based on Predefined Attack Scenarios

An attack scenario usually is a sequence of individual attack steps linked together to show an aggregated or global view of security threats. To build these attack sequences, a straightforward way is to first predefine some attack scenario templates. For example, we may specify an attack sequence template where *IP_Scan* is followed by *TCP_Port_Scan* and then by *FTP_Buffer_Overflow*. Next, individual alerts reported by IDSs are matched to these scenario templates to construct attack scenarios. These approaches can help security officers to discover all scenarios where their corresponding patterns are aware of and predefined. However, sometimes it is not easy to exhaustively list all attack sequence templates. Another limitation of these methods is that once some novel attack patterns are created by attackers, the corresponding attack scenarios may not be recognized. In the following, we present a few representative approaches in this category.

3.1 Aggregation and Correlation in IBM/Tivoli Systems

In 2001, Debar and Wespi [11] proposed an approach to performing aggregation and correlation to intrusion alerts. The purpose of this paper is to address the current IDSs' limitations such as alert flooding and false alerts. Various issues have been discussed, for example, the architecture of combing IDSs with aggregation and correlation components, alert data model, and *aggregation and correlation components* (ACC). In this subsection, we focus on ACC, which is a component in IBM/Tivoli Systems.

The main functionality of ACC is to group alerts based on predefined relationships between alerts. ACC mainly identify two types of relationships: *correlation relationship* and *aggregation relationship*, where correlation relationships are used to discover the same *attack trend* through identifying *duplicates* and *consequences*, and aggregation relationships aggregate alerts based on the predefined *situation* criteria. Alert processing in ACC can be divided into three steps.

The first step is alert preprocessing. The basic functionality of this preprocessing is to provide a unified alert data model for the later correlation and aggregation analysis. In this step, several tasks are performed. For example, common attributes of IDS alerts are extracted, obviously incorrect information about alerts are identified, time information is synchronized, and the mapping between network service names and port numbers is established.

The second step is alert correlation, where two types of correlation relationships, *duplicates* and *consequences*, are identified. An example of duplicate alerts is those alerts flagged when multiple IDSs detect the same attack. The identification of duplicate relationships is similar to those similarity based correlation approaches discussed in Section 2. Alert type information as well as attribute values from different alerts are examined to see if they match. New severity levels will also be computed for the duplicates. On the other hand, *consequence relationships* are used to model

```
chronicle EX1[?source, ?target]
{
        event(alert[port_scan, ?source, ?target], t1)
        event(alert[ftp_overflow, ?source, ?target], t2)
        event(alert[remote_access, ?source, ?target], t3)

        t1 < t2 < t3

        when recognized {
             emit event(alert[ftp_scenario, ?source, ?target], t2);
        }
}
```

Fig. 1 An example of chronicles

if one security event is the consequence of an earlier event. A sequence of consequence relationships can describe a chain of attack steps in an attack scenario. To specify consequence relationships between alerts, *initial alert type*, *consequence alert type*, attributes to be matched, severity levels, and the timestamp difference between initial and consequence alerts, will be considered.

The third step is alert aggregation, where a group of alerts are aggregated based on *situations*. Here situations specify certain constraints that a group of alerts should satisfy. Situation specification is based on alert types, attribute values, as well as severity levels. In this paper, Debar and Wespi define seven situations. For example, Situation 1 requires all alerts in a group should have the identical alert types, and the same source IP addresses and destination IP addresses.

ACC has been implemented as a prototype system based on Tivoli Enterprise Console (TEC). Debar and Wespi also did experiments to evaluate their techniques. For example, they deployed a Web IDS and RealSecure network sensor to monitor a Web server. PHF attacks against the Web server were detected by both IDSs. Through examining the alert messages as well as attribute values, duplicate relationships were identified.

3.2 Chronicles Based Approach

In 2003, Morin and Debar [23] proposed an alert correlation through chronicles formalism. In a dynamic system, chronicles provide a mechanism to model event temporal patterns and monitor the system's evolution. Chronicles are widely used in telecommunication systems. Morin and Debar adapt this technique to monitor security events and perform alert correlation, which may potentially reduce the overall volume of alerts, and improve the certainty of false alerts.

To specify a chronicle model, event patterns, related timestamp information, time constraints among events, as well as other patterns and actions will be used for modeling. Figure 1 shows an example of chronicles.

In this chronicle, three events are considered *port_scan*, *ftp_overflow*, and *remote_access*, where their corresponding timestamps should be in increasing order (i.e., $t_1 < t_2 < t_3$), and their corresponding domain attributes (i.e., source and target) should be equal. If all these patterns as well as constraints are satisfied, then this chronicle is recognized and a synthetic alert is generated. Notice that usually only synthetic alerts will be reported to security officers. So this may significantly reduce the workload for security officers.

In addition to mitigating the alert flooding problem, chronicles can also improve the capability of identifying false or true positives. This may be achieved through examining *contextual events* (i.e., related events in the event pattern) in the chronicle. Notice that benign events can also be included in chronicle models. An example illustrated by Morin and Debar on how to improve the certainty of false positives is that two FTP related benign events and one shell code related event are specified in a chronicle. Shell code related event itself may imply some buffer overflow attacks. However, under the context of some FTP activities, shell code related events are very likely to be normal FTP activities. So if this chronicle is properly defined, and then recognized based on events reported, security officers may consider that shell code related alert in this chronicle has high possibility to be the false positive.

At the time of publishing this paper, this alert correlation approach based on chronicles has not been fully implemented and tested. However, Morin and Debar did do some experiments to test the effectiveness of their approach through some alert logs generated in their networks.

4 Approaches Based on Prerequisites and Consequences of Attacks

It is usually the case that when adversaries attack some networks and hosts, they may use earlier attacks to prepare for the later ones. For example, attackers may first launch IP sweep to find live hosts in a network, then they may scan open ports on these live hosts to find vulnerable services, and finally launch buffer overflow attacks against those vulnerable services on those live machines. This means that there are logical connections (may also be called as *causal relationships*) between individual attack steps. Linking these connections may lead to building attack scenarios.

Prerequisites and consequences based correlation approaches can help construct attack scenarios so security officers will have more complete views about security threats. Generally speaking, the *prerequisite* of an attack (also called as the *precondition*) is the necessary condition to launch an attack successfully. For example, to launch an *Ftp_Glob_Expansion* attack, the victim host should have a vulnerable FTP service. The *consequence* of an attack (also called as *post-condition*) is the possible outcome if the attack does succeed. For example, if an *Ftp_Glob_Expansion* attack is launched successfully, the attacker may gain the administrator's privilege on the victim host. The modeling of prerequisites and consequences can be achieved through first order logic or some attack modeling languages such as LAMBDA

[8]. For example, we may use predicates *ExistVulService(VictimIP, VictimPort)* and *GainAdminAccess(VictimIP)* to model attack *Ftp_Glob_Expansion*'s prerequisite and consequence, respectively.

The rationale of attack scenario construction is to discover if the success of some earlier attacks may *contribute* to the success of some later attacks. After attack modeling, to perform correlation, different mechanisms exist. For example, in [25], the prerequisites and consequences can be instantiated through introducing alert attribute values reported by IDSs. Next, the instantiated prerequisites and consequences in different alerts are examined to see possible match or at least partial match. Alerts with (partially) matching prerequisites and consequences are linked together to build attack scenarios. These scenarios can help security officers understand the logical connections between individual alerts.

Notice that in order to make these correlation approaches practical to production networks, a comprehensive knowledge base about different attacks as well as the corresponding prerequisites and consequences are critical. Also notice that since attack scenarios can be discovered through matching prerequisites and consequences, these approaches do not need to have any scenario templates. This means that novel attack scenarios can be discovered. In the following, we survey a few typical approaches in this category.

4.1 Pre-condition/Post-condition Based Approach in MIRADOR Project

In 2002, Cuppens and Miège [7] proposed an approach to correlate alerts from multiple, cooperative IDSs. This work is a further extension to [6], which is discussed in Section 2. In [6], Cuppens focuses on alert base management, alert clustering, and alert merging. While in [7], alert correlation, as the next step to alert merging, is the major focus.

This paper proposes to build attack scenarios based on pre-conditions and post-conditions of attacks. Each attack is modeled through attack modeling language LAMBDA [8] (LAMBDA uses first order logic to model attacks). Each pre-condition/post-condition has a set of predicates to define what is the condition to be satisfied in order to launch an attack successfully, or the possible effect if the attack succeeds. These predicates specify access privileges of attackers, source and target systems' status, and so forth. Examples of these predicates include *access_level(user1, targetIP, local)* and *use_service(targetIP, vul_service)*.

This paper further proposes to automatically extract correlation rules based on LAMBDA attack specification. Correlation rule generation can be divided into two cases: *direct correlation* and *indirected correlation* [7].

- *Direct Correlation.* Given two attacks A_1 and A_2, assume the post-condition of A_1 is *Post*(A_1), and the pre-condition of A_2 is *Pre*(A_2). Direct correlation, simply speaking, is to examine predicates in *Post*(A_1) and *Pre*(A_2), to see if they are *unifiable* through a most general unifier θ. (Notice that special attention need to be given when predicates involve *knows*.)

- *Indirect Correlation*. In this case, ontological rules are specified to denote the relations between predicates. For example, as illustrated by Cuppens and Miège, port 139 is open may suggest that the corresponding host has a Windows system. Two attacks can be correlated based on a sequence of ontological rules through a corresponding sequence of most general unifiers $\theta_0, \theta_1, \cdots, \theta_n$.

After all correlation rules have been derived, alert correlation is straightforward. In this procedure, alert data such as alert types (i.e., the corresponding attack classification), attribute values, as well as timestamps are extracted and evaluated based on correlation rules (conditions). A sequence of correlated alerts result in an attack scenario.

In addition to alert correlation, Cuppens and Miège also briefly discuss how to deal with false negative problems. False negatives are those attacks that beyond the capability of an IDS, so the IDS cannot detect them. Cuppens and Miège propose to use *abductive correlation* to address this problem. The basic idea is to hypothesize some *virtual* alerts based on correlation functions. But the details on correlation functions performing hypotheses is not clear in this paper. After generating virtual alerts, existing alerts as well as virtual alerts are correlated through the aforementioned correlation techniques.

The correlation method proposed in this paper is a part of CRIM, a cooperative module for intrusion detection systems. CRIM has been implemented and developed in MIRADOR project. To evaluate the proposed approach, Cuppens and Miège did experiments using two IDSs: Snort and e-Trust.

4.2 A Prerequisite and Consequence Based Approach

In the recent a few years, Ning el al. [25, 26] have systematically studied the alert correlation problem and several papers have been published. In this section as well as later sections, we will selectively present these methods. At this subsection, we focus on [25, 26].

As mentioned earlier, each attack has several attributes such as *SourceIP* and *DestIP*. And the *prerequisite* of an attack is the necessary condition to launch the attack successfully, and the *consequence* of an attack is the possible outcome (effect) if the attack succeeds. First order logic is used to describe prerequisites and consequences. In [25, 26], formally speaking, an alert type (which may be defined as attack classification in some other papers) is a triple (*attr, prereq, conseq*), where *attr* is a list of attributes to describe the related attack, *prereq* is a logical formula to represent the prerequisite, and *conseq* uses a set of predicates to denote the consequence. As an example, given an alert type *Ftp_Glob_Expansion*, its attribute list is {*SourceIP, SourcePort, DestIP, DestPort, StartTime, EndTime*}, its prerequsite is *ExistVulService(DestIP, DestPort)*, and its consequence is {GainAdminAccess(DestIP)}.

For each alert, we can instantiate the corresponding prerequisite and consequence through replacing attribute names in the predicates with their attribute values. To continue the above example, if an *Ftp_Glob_Expansion* alert has *DestIP=10.10.2.1* and *DestPort=21*, the instantiated prerequisite and consequence are *ExistVulService(10.10.2.1, 21)* and {GainAdminAccess(10.10.2.1)}, respectively.

After deriving all the instantiated prerequisites and consequences for the given alerts, alert correlation is to examine these instantiated prerequisites and consequences to see the possible (partial) match. The logical connections between alerts are modeled as *prepare-for* relations in [25, 26]. Formally, given two alerts a_1 and a_2, a_1 *prepares for* a_2 if (1) one of the instantiated predicates in a_1's consequence implies one of the instantiated predicates in a_2's prerequisite, and (2) a_1.*EndTime*$<$ a_2.*StartTime*.

Based on prepare-for relations, Ning et al. further define *correlation graphs* to model attack scenarios. A correlation graph is a directed acyclic graph G, where vertices in G represent individual alerts, and the edges denote the prepare-for relations between the corresponding vertices.

The techniques proposed in [25, 26] has been implemented and integrated into a *Toolkit for Intrusion Alert Analysis (TIAA)* [1]. This toolkit can be downloaded from `http://discovery.csc.ncsu.edu/software/correlator/`. Several data sets have been used to test the effectiveness of this correlation method. As a result from [25, 26], Figure 2 shows a correlation graph generated using one of the data sets (Scenario LLDOS 1.0) in 2000 DARPA intrusion detection scenario specific data sets [22]. Notice that those alerts in the figure are reported by RealSecure network sensors. The string in each node is the alert type followed by an ID number. This correlation graph clearly discloses a multi-stage attack scenario: the adversaries first use *Sadmind_Ping* to probe vulnerable sadmind services, then *Sadmind_Amslverify_Overflow* attacks are launched to get root privileges, next *mstream DDoS* softwares are installed and run through *Rsh*, and finally the mstream components communicate with each other (*Mstream_Zombie*) and DDoS attacks (*Stream_DoS*) are launched. In addition to attack scenarios, Ning et al. also computed many measures (e.g., false alert rates and detection rates) to evaluate their methods.

4.3 Attack Hypothesizing and Reasoning Techniques

Under the framework of prerequisites and consequences based methods [25, 26], Ning and Xu [27] propose an approach to addressing false negative problems. False negatives are those attacks missed by IDSs, which may be critical for security officers to understand security threats.

To address this problem, Ning and Xu propose to hypothesize and reason about missed attacks (or the unknow variations of known attacks). This approach is based on their observation that when some intermediate attacks in a scenario are missed by IDSs, this attack scenario may be split into multiple attack scenarios. However,

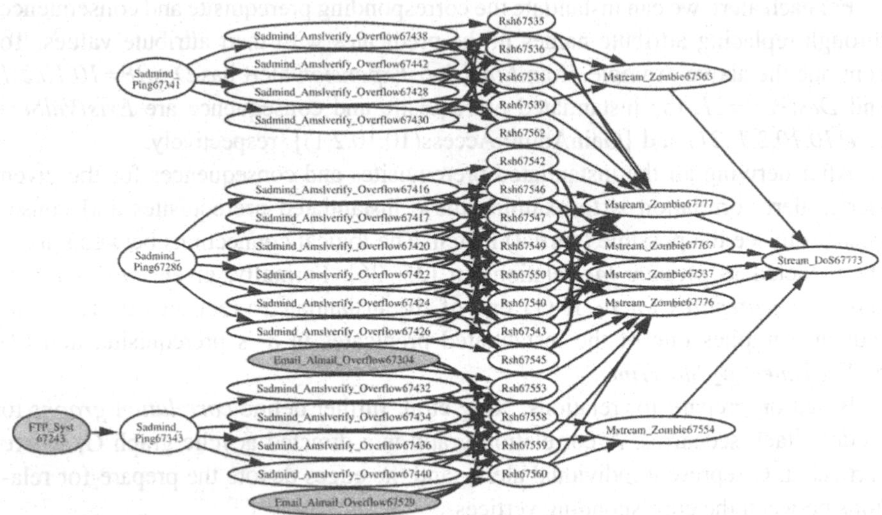

Fig. 2 An alert correlation graph discovered in LLDOS 1.0 (cited from [25, 26]).

the alerts in these multiple scenarios may still satisfy certain constraints. If these constraints can be specified, those alerts in different scenarios will be tested against these constraints. Once certain constraints are satisfied, the possibly missed attacks will be hypothesized, and the attribute values about these hypothesized attacks will be derived. In addition, these hypothesized attacks are validated/invalidated based on the original audit data; invalidated hypotheses are filtered out. Finally, based on the existing alerts as well as hypothesized attacks, the hypothesized attacks are consolidated and concise attack scenarios are constructed.

Simply speaking, a series of techniques are proposed in [27], which include attack constraints extraction, attack hypothesizing, attribute inference, hypothesized attack filtering, and hypothesized attack consolidation.

Attack constraints extraction is based on all attacks types that can be detected by certain IDSs. These attacks are modeled through specifying their attributes, prerequisites and consequences. Intuitively, given two attacks T_1 and T_2, an alert a_1 of type T_1 may have a chance to prepare for another alert a_2 of type T_2 if one of the predicates in T_1's consequence may imply one of the predicates in T_2's prerequisite. This is defined as T_1 *may prepare for* T_2 in [27]. Additionally, if T_1 and T_2 are connected through a chain of may-prepare-for relations, this is defined as T_1 *may indirectly prepare for* T_2. A further analysis of these may-prepare-for or may-indirectly-prepare-for relations can help to discover the *equality constraints* between the corresponding attacks. Informally, an equality constraint between attacks T_1 and T_2 is the equality relationship between T_1 and T_2's attributes, which can be derived through matching predicate names and checking attributes. For example, an equality constraint between T_1 and T_2 may be $T_1.DestIP = T_2.DestIP \wedge T_1.DestPort = T_2.DestPort$.

In the stage of attack hypothesizing, each pair of alerts spreading in different attack scenarios are evaluated to see if they satisfy certain equality constraints. If constraints are satisfied, this means the corresponding pair of attacks have may-indirectly-prepare-for relations. Thus those intermediate attacks between them are hypothesized. These hypothesized attacks are the candidate attacks that may be missed by IDSs.

After attack hypothesizing, attribute inference for these hypothesized attacks is performed. The inference is based on the equality constraints between attacks. For example, given an alert a_1 with attack type T_1, and a hypothesized attack a_2 with type T_2, assume that the equality constraint between T_1 and T_2 is $T_1.DestIP = T_2.DestIP \wedge T_1.DestPort = T_2.DestPort$. If we know that $a_1.DestIP$ = *10.10.3.1* and $a_1.DestPort$ =*21*, then it is straightforward to derive that $a_2.DestIP$ = *10.10.3.1* and $a_2.DestPort$ = *21*. In addition, the possible range of timestamp information about hypothesized attacks may also be derived.

Hypothesized attack filtering is used to rule out some incorrect hypotheses. This is achieved through examining the audit data to see if there is any evidence to support or invalidate such hypotheses. For example, if an *Ftp_Glob_Expansion* attack is hypothesized, and attribute values as well as the timestamp range are also derived, but if there are no FTP activities during the related time frame, then this hypothesis will be invalidated.

The last stage is to consolidate hypothesized attacks to build concise attack scenarios. It is noticed that the same attack may be hypothesized many times under different contexts, which may introduce too many hypothesized attacks when we combining different, partial attack scenarios. Ning and Xu propose to consolidate hypothesized attacks if they are of the same attack type, their attribute values do not conflict with each other, and their timestamps overlap. This technique can greatly reduce the number of hypothesized attacks. For example, in one experiment, 137 hypothesized attacks were consolidated into 5.

Similar as those techniques proposed in [25, 26], the techniques proposed in [27] also have been implemented and integrated into a *Toolkit for Intrusion Alert Analysis (TIAA)* [1]. In the experiments, 2000 DARPA intrusion detection scenario specific data sets [22] were used. RealSecure network sensors were deployed to detect attacks. In order to test the hypothesizing and reasoning techniques, *Sadmind_Amslverify_Overflow* attacks were deliberately dropped in the alert data sets. Thus it is possible that one complete attack scenario may be split into multiple scenarios. For example, as demonstrated in [27], in the data set of LLDOS 1.0 inside part, one scenario (which is shown in Figure 2) was split into four. After applying the techniques proposed in this paper, these four attack scenarios have been integrated back into one, which is shown in Figure 3. This figure demonstrates that the proposed techniques are effective because *Sadmind_Amslverify_Overflow* attacks are correctly hypothesized.

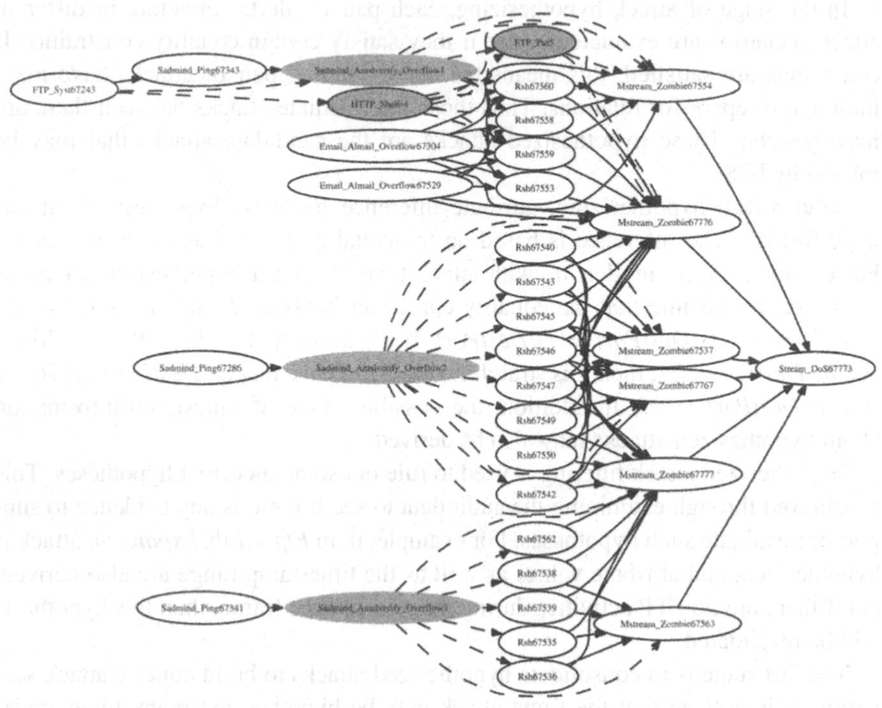

Fig. 3 An integrated correlation graph built from LLDOS 1.0 inside part (cited from [27])

5 Approaches Based on Multiple Information Sources

To protect digital assets, it is usually considered as a good practice to deploy multiple, complementary security systems into networks and hosts. These security systems may include firewalls, authentication services, antivirus tools, vulnerability scanners, and intrusion detection systems. Generally, different systems have different capabilities, and combing them can potentially provide better protection to our networks and hosts.

The potentially better protection with multiple, heterogeneous security systems also bring challenging problems to security officers. Specifically, as we mentioned in the Introduction, one IDS may report thousands of alerts everyday, and multiple security systems can make this situation much worse. Security officers will be overwhelmed by such a high volume of alerts. In addition, different systems usually run and act independently, and lack of the cooperation among them makes incidents investigation very difficult. In other words, how to perform correlation analysis among tons of security events reported by different systems is quite challenging.

To address this challenging problem, many approaches have been proposed. For example, Porras, Fong, and Valdes [30] propose a mission-impact-based approach, where incidents are ranked according to their impact to the networks and hosts.

Morin et al. [24] propose to define a unified data model to formalize different information sources such as networks, hosts, vulnerability information, security systems, and security events and alerts, which may greatly facilitate correlation analysis. Xu and Ning [36] propose to combine similarity based method with prerequisites and consequences based approach to perform alert correlation. The details of these methods will be given in the following subsections.

5.1 Mission-Impact-Based Approach

In 2002, Porras, Fong, and Valdes [30] proposed a mission-impact-based approach to automating the correlation of alerts from different systems such as firewalls and IDSs. Central to this approach is two knowledge bases (databases) *incident handling fact base* and *topology map of the protected network and hosts*, and a sequence of alert processing steps including *alert filtering*, *topology vetting*, *priority computation*, *incident ranking*, and *alert clustering/aggregation*.

The two aforementioned knowledge bases are very important to topology vetting. *Incident handling fact base* is a comprehensive repository including all the necessary information about attacks, vulnerabilities, and so forth. For example, in the fact base developed by Porras, Fong, and Valdes, over 1000 different attacks that can be detected by RealSecure, Snort, or EMERALD [46] are included. Vulnerability information includes incident descriptions, related hardware platforms and application versions, operating system versions, network service information, and so on.

Topology map of the protected networks and hosts includes topological and configuration information about the network, for example, host IP addresses and names, network services run by each host, operating systems versions, and hardware platforms. The topology map should be updated dynamically, which may be done by *NAMP* [13].

In the stage of alert filtering, users choose to subscribe the alerts that are important to their networks and hosts. Based on the mission of networks, users can also dynamically update their subscription, which may reduce the workload of alert processing for their networks.

In the stage of topology vetting, based on incident handling fact base and topological map of protected networks and hosts, a *relevance score* is computed for each alert, which represents the degree of dependency between the incident (represented as an alert) and the related network and host configurations. For example, if the incident requires the target machine to be a Windows system, but the network and host configurations show that the only operating system in this machine is Linux, then the relevance score for the corresponding alert should be low. In this paper, relevance scores are in the range of 0 to 255.

Priority computation shows the degree that an incident affects the *mission* of the networks. As defined in [30], "the *mission* is the underlying objective for which the computing resources and data assets of the monitored network are brought together and used." Based on this definition, priority score computation needs to consider two factors:

- the computing resources and data assets, and
- security incidents that greatly affect networks.

In a network, the computing resources and data assets can include web servers, file servers, database management systems, important data files (e.g., the source code of a program), and user accounts. In addition, security officers also need to specify in what security incidents they are interested, for example, the incidents performing *PRIVILEGE_VIOLATION* or *DENIAL_OF_SERVICE*.

In the stage of incident ranking, for each alert, an *incident rank* is computed to represent the overall impact that the incident brings to target networks, as well as the probability that the incident is successful. This computation is performed through Bayes networks, where *relevance*, *priority*, and other related factors are all involved.

Alert clustering is the last stage of alert processing in this paper. Notice that here clustering analysis is performed through the *clustering policy*. For example, several alerts may be grouped if they are of the same incident types, and with the same source IP addresses and destination IP addresses. This stage is similar to those similarity based alert correlation.

The proposed techniques have been developed as a prototype system *Mission Impact Intrusion Report Correlation System (M-Correlator)*. To test the effectiveness of M-Correlator, experiments were conducted in a simulated network, where multiple security systems were deployed such as RealSecure, eBayes-TCP, eXpert-Net, and Checkpoint firewalls. In one of the experiments, 79 alerts were produced by security systems, and after a sequence of processing, only 4 clusters were generated in alert clustering/aggregation.

5.2 A Data Model M2D2 for Alert Correlation

To facilitate alert correlation and threat analysis, Morin et al. [24] proposed a formal data model *M2D2* in 2002. In M2D2, four types of information are formalized: the features of networks and hosts under monitoring and protection, vulnerability information, security systems and tools, and events, alerts and scans (generated by vulnerability scanners). M2D2 is presented using Z and B formal methods [24].

In the formal specification about the features of networks and hosts, network topology, products (e.g., operating systems, and software applications) and other information are included. To model network topology, hypergraph model [35] has been extended, and other information such as host IP address and name mapping is also included. To formalize product information, vendor names, product names, product versions, and product types are necessary.

Vulnerabilities usually are specific to certain network and host configurations. For example, a vulnerability may only exist if a specific version of FTP servers are installed in Windows machines. Other related information include vulnerability names, privilege requirement to exploit vulnerabilities, and the possible effect if a vulnerability is exploited successfully (e.g., privilege escalation, and denial of service). These are all modeled in [24].

In the modeling of security systems and tools, Morin et al. focus on IDSs and vulnerability scanners. IDS detection methods (misuse detection or anomaly detection), detection capability (e.g., how many different signatures used in detection), as well as other necessary information (e.g., messages reported when certain attacks detected) may be included in the modeling.

Events usually are low-level activities observed by systems. In [24], five types of events are modeled: *IP events*, *UDP events*, *TCP events*, *HTTP events*, and *web log events*. Necessary information such as timestamps are also involved. Alerts are reported by IDSs, and scans are generated by vulnerability scanners. Their related information such as reported messages, source and target IP addresses may also be included in their modeling.

To demonstrate that M2D2 can facilitate alert correlation, several examples of alert correlation methods have been enumerated. In one example, the alerts reported by host based IDS and network based IDS are aggregated if their target hosts are the same.

5.3 Triggering Events and Common Resources Based Approach

In 2004, Xu and Ning [36] proposed to correlate alerts from multiple security systems through *triggering events* and common *resources*. This approach is based on the observations that (1) though different alerts may be reported by different security systems, the underlying events that trigger these alerts usually are the same; (2) network and host configurations can help assess the severity of alerts; (3) in the prerequisites and consequences based correlation approach, the specification of prerequisites and consequences are time-consuming and sometimes even error-prone. This situation can be improved if network and computer resources (e.g., network services) are introduced into attack modeling.

Based on the aforementioned key observations, the correlation approach in [36] can be divided into three steps: alert clustering through triggering events, alert severity evaluation through examining if alerts are *consistent* with the corresponding network and host configurations, and attack scenario construction through *input* and *output resources*.

Given an alert, *Triggering events* are low level events (e.g., an FTP connection) that trigger this alert. For example, a *malicious sadmind NETMGT_PROC_SERVICE Request* event may trigger *Sadmind_Amslverify_Overflow* alert for RealSecure network sensors. Notice that to describe a triggering event, attribute values are necessary, for example, source IP addresses, destination IP addresses, timestamps, and so on. To perform alert clustering, all the triggering events are discovered for each alert in the data set. Next, the alerts with *similar* triggering events are grouped, where *similar* events mean that either events are the same, or one event can imply another (e.g., the recursive deletion of a directory */user/Alice/programs* implies the deletion of a file */user/Alice/programs/HelloWorld.c*).

In the next stage, the severity of alerts in clusters are assessed through *consistency* (or *inconsistency*) evaluation between alerts and their network and host configurations. Intuitively, an alert is *consistent* with a related host configuration, if the corresponding attack may be successful based on the host configuration information. For example, if an attack *HTTP_IIS_URL_Decoding* is targeting a host 10.10.5.1 on port 80, while this host does not have any IIS applications and port 80 is not open, then this attack is not consistent with the host configuration, and cannot be successful. This also means the corresponding alert is of low severity and possibly is a false positive.

In the third stage, attack scenarios are built through input and output resources. Intuitively, *input resources* are the necessary resources to launch an attack successfully, and *output resources* are the resources that an attack can provide if it succeeds. Resources include network services, access privilege, important files, and so on. As an example, the input resource of an attack *Ftp_Glob_Expansion* is a vulnerable FTP service on a victim host, and the output resource is the administrative privilege on the victim host. The correlation model in [25, 26] has been extended to accommodate input and output resources. To find logical connections in alerts, input and output resources for each alert are first enumerated. Next, output and input resources are examined, and if one of the output resources in an earlier alert can imply one of the the input resources in a later alert, the two corresponding alerts will be connected. A sequence of these connections can result in an attack scenario.

The proposed techniques are evaluated through DARPA Cyber Panel Program Grand Challenge Problem Release 3.2 (GCP) [10], where 10 different security systems are involved. In one data set, 529 alerts were generated. And clustering analysis resulted in 512 clusters. The next step of severity evaluation identified several low severity alerts. Finally attack scenario construction brought 10 scenario graphs.

6 Privacy Issues in Alert Correlation

In recent years, the threat from large scale attacks such as worms and distributed denial of service attacks is increasing. For example, as estimated by *Computer Economics*, *Code Red* has resulted in an economic loss of about $ 2.6 billion [4]. To defend against these attacks, it is desirable that different organizations and companies cooperate in sharing attack related data and performing correlation analysis. At present, there are a few organizations or projects that focus on collecting data over the Internet, and then performing analysis. Examples include *DShield* [33], *PREDICT* [28], and *Cyber-TA* [16].

When security data is collected from different companies and organizations, the privacy concerns from those different data owners have to be satisfied before data can be shared. Thus the appropriate data sanitization techniques that can fulfill data owners' requirement are necessary. As an effort to address privacy concerns,

DShield allows data contributors to perform partial or complete obfuscation to destination IP addresses in their data sets. Partial obfuscation changes the first byte of an IP addresses to decimal 10, and complete obfuscation replaces a whole IP address to a fixed value.

Beside privacy concerns from data owners, security analysts are also interested in the utility of sanitized data sets. To be more specific, the correlation analysis of sanitized data sets should still provide useful information to help them understand security threats. However, since data sanitization usually bring negative impact to the later correlation analysis, appropriate techniques that can preserve the utility of sanitized data are equally important.

To address these challenges, several privacy-preserving alert sharing and correlation techniques have been proposed in recent years [21, 37, 38]. In this section, we give an overview of these techniques.

6.1 An Approach on Alert Sharing and Correlation

In 2004, Lincoln, Porras, and Shmatikov [21] proposed an approach to perform privacy-preserving alert sharing and correlation. Several issues have been discussed in [21] including the threat model to alert sharing, alert sharing and sanitization, possible analysis of sanitized alerts, and performance issues.

Alert data can be generated from many security systems, and firewalls, IDSs, and antivirus tools are the main focus in [21]. Alert attributes reported by these systems include source IP addresses, destination IP addresses, port numbers, timestamps, virus infected files, and so on. Many attributes are considered sensitive and need to be sanitized, for example, IP addresses in an organization's network, and critical files. Other information such as network and host configurations may also be considered as sensitive. Notice that in order to achieve alert sharing and correlation, alert data repositories, where data is obtained from many data owners, are assumed to be at least partially available to different users including attackers. In addition, the threat model in [21] also lists several potential attacks to this alert sharing scheme, for example, dictionary attacks to guess the original values of sanitized attributes, probe-response attacks to learn the details of some networks, and even data repository corruption attacks. The threat model can help us justify why certain techniques are necessary (e.g., different methods for alert sanitization).

To perform alert data sharing, different data contributors can submit their data to a single repository they choose, or spread alert data into multiple repositories. To better protect data submission, *randomized alert routing* is proposed, which can improve the anonymity for data sources (data contributors). But before data contributors send out alert data, alert sanitization should be performed. In other words, sensitive attributes in an alert should be protected and their values are not published in alert repositories. [21] proposes several options to santize attributes, for example, mapping to random values, removing certain parts of data, performing hash functions (e.g., SHA-1) and keyed hash functions (e.g., HMAC), introducing randomization to some threshold values, and so on. What sanitization methods should be chosen is decided by privacy policy. As a special case, the authors suggest to perform keyed hash functions to IP addresses inside data owners' networks, while perform hash functions to outside IP addresses.

After alert sanitization, another critical task is to perform correlation to sanitized alerts. In [21], several different analyses are discussed such as *trend analysis*, *intensity analysis*, and *alert aggregation*. To what degree these analyses can be performed are closely related to the corresponding sanitization techniques. For example, to discover how many different IP addresses are involved in certain attacks, if only hash functions are performed to these IP addresses, then counting different hash values may get the answer.

Considering many security systems may contribute alerts, the number of alerts submitted to data repositories can be very large. This requires that alert sharing and sanitization to be efficient. This performance issue has been discussed in [21]. And experiments were conducted. In their experiments, two data sets were used: one was collected in their own network with 4,224,122 alerts, and the other was from DShield with 19,146,346 alerts. Experimental results show that hashing or keyed hashing to IP addresses can be finished in about 30 seconds for every 1 million alerts.

6.2 Generalization and Perturbation Based Approaches

In 2005 and 2006, Xu and Ning [37, 38] proposed privacy-preserving correlation approaches through applying attribute generalization and perturbation techniques. They mainly focus on two problems, one is how to perform alert sanitization, and the other is how to perform correlation to sanitized alerts. For the first problem, attribute generalization as well as perturbation are proposed. For the second problem, probability based approach is presented.

Xu and Ning propose one generalization and three perturbation based schemes to sanitize alerts. These schemes are independent to each other, but can also be combined together. In the generalization based scheme, original attribute values are generalized to appropriate high level concepts (i.e., general values). For example, IP addresses (e.g., *10.10.5.2*) can be generalized to their corresponding /24 network addresses (e.g., *10.10.5.0/24*), and processing time (e.g., 56 seconds) can be generalized to an interval (e.g., $(50, 75]$).

To perform generalization for an attribute, a *concept hierarchy* for this attribute is usually necessary. Intuitively, a concept hierarchy is a way to organize different concepts (including original attribute values) into different abstraction levels. Alert attributes can be categorical (e.g., IP addresses) or continuous (e.g., processing time). As an example concept hierarchy for categorical attributes, individual IP addresses can be first generalized into /24 networks, and then to /16 networks. For a continuous attribute, to design a concept hierarchy, the attribute domain can be partitioned into different intervals and organized into different levels. For example, a domain of $[0,100]$ can be first divided into 4 intervals $[0,25]$, $(25,50]$, $(50,75]$, and $(75,100]$, and then $[0,25]$ and $(25,50]$ can be combined into $[0,50]$, and $(50,75]$ and $(75,100]$ can be combined into $(50,100]$.

In the generalization based sanitization, an appropriate general value has to be chosen to replace the original value. This process is guided through *entropy* (for categorical attributes such as IP addresses) or *differential entropy* (for continuous attributes such as processing time) [37, 38, 5].

- Given a concept hierarchy for a categorical attribute a, assume an original value v_o is sanitized to a general value v_g. The entropy of attribute a with respect to v_g is defined as $H_a(v_g) = -\sum_{i=1}^{n} p(a = v_i) \log_2 p(a = v_i)$, where n is the number of original values under v_g in the concept hierarchy.
- Given a concept hierarchy for a continuous attribute a, assume an original value v_o is sanitized by an interval v_g. The differential entropy of attribute a with respect to v_g is defined as $H_a(v_g) = -\int_{v_g} f(a) \log_2 f(a) da$, where $f(a)$ is the probability density function for attribute a over interval v_g.

Entropy or differential entropy values can be computed based on attribute distributions, then appropriate general values can be chosen based on entropy value requirement specified by privacy policy.

In the perturbation based sanitization, three schemes are proposed in [37, 38]. In the first scheme, artificial alerts are injected into the original data set to hide original attribute values. Sensitive attribute values in artificial alerts are generated through randomization based on concept hierarchies and attribute distributions. In the second scheme, the original values of sensitive attributes are randomized through concept hierarchies. For example, an IP address 10.10.5.3 may be randomized to 10.10.5.99 under the same /24 network. Notice that in this scheme, to improve the data utility, if original attribute values are the same, then their randomized values are also identical. In the third scheme, a data set can be partitioned into multiple subsets based on timestamp information, and then each subset is randomized independently. Thus in this scheme, the same original attribute values in different subsets may not be randomized to the identical values. This scheme may reduce the impact of potential probe-response attacks.

After alert sanitization, the next step is correlation analysis of sanitized alerts. Two issues are discussed in [37, 38]: one is how to compute the similarity values between sanitized attributes, and the other is how to build attack scenarios for sanitized data sets. To address similarity computation, a probability based approach is proposed. Given two sanitized values, the basic idea is to calculate the probability that how possible the sanitized attributes may have the same original values, and then use this probability value as their similarity value. For example, if both sanitized IP addresses are 10.10.5.0/24, and IP addresses are in uniform distribution in subnet 10.10.5.0/24, then the similarity between these two sanitized attributes is $\frac{1}{256}$. To build attack scenarios for sanitized data sets, Xu and Ning extend their previous work on building attack scenarios for original data sets [25, 26], and propose a probability based approach. Specifically, this approach identifies logical connections between sanitized alerts as long as there is a chance that the corresponding original alerts may have *prepare-for* relations.

To evaluate the proposed privacy-preserving alert correlation approach, Xu and Ning did experiments using 2000 DARPA intrusion detection scenario specific data sets [22]. They sanitized the destination IP address in each alert to the corresponding /24 network address. Similarity values were computed, attack scenarios were constructed, and different measures such as false alert rates and detection rates were also calculated.

7 Summary

In this chapter, we have discussed the alert correlation approaches proposed by different researchers in recent years. We divide these approaches into four categories: similarity based methods, predefined attack scenario based methods, prerequisites and consequences based methods, as well as multiple information sources based methods. In each category, representative approaches are presented. In addition, privacy issues in the field of alert correlation are also addressed.

References

1. TIAA: A toolkit for intrusion alert analysis. `http://discovery.csc.ncsu.edu/software/correlator/`, 2004.
2. J. P. Anderson. Computer security threat monitoring and surveillance. Technical report, James P. Anderson Co., Fort Washington, PA, 1980.
3. Brian Caswell and Marty Roesch. Snort: The open source network intrusion detection system. `http://www.snort.org`.
4. CERT Coordinate Center. Overview of attack trends. `http://www.cert.org/archive/pdf/attack_trends.pdf`, 2002. Accessed in August 2004.
5. T. Cover and J. Thomas. *Elements of Information Theory*. John Wiley & Sons, Inc., 1991.
6. F. Cuppens. Managing alerts in a multi-intrusion detection environment. In *Proceedings of the 17th Annual Computer Security Applications Conference*, December 2001.
7. F. Cuppens and A. Miege. Alert correlation in a cooperative intrusion detection framework. In *Proceedings of the 2002 IEEE Symposium on Security and Privacy*, May 2002.
8. F. Cuppens and R. Ortalo. LAMBDA: A language to model a database for detection of attacks. In *Proc. of Recent Advances in Intrusion Detection (RAID 2000)*, pages 197–216, September 2000.
9. D. Curry and H. Debar. Intrusion detection message exchange format data model and extensible markup language (xml) document type definition. Internet Draft, draft-ietf-idwg-idmef-xml-03.txt, February 2001.
10. DARPA Cyber Panel Program. DARPA cyber panel program grand challenge problem. `http://www.grandchallengeproblem.net/`, 2003.
11. H. Debar and A. Wespi. Aggregation and correlation of intrusion-detection alerts. In *Recent Advances in Intrusion Detection*, LNCS 2212, pages 85 – 103, 2001.
12. DEFCON. Def con capture the flag (CTF) contest. http://www.defcon.org/html/defcon-9/defcon-9-pre.html, July 2001.
13. Fyodor. Nmap free security scanner. `http://www.insecure.org/nmap`, 2003.

14. C. Granger. Investigating causal relations by econometric methods and cross-spectral methods. *Econometrica*, 34:424–428, 1969.
15. J. Han and M. Kamber. *Data Mining: Concepts and Techniques*. Morgan Kaufmann, 2000. ISBN 1-55860-489-8.
16. SRI International. Cyber-threat analytics (Cyber-TA). `http://www.cyber-ta.org/`.
17. Internet Security Systems. RealSecure intrusion detection system. `http://www.iss.net`.
18. K. Julisch. Clustering intrusion detection alarms to support root cause analysis. *ACM Transactions on Information and System Security*, 6(4):443–471, Nov 2003.
19. K. Julisch and M. Dacier. Mining intrusion detection alarms for actionable knowledge. In *The 8th ACM International Conference on Knowledge Discovery and Data Mining*, July 2002.
20. L. Kaufman and P. J. Rousseeuw. *Finding Groups in Data: An Introduction to Cluster Analysis*. John Wiley and Sons, 1990.
21. P. Lincoln, P. Porras, and V. Shmatikov. Privacy-preserving sharing and correlation of security alerts. In *Proceedings of 13th USENIX Security Symposium*, August 2004.
22. MIT Lincoln Lab. 2000 DARPA intrusion detection scenario specific datasets. `http://www.ll.mit.edu/IST/ideval/data/2000/2000_data_index.html`, 2000.
23. B. Morin and H. Debar. Correlation of intrusion symptoms: an application of chronicles. In *Proceedings of the 6th International Conference on Recent Advances in Intrusion Detection (RAID'03)*, September 2003.
24. B. Morin, L. Mé, H. Debar, and M. Ducassé. M2D2: A formal data model for IDS alert correlation. In *Proceedings of the 5th International Symposium on Recent Advances in Intrusion Detection (RAID 2002)*, pages 115–137, 2002.
25. P. Ning, Y. Cui, and D.S. Reeves. Constructing attack scenarios through correlation of intrusion alerts. In *Proceedings of the 9th ACM Conference on Computer and Communications Security*, pages 245–254, Washington, D.C., November 2002.
26. P. Ning, Y. Cui, D.S. Reeves, and D. Xu. Tools and techniques for analyzing intrusion alerts. *ACM Transactions on Information and System Security*, 7(2):273–318, May 2004.
27. P. Ning and D. Xu. Hypothesizing and reasoning about attacks missed by intrusion detection systems. *ACM Transactions on Information and System Security*, 7(4):591–627, November 2004.
28. The Department of Homeland Security Science and Technology directorate. PREDICT - protected repository for the defense of infrastructure against cyber threats. `https://www.predict.org`.
29. P. A. Porras and P. G. Neumann. EMERALD: Event monitoring enabling response to anomalous live disturbances. In *Proceedings of the 20th National Information Systems Security Conference*, National Institute of Standards and Technology, 1997.
30. P.A. Porras, M.W. Fong, and A. Valdes. A mission-impact-based approach to INFOSEC alarm correlation. In *Proceedings of the 5th International Symposium on Recent Advances in Intrusion Detection (RAID 2002)*, pages 95–114, 2002.
31. X. Qin and W. Lee. Statistical causality analysis of infosec alert data. In *Proceedings of The 6th International Symposium on Recent Advances in Intrusion Detection (RAID 2003)*, Pittsburgh, PA, September 2003.
32. S. Staniford, J.A. Hoagland, and J.M. McAlerney. Practical automated detection of stealthy portscans. *Journal of Computer Security*, 10(1/2):105–136, 2002.
33. J. Ullrich. DShield - distributed intrusion detection system. `http://www.dshield.org`.
34. A. Valdes and K. Skinner. Probabilistic alert correlation. In *Proceedings of the 4th International Symposium on Recent Advances in Intrusion Detection (RAID 2001)*, pages 54–68, 2001.
35. G. Vigna and R. A. Kemmerer. NetSTAT: A network-based intrusion detection system. *Journal of Computer Security*, 7(1):37–71, 1999.
36. D. Xu and P. Ning. Alert correlation through triggering events and common resources. In *Proceedings of the 20th Annual Computer Security Applications Conference (ACSAC '04)*, December 2004.

37. D. Xu and P. Ning. Privacy-preserving alert correlation: A concept hierarchy based approach. In *Proceedings of the 21st Annual Computer Security Applications Conference (ACSAC '05)*, December 2005.
38. D. Xu and P. Ning. A flexible approach to intrusion alert anonymization and correlation. In *Proceedings of 2nd IEEE Communications Society/CreateNet International Conference on Security and Privacy in Communication Networks (SecureComm 2006)*, August 2006.
39. Y. Zhai, P. Ning, P. Iyer, and D.S. Reeves. Reasoning about complementary intrusion evidence. In *Proceedings of the 20th Annual Computer Security Applications Conference (ACSAC '04)*, December 2004.

An Approach to Preventing, Correlating, and Predicting Multi-Step Network Attacks

Lingyu Wang[1] and Sushil Jajodia[2]

Abstract To protect networks from malicious intrusions, it is necessary to take steps to prevent attacks from succeeding. At the same time, it is important to recognize that not all attacks can be averted at the outset; attacks that are successful to some degree must be recognized as unavoidable and comprehensive support for identifying and responding to attacks is required. This essay will describe the recent research on attack graphs that represent known attack sequences attackers can use to penetrate computer networks. It will show how attack graphs can be used to compute actual sets of hardening measures that guarantee the safety of given critical resources. Attack graphs can also be used to correlate received alerts, hypothesize missing alerts, and predict future alerts, all at the same time. Thus, they offer a promising solution for administrators to monitor and predict the progress of an intrusion, and take appropriate countermeasures in a timely manner.

1 Introduction

Real threats to a network usually come from skilled attackers who employ multiple attacks to evade security measures and to gradually gain privileges. Such multi-step network intrusions can often infiltrate a seemingly well guarded network. Most existing vulnerability scanners and intrusion detection systems (IDSs) can only report isolated vulnerabilities and attacks, which may not seem to be serious threats until

Concordia Institute for Information Systems Engineering
Concordia University
Montreal, QC H3G 1M8, Canada
e-mail: wang@ciise.concordia.ca

Center for Secure Information Systems
George Mason University
Fairfax, VA 22030-4444, USA
e-mail: jajodia@gmu.edu

they are cleverly combined by attackers. A penetration test may raise alarms about potential multi-step intrusions, but the effectiveness of such a test heavily depends on the capability of red team and the results are prone to human errors. Attack response based on isolated alerts is generally impractical due to the well-known impreciseness of IDSs.

In this essay, we describe a comprehensive approach to preventing, correlating, and predicting multi-step network intrusions. The approach is based on *attack graph*, which encodes knowledge about the network to be protected. More specifically, an attack graph represents all possible sequences of vulnerabilities that attackers may exploit during a multi-step intrusion. Attack graphs can be obtained through existing tools, such as the Topological Vulnerability Analysis (TVA) system [16] that can model 37,000 vulnerabilities taken from 24 information sources including X-Force, Bugtraq, CVE, CERT, Nessus, and Snort.

Although attack graphs reveal the threats, they do not directly provide a solution to prevent attackers from realizing such threats. In the first part of the essay, we describe a method to compute optimal network hardening solutions [25, 47]. Specifically, we view each vulnerability as a Boolean variable, and we derive a logic proposition to represent the negation of given critical resources in terms of initially satisfied security-related conditions. This proposition is thus the necessary and sufficient condition for protecting the critical resources. To make hardening options explicit, we transform this logic proposition into its disjunctive normal form (DNF). Each disjunction in the DNF provides a different option in hardening the network. We then choose options with the minimum cost based on given assumptions on the cost of initial conditions.

This approach to preventing multi-step intrusions by hardening the network has advantages over previous approaches of computing the minimal cut set of an attack graph [38, 17]. The key difference lies in that a minimal cut set of an attack graph does not capture the interdependency between vulnerabilities, whereas this approach does. This is important because a solution based on minimal cut sets is not directly enforceable, since some of the vulnerabilities are consequences of exploiting other vulnerabilities, and the consequences cannot be removed without first removing the causes. For example, the solution may require an FTP-related vulnerability to be removed, but the vulnerability cannot be removed without first removing another vulnerability that enables attackers to install the vulnerable FTP service.

Although off-line network hardening is an ideal solution in preventing multi-step intrusions, it is not always an option due to its costs and potential impact on availability. In practice, we may need to live with some of the vulnerabilities, and to take countermeasures only when a multi-step intrusion is actually happening. We thus need real-time detection and prediction methods for multi-step intrusions. In the second part of the essay, we describe a method to correlate isolated attacks into attack scenario and predict possible future attacks in real time [45, 46]. The method can thus help administrators to monitor and predict the progress of a multi-step intrusion, and take appropriate countermeasures in a timely manner.

Most previous alert correlation methods are designed for off-line applications, such as computer forensics. The defense against multi-step intrusions in real time brings new challenge to those methods. Those methods typically have a computational complexity and memory requirement both linear in the number of received alerts. This implies the number of alerts that can be processed for correlation will be limited by available resources, such as memory. This may be okay for an off-line application where the number of alerts is already known and resources can be allocated accordingly. However, a *live* attacker aware of this fact can prevent two attack steps from being correlated by either passively delaying the second step or actively injecting bogus alerts between the two steps. In either case, the correlation effort is completely defeated.

To address the above limitation of previous methods, we propose a novel method for efficiently correlating isolated attacks into attack scenario. We only keep the last alert matching each of the known vulnerabilities. The correlation between a new alert and these alerts is explicitly recorded, whereas the correlation with other alerts is implicitly represented using the temporal order between alerts. The time complexity and memory requirement of this method are both independent of the number of received alerts, meaning the efficiency does not decrease over time. This approach can correlate two alerts that are separated by arbitrarily many others. It is thus immune to deliberately slowed intrusions and injected bogus attacks.

We then extend the method for the hypothesis and prediction of intrusion alerts. The method compares *knowledge* encoded in a queue graph with *facts* represented by correlated alerts. An inconsistency between the knowledge and the facts implies potential attacks missed by IDSs, whereas extending the facts in a consistent way with respect to the knowledge indicates potential future attacks. The result of the analysis is represented in a compact way, such that all transitive edges are removed, and those alerts that are *indistinguishable* in terms of correlation are aggregated. Empirical results indicate that this method can fulfill all the tasks in one pass and faster than the IDS can report alerts.

The rest of this chapter is organized as follows. The next section reviews related work. Section 3 states basic concepts and assumptions. Section 4 discusses the network hardening method. Section 5 devises the queue graph-based methods for alert correlation, hypothesis, and prediction. Section 6 concludes the chapter.

2 Related Work

Alert correlation techniques aim to reconstruct attack scenarios from isolated alerts reported by IDSs, using prior knowledge about attack strategies [7, 9, 4, 11, 41] or alert dependencies [3, 21, 23]. Some techniques aggregate alerts with similar attributes [2, 6, 39, 44] or similar statistical patterns [18, 30]. Hybrid approaches combine different techniques for better results [23, 31, 51]. Alert correlation techniques are also used for other purposes rather than analyzing multi-step intrusions, such as to relate alerts to the same thread of attacks [15]. The privacy issue of alert correlation has recently been investigated [52]. Alert correlation is employed to deal with insider attacks [34, 32].

A number of tools are available for scanning network vulnerabilities, such as Nessus [10], but most of them can only report isolated vulnerabilities. On the research front, attack graphs are constructed by analyzing the inter-dependency between vulnerabilities and security conditions that have been identified in the target network [12, 53, 29, 5, 26, 35, 40, 36, 1, 38, 16]. Such analysis can be either forward starting from the initial state [29, 40] or backward from the goal state [35, 38]. Model checking was first used to analyze whether the given goal state is reachable from the initial state [35, 33] but later used to enumerate all possible sequences of attacks between the two states [38, 17].

The explicit attack sequences produced by a model checker face a serious scalability issue, because the number of such sequences is exponential in the number of vulnerabilities multiplied by the number of hosts. To avoid such combinatorial explosion, a more compact representation of attack graphs was proposed in [1]. The *monotonicity assumption* underlies this representation, i.e., an attacker never relinquishes any obtained capability. This newer representation can thus keep exactly one vertex for each exploit or security condition, leading to an attack graph of polynomial size (in the total number of vulnerabilities and security conditions). In this chapter we shall assume such a compact representation of the attack graph.

Algorithms exist to find the set of exploits from which the goal conditions are reachable [1]. This eliminates some irrelevant exploits from further consideration because they do not contribute to reaching the goal condition. However, this result may still include many irrelevant exploits, even though the goal condition is reachable from them. The reason lies in that the reachability is a necessary but not sufficient condition for an exploit to actually contribute to reaching the goal condition. On the other hand, this solution is necessary and sufficient for a goal condition to be satisfied.

The *minimal critical attack set* is a minimal set of exploits in an attack graph whose removal prevents attackers from reaching any of the goal states [38, 17, 1]. The minimal critical attack set thus provides solutions to harden the network. However, the method ignores the critical fact that consequences cannot be removed without removing the causes. The exploits in their solutions usually depend on other exploits that also need to be disabled. The solution is thus not directly enforceable. Moreover, after taking into account those implied exploits the solution is no longer minimal. To support interactive analysis of attack graphs, a relational model for encoding attack graphs and corresponding queries is proposed [50]. Preliminary efforts on quantifying vulnerabilities are described in [49, 48].

Attack scenarios broken by missed attacks are reassembled by clustering alerts with similar attributes [24], and those caused by incomplete knowledge are pieced together through statistical analyses [31, 30]. Instead of repairing a broken scenario afterwards, this method can tolerate and hypothesize missed attacks at the same time of correlation. Real-Time detection of isolated alerts is studied in [19, 28]. Some products claim to support real-time analyses of alerts, such as the Tivoli Risk Manager [14]. Designed for a different purpose, the RUSSEL language is similar to this approach in that the analysis of data only requires one-pass of processing [13].

3 Preliminaries

Our discussions will involve concepts in both topological vulnerability analysis and intrusion alert correlation. This chapter reviews relevant concepts and states our assumptions. First, Section 3.1 discusses attack graphs. Section 3.2 then discusses intrusion alerts and their correlation.

3.1 Attack Graph

Attack graphs represent prior knowledge about network connectivity and the dependency between vulnerabilities. There have been two different representations for an attack graph. First, an attack graph can explicitly enumerate all possible sequences of vulnerabilities that an attacker can follow, that is *attack paths* [38, 17]. However, such graphs are subject to inherent combinatorial explosion in the number of attack paths.

Second, an attack graph can be represented by the dependency relationships among vulnerabilities, and attack paths are encoded implicitly [1]. This representation does not lose any information under the monotonicity assumption, which states that an attacker never need to relinquish any obtained capability. The resulting attack graph has no duplicate vertices, and hence has a polynomial size in the number of vulnerabilities multiplied by the number of connected pairs of hosts. We shall assume this latter notion of attack graphs.

An attack graph is usually represented as a directed graph with two type of vertices, *exploits* and *security conditions* (or simply *conditions* when no confusion is possible). We denote an exploit as a tuple (v, h_s, h_m, h_d). This indicates an exploitation of the vulnerability v on the destination host h_d, initiated from the source host h_s and through an intermediate host h_m. For exploits involving two hosts (no intermediate host) or one (local) host, we use (v, h_s, h_d) and (v, h), respectively.

Similarly, a security condition is a triple (c, h_s, h_d) that indicates a security-related condition c involving the source host h_s and the destination host h_d. When a condition involves a single host, we simply write (c, h). Examples of security conditions include the existence of a vulnerability or the connectivity between two hosts. While there might be abundant security conditions in each host, we only include those that are relevant to at least one exploit in the attack graph.

Two types of directed edges inter-connect exploits and conditions (no edge exists directly between exploits, nor between conditions). First, an edge can point from a condition to an exploit. Such an edge denotes the *require* relation, which means the exploit cannot be executed unless the condition is satisfied. Second, an edge pointing from an exploit to a condition denotes the *imply* relation, which means executing the exploit will satisfy the condition. For example, an exploit usually requires the existence of the vulnerability on the destination host and the connectivity between the two hosts. We formally characterize attack graphs in Definition 0.1.

Definition 0.1. Given a set of exploits E, a set of conditions C, a **require** relation $R_r \subseteq C \times E$, and an **imply** relation $R_i \subseteq E \times C$,

- We call the directed graph $G(E \cup C, R_r \cup R_i)$ an **attack graph** ($E \cup C$ is the vertex set and $R_r \cup R_i$ the edge set).
- We use $\rightarrow$ for the **prepare-for** relation $R_i \circ R_r$ ($\circ$ denotes the composition).

Example 0.1. Figure 1 depicts a simplified example of attack graph. The vertices in plaintext denote security conditions, and those inside ovals denote exploits. The attack graph shows an attacker having user privilege on host $h3$ can exploit the *SADMIND BUFFER OVERFLOW* (Nessus ID 11841) vulnerability on hosts $h1$ and $h2$ and obtain user privilege on the destination hosts. We can see that after an attacker has obtained user privilege on host $h1$ (or $h2$), he/she can then exploit host $h2$ (or $h1$) from either host $h3$ or host $h1$.

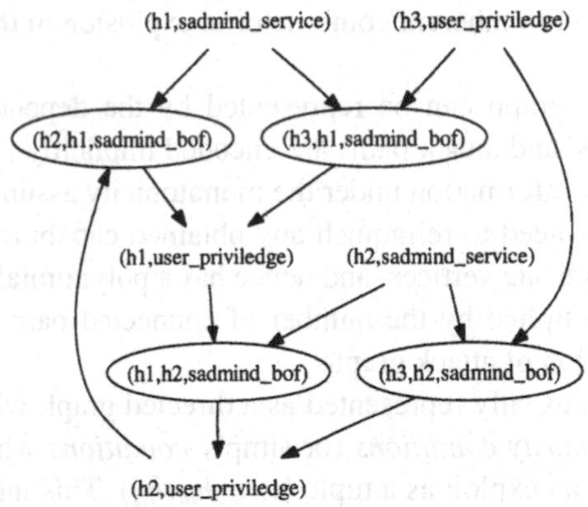

Fig. 1 An Example of Attack Graph

One important aspect of attack graphs is that the require relation is always conjunctive, whereas the imply relation is always disjunctive. More specifically, an exploit cannot be realized until *all* of its required conditions have been satisfied, whereas a condition is satisfied if *any* of the realized exploits implies the condition. Exceptions to the above requirements do exist. First, an exploit with multiple variations may require different sets of conditions, whence the require relation for this exploit is disjunctive (between these sets of conditions). This case can be handled by having a separate vertex for each variation of the exploit such that the require relation for each variation is still strictly conjunctive.

On the other hand, a collection of exploits may jointly imply a condition whereas none of them alone can do so, whence the imply relation becomes conjunctive for this condition. This case can be handled by inserting dummy conditions and exploits to capture the conjunctive relationship. For example, suppose both e_1 and e_2 are required to make a condition c satisfied. We insert two dummy conditions c_1 and c_2

and a dummy exploit e_3 into the attack graph. The edges are inserted such that e_1 and e_2 imply c_1 and c_2, respectively, and c_1 and c_2 are required by e_3, which in turn implies c. Now the conjunctive relationship that both e_1 and e_2 are required for c to be satisfied is encoded in the fact that e_3 requires both c_1 and c_2.

We assume attack graphs can be obtained with existing tools, such as the aforementioned Topological Vulnerability Analysis (TVA) system [16]. We assume the attack graph is updated in a timely fashion upon changes in network topology and configuration. We assume the attack graph can be placed in memory. For a given network, the size of an attack graph can usually be estimated and the required memory can be accordingly allocated. We do not assume external host addresses to be trustful and use wildcards to match them. This may cause false correlations when multiple attackers concurrently launch similar attacks while they do not intend to cooperate with each other.

3.2 Intrusion Alert and Correlation

Intrusion alerts are reported by IDS sensors placed in a network, and they typically have attributes like the type of events, the address of the source and destination host, the time stamp, and so on. Our discussion does not depend on specific format of alerts, so we simply regard each alert as a relational tuple with a given (usually implicit) schema. For example, with the schema *(event type, source IP, destination IP, time stamp)*, an alert will have the form *(RPC portmap sadmind request UDP, 202.77.162.213, 172.16.115.20, 03/07-08:50:04.74612)*.

We adopt a vulnerability-centric correlation approach, which first matches alerts with exploits and then correlate them using the knowledge encoded in an attack graph. To match alerts with exploits, the event type attributes of alerts need to be mapped to the vulnerability attributes of exploits using domain knowledge, such as the correspondence between Snort identifiers and Nessus identifiers [27]. For simplicity, we denote the matching between alerts and exploits as a function $Exp()$ from the set of alerts A to the set of exploits E (in some cases an event type matches multiple vulnerabilities, which will be handled by creating a copy of alert for each matched exploit, indicating an simultaneous exploitation of multiple vulnerabilities).

Starting from the knowledge about one's own network, the vulnerability-centric correlation approach can mitigate the negative impact of disruptive alerts. For example, if the attacker blindly launches some Windows-specific attacks on UNIX machines, then the reported alerts will be ignored by the approach. On the other hand, the limitation lies in that relevant alerts do not always match exploits. For example, an ICMP PING matches no vulnerability, but it may signal the probing preparation for following attacks. Such relevant alerts can be identified based on attack graphs and the knowledge about alert types. We extend the concept of exploits to include alert types in the place of vulnerability attributes. Such special *exploits* are added to attack graphs and the function *Exp* is extended accordingly.

As we shall discuss in Section 5, the correlation methods critically depend on temporal characteristics of alerts, such that the order of arrivals and timestamps. In practice, those characteristics will exhibit much uncertainty due to various delays in hosts and network, especially when alerts are collected from multiple sensors placed differently in a network. We shall address such temporal impreciseness in more details in later sections. We assume the clocks of IDS sensors are loosely synchronized with the correlation engine. This can be achieved in many different ways depending on specific IDS systems. For example, Snort has built-in support of automatic time synchronization through the network time protocol (NTP) [37]. We leave the case where attackers may temper with the clocks as future work.

4 Hardening Network To Prevent Multi-Step Intrusions

This section discusses how to prevent multi-step intrusions through hardening the network. First, Section 4.1 gives intuitions via examples. Section 4.2 then formalizes the hardening problem and provides a graph-based algorithm to find possible hardening options. Finally, Section 4.3 studies how to pick a option with the minimal cost.

4.1 A Motivating Example

Ideally, we want to prevent all sequences of multi-step attacks that may endanger given important resources in a network. We can achieve this goal through hardening the network, such as removing vulnerabilities and modifying network configurations. However, each such network hardening option will incur a cost, and it is desirable to keep overall costs as low as possible. The optimal solution should provably prevent any attacker from reaching a given goal (corresponding to the resources to be guarded) and yet incur the lowest cost. Such a desired solution is usually not apparent from the attack graph itself. This is true even for relatively simple scenario, due to multiple interleaved attack paths leading to the goal condition. To illustrate, consider the following example.

Example 0.2. An attack graph similar to those in [38, 1, 17] is given in Figure 2. Notice that some modeling simplifications have been made, such as combining connectivity at different layers. The details of the attack scenario (for example, network topology, services, and operating systems) are also omitted here. In the figure, exploits appear as ovals, and conditions as plain text (with the goal condition shaded).

As an example of attack paths, the attacker can first establish a trust relationship from his machine host 0 to host 2 (the condition $(trust\_0,2)$) via the ftp .rhosts vulnerability on host 2 (the exploit $(ftp\_rhosts,0,2)$), then gain user privilege on host 2 (the condition $(user,2)$) with an rsh login (the exploit $(rsh,0,2)$), and finally achieve the goal condition $(root,2)$ using a local buffer overflow attack on host 2 (the exploit $(local\_bof, 2)$). The following are some of the valid attack paths that can be generated using existing algorithms [1].

- $(ftp\_rhosts, 0, 2), (rsh, 0, 2), (local\_bof, 2)$
- $(ftp\_rhosts, 0, 1), (rsh, 0, 1), (ftp\_rhosts, 1, 2), (rsh, 1, 2), (local\_bof, 2)$
- $(sshd\_bof, 0, 2), (ftp\_rhosts, 1, 2), (rsh, 1, 2), (local\_bof, 2)$

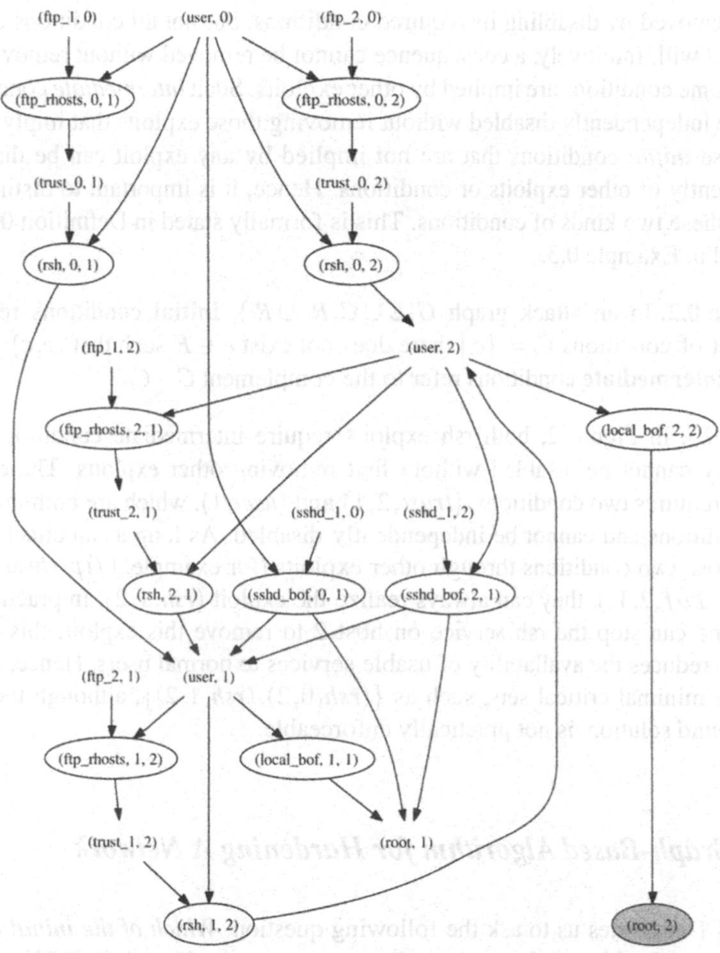

Fig. 2 An Example Attack Graph

Intuitively, to safeguard the goal condition, we want to *break* all the attack paths leading to the goal. This intuition was captured by the concept of *critical set*, that is, a set of exploits (and corresponding conditions) whose removal from the attack graph will invalidate all attack paths [38, 17]. It has also been shown that finding critical sets with the minimum cardinality is NP-hard, whereas finding a minimal critical set (that is, a critical set with no proper subset being a critical set) is polynomial. Based on the above attack paths, there are many minimal critical sets, such as $\{(rsh,0,2),(rsh,1,2)\}$, $\{(ftp\_rhosts,0,2)\},(rsh,1,2)\}$, $\{(ftp\_rhosts,1,2),(rsh,0,2)\}$, and so on. If any of those sets of exploits could be completely removed, all the attack paths will become invalid, and hence the goal condition is safe.

Unfortunately, this solution based on critical set ignores an important fact. That is, Not all exploits are under the direct control of administrators. An exploit can only be removed by disabling its required conditions, but not all conditions can be disabled at will. Intuitively, a consequence cannot be removed without removing its causes. Some conditions are implied by other exploits. Such *intermediate* conditions cannot be independently disabled without removing those exploits that imply them. Only those *initial* conditions that are not implied by any exploit can be disabled independently of other exploits or conditions. Hence, it is important to distinguish between these two kinds of conditions. This is formally stated in Definition 0.2 and illustrated in Example 0.3.

Definition 0.2. In an attack graph $G(E \cup C, R_r \cup R_i)$, **initial** conditions refer to the subset of conditions $C_i = \{c \mid \text{there does not exist } e \in E \text{ such that } (e,c) \in R_i\}$, whereas **intermediate** conditions refer to the complement $C - C_i$.

Example 0.3. In Figure 2, both rsh exploits require intermediate conditions, and hence they cannot be disabled without first removing other exploits. The exploit $rsh(1,2)$ requires two conditions, $(trust,2,1)$ and $(user,1)$, which are both intermediate conditions and cannot be independently disabled. As long as an attacker can satisfy those two conditions through other exploits (for example, $(ftp\_rhosts,1,2)$ and $(sshd\_bof,2,1)$), they can always realize the exploit $(rsh,1,2)$. In practice, although one can stop the rsh service on host 2 to remove this exploit, this action adversely reduces the availability of usable services to normal users. Hence, any of the above minimal critical sets, such as $\{(rsh,0,2),(rsh,1,2)\}$, although theoretically a sound solution, is not practically enforceable.

4.2 A Graph-Based Algorithm for Hardening A Network

Section 4.1 motivates us to ask the following question: *Which of the initial conditions must be disabled, if the goal conditions are never to be satisfied?* The answer to this question comprises an enforceable solution, because initial conditions can be independently disabled. To more formally state the above problem, it is convenient to interpret an attack graph as a simple logic program as follows. Each exploit or condition in the attack graph is interpreted as a logic variable. The interdependency between exploits and conditions now becomes logic propositions involving the two connectives *AND* and *OR*, with *AND* between the conditions required by each exploit and *OR* between the exploits implying each condition.

All the variables in the logic program are Boolean. A true initial condition means the condition is satisfied and a false one means it has been disabled by security measures. A true exploit means it has been realized. A true intermediate condition means it has been satisfied by at least one realized exploit implying that condition. With this logic program, the *network hardening* problem is simply to find value assignments to the initial conditions satisfying that a given set of goal conditions are all false. The above description is more formally stated as Definition 0.3 and illustrated in Example 0.4.

Definition 0.3. Given an attack graph $G(E \cup C, R_r \cup R_i)$ and the goal conditions $C_g \subseteq C$, let $P(G)$ denote a logic program comprised of the following clause for each $e \in E$:

$$e \leftarrow c_1 \wedge c_2 \wedge \dots c_n$$

$$c_1, c_2, \dots, c_n \in R_r(e)$$

and the collection of clauses for each $c \in C$:

$$c \leftarrow e_1$$

$$c \leftarrow e_2$$

$$\dots$$

$$c \leftarrow e_m$$

$$e_1, e_2, \dots, e_m \in R_i(c)$$

The **network hardening** problem is to satisfy the goal $\neg c_1 \wedge \neg c_2 \wedge \cdots \neg c_l$ where each $c_1, c_2, \dots, c_l \in C_g$.

Example 0.4. For the attack graph G shown in Figure 2, the following are examples of clauses in $P(G)$

$$ftp\_rhosts(0,1) \leftarrow ftp(0,1) \wedge user(0)$$

$$rsh(0,1) \leftarrow trust(1,0) \wedge user(0)$$

$$user(1) \leftarrow rsh(0,1) \vee rsh(2,1) \vee sshd\_bof(0,1) \vee sshd\_bof(2,1)$$

$$root(2) \leftarrow local\_bof(2)$$

To harden the network, we ony need to find a value assignment to the initial conditions such that the goal $\neg root(2)$ is true.

By its very definition, the hardening problem can certainly be solved by logic programming techniques. However, considering the simplicity of the logic program, we shall instead resolve to a simpler solution based on graph searches. Roughly speaking, we start from the goal conditions to traverse the attack graph backwards by following the directed edges in the reverse direction. During the traversal we make logical inferences. At the end of the graph traversal, a logic proposition of the initial conditions is derived to be the necessary and sufficient condition for making the goal true.

Procedure *Network_Hardening*
Input: An attack graph $G(E \cup C, R_r \cup R_i)$ and the goal conditions $C_g \subseteq C$
Output: A solution L to the goal $\bigwedge_{c \in C_g} \neg c$
Method:

1. **Let** $L = \bigwedge_{c \in C_g} \neg c$ //The initial goal
2. **For** each $e \in E$ and $c \in C$
3.   **Let** $Pre(e) = \{e\}$ and $Pre(c) = \{c\}$ //Initialize the predecessor list
4. **Do** a breadth-first search in G starting from C_g
5.   **For** each encountered condition c //Each exploit e is handled similarly
6.   **Let** $S_e = \{e_1, e_2, \ldots, e_n\}$ be the exploits pointing to c in G
7.   **Let** $T = (e_1 \vee e_2 \vee \ldots e_n)$ //Temporary variable
8.   **For** each $e_i \in S_e \cap Pre(c)$
9.   **Replace** e_i with *FALSE* in T //Break a cycle
10.   **Replace** c with T in L //Expand on the condition
11.   **For** each $e_i \in S_e - Pre(c)$
12.   **Let** $Pre(e_i) = Pre(e_i) \cup Pre(c)$ //Update the predecessor list
13. **Return** L

Fig. 3 A Procedure for Solving The Network Hardening Problem

Figure 3 shows a procedure *Network_Hardening* that more precisely describes this process. The first three lines of procedure *Network_Hardening* initialize the result L and a *predecessor set* for each vertex (an exploit or a condition) that used to avoid cycles. The procedure then searches the attack graph backwards in a breadth-first manner (strictly speaking, this is not a breadth-first search, since each vertex may be visited more than once).

For each condition c the procedure encounters (each exploit is handled in a similar way, and hence is omitted.), it substitutes c in the result L with a logically equivalent proposition, that is, the conjunction of those exploits that imply condition c (line 6 through line 10). It adds the vertices reachable from the current vertex to the predecessor set of that vertex (line 11-12). The procedure avoids running into cycles by only expanding the search towards those vertices not reachable from the current vertex (line 8-9) and thus avoids introducing logic loops into the final result.

Consider Figure 2 again. Because the procedure will only search among the vertices from which the goal condition is reachable, we can safely remove from further consideration the exploit $local\_bof(1)$ and the condition $root(1)$, together with corresponding edges. The condition $user(0)$, which denotes the attacker's privilege on his/her own machine, can also be removed because it is beyond the control of administrators. The simplified version of the attack graph is shown in Figure 4.

The Procedure *Network_Hardening* traverses this attack graph as follows (for clarity purposes, we shall describe it in a depth-first manner and ignore the result collection for the time being). It starts from the goal condition $(root, 2)$ and

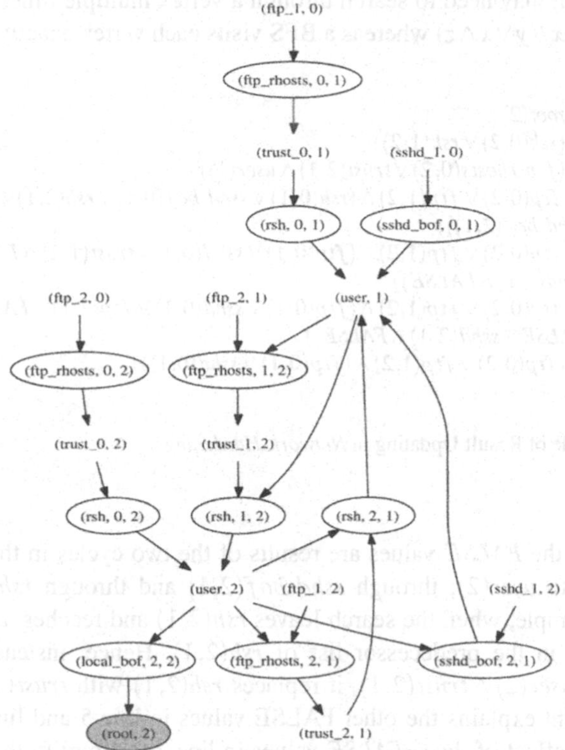

Fig. 4 Illustration of The Procedure *Network_Hardening*

advances to $(user,2)$ through $(local\_bof,2,2)$. It then branches and reaches both $(rsh,0,2)$ and $(rsh,1,2)$. The advance of the branch at $(rsh,0,2)$ is straightforward. For the branch at $(rsh,1,2)$, it reaches $(user,1)$ twice, one directly from $(rsh,1,2)$ and the other through $(trust\_1,2)$ and $(ftp\_rhosts,1,2)$. The advance from $(user,1)$ branches upwards to $(rsh,0,1)$ and $(sshd\_bof,0,1)$, and also downwards to $(rsh,2,1)$ and $(sshd\_bof,2,1)$. The advance of the first two branches is straightforward. The two downward branches loop back to $(user,2)$ and both terminate there, because $(user,2)$ is included by the predecessor set of $(rsh,2,1)$, $(ftp\_rhosts,2,1)$, and $(sshd\_bof,2,1)$).

The result L is initially $\neg(root,2)$ and is subsequently updated as in Figure 5. Some straightforward steps are omitted for simplicity. The condition $(user,1)$ actually appears twice in the proposition, one required by $(rsh,1,2)$ in line 3 and the other required by $(ftp\_rhosts,1,2)$. The second appearance should be included in line 4 but we have omitted it for simplicity since $(user,1) \wedge (user,1)$ is logically equivalent to $(user,1)$. Notice, however, such simplification is not always possible (for example, in the case of $x \wedge y \vee x \wedge z$, both copies of x must be kept), and it is not part of the procedure. Indeed, the procedure differs from normal breadth-first search

(BFS) because it may need to search through a vertex multiple times (for example, x in the case of $x \wedge y \vee x \wedge z$) whereas a BFS visits each vertex exactly once.

1. $L = \neg root(2)$
2. $= \neg(rsh(0,2) \vee rsh(1,2))$
3. $= \neg(ftp\_rhosts(0,2) \vee trust(2,1) \wedge user(1))$
4. $= \neg(ftp(0,2) \vee ftp(1,2) \wedge (rsh(0,1) \vee sshd\_bof(0,1) \vee rsh(2,1) \vee sshd\_bof(2,1)))$
5. $= \neg(ftp(0,2) \vee ftp(1,2) \wedge (ftp(0,1) \vee sshd(0,1) \vee trust(1,2) \wedge FALSE \vee sshd(2,1) \wedge FALSE))$
6. $= \neg(ftp(0,2) \vee ftp(1,2) \wedge (ftp(0,1) \vee sshd(0,1) \vee ftp(2,1) \wedge FALSE \wedge FALSE \vee sshd(2,1) \wedge FALSE))$
7. $= \neg(ftp(0,2) \vee ftp(1,2) \wedge (ftp(0,1) \vee sshd(0,1)))$

Fig. 5 An Example of Result Updating in *Network_Hardening*

In Figure 5, the *FALSE* values are results of the two cycles in the attack graph (from $user(1)$ to $user(2)$, through $sshd\_bof(2,1)$ and through $rsh(2,1)$, respectively). For example, when the search leaves $rsh(2,1)$ and reaches $user(2)$, it finds that $user(2)$ is in the predecessor list of $rsh(2,1)$. Hence, instead of replacing $rsh(2,1)$ with $user(2) \wedge trust(2,1)$, it replaces $rsh(2,1)$ with $trust(1,2) \wedge FALSE$. Similar argument explains the other FALSE values in line 5 and line 6. Although we remove the effect of those *FALSE* values in line 7 to simplify the result, this is not part of the procedure.

4.3 Minimum-Cost Solutions

The procedure *Network_Hardening* returns the necessary and sufficient condition for hardening the network such that none of the goal conditions can be satisfied. However, such a proposition usually implies multiple options. It is not always clear which option is the best. Therefore, we need to simplify the proposition and choose optimal solutions with respect to given cost metrics. As the first step, we convert the proposition L returned by the Procedure *Network_Hardening* to its disjunctive normal form (DNF). Each disjunction in the DNF thus represents a sufficient option in hardening the network. Each disjunction in the DNS is the conjunction of negated initial conditions, meaning these initial conditions must be disabled.

Example 0.5. In Figure 5, by applying the tautology $A \vee B \wedge C \leftrightarrow (A \vee B) \wedge (A \vee C)$ and De Morgan's law [20], we can simplify the result as follows.

$$L = \neg(ftp(0,2) \vee ftp(1,2) \wedge (ftp(0,1) \vee sshd(0,1)))$$
$$\equiv \neg((ftp(0,2) \vee ftp(1,2)) \wedge (ftp(0,2) \vee ftp(0,1) \vee sshd(0,1)))$$
$$\equiv \neg ftp(0,2) \wedge \neg ftp(1,2) \vee \neg ftp(0,2) \wedge \neg ftp(0,1) \wedge \neg sshd(0,1)$$

From this DNF, we can see clearly the two options in hardening the network: one is to disable both $ftp(0,2)$ and $ftp(1,2)$, the other is to disable the three conditions $ftp(0,2)$, $ftp(0,1)$, and $sshd(0,1)$.

Although any of the disjunctions in the DNF of the result is a sufficient option for hardening the network, the cost of those options may be different. First, the set of initial conditions involved in one option may be a proper super set of those involved in another option. The cost incurred by the latter is clearly no greater than that by the former, and hence the former can be removed from further consideration. Theoretically, the DNF of L may have an exponential size in the number of initial conditions (after the above reduction, this number of options will be bound by the number of incomparable subsets of n initial conditions, which is known as the binomial coefficient $\binom{n}{\lfloor n/2 \rfloor}$ by Sperner's Theorem).

We are now left with options involving mutually incomparable subsets of initial conditions. The options that incur the minimum cost can be easily chosen, if the cost of disabling each initial condition has been assigned by administrators. In such a case, the cost of an option is simply equal to the summation of the cost of all the initial conditions involved by the option. Although it is usually difficult to assign precise cost to each condition, the conditions can always be partially ordered based on their costs. Consequently, the options can also be partially ordered based on the cost of conditions. An option with a cost no greater than any other options can thus be chosen based on the partial order.

Example 0.6. Consider the two options we have derived from the last example, that is either to disable both $ftp(0,2)$ and $ftp(1,2)$, or to disable the three conditions $ftp(0,2)$, $ftp(0,1)$, and $sshd(0,1)$. The condition $ftp(0,2)$ must be disabled in either case, and hence it can be ignored in considering relative costs. Since the condition $sshd(0,1)$ can be disabled by patching the buffer overflow vulnerability in the sshd service, the cost may be relatively low. On the other hand, the conditions involving the ftp service incurs more costs, because the ftp service is properly functioning, and is simply used by the attacker in a clever way. Moreover, disabling $ftp(0,2)$ may mean stopping the ftp service on host 2 to all external hosts, which may incur a higher cost than stopping the ftp service between two internal hosts 1 and 2 (they may still communicate files via other services). Based on those assumptions, the first option has a lower cost than that of the second and thus should be chosen as the solution.

5 Correlating and Predicting Multi-Step Attacks

The previous section shows that multi-step attacks can be avoided, if we can harden the network by removing vulnerabilities and reconfiguring the network. However, network hardening is not always feasible due to its incurred costs. Hence, this section discusses another option in defending a multi-step intrusion, that is to monitor and predict its progress in real time, and to take appropriate actions accordingly. First, Section 5.1 gives the motivation. Section 5.2 then describes our queue graph-based approach to alert correlation. Section 5.3 extends the approach to hypothesize and predict alerts. Finally, Section 5.4 discusses how to compress the result of these analyses.

5.1 Motivation

Roughly speaking, when an alert correlation engine receives a new alert, it searches through the received alerts to find those that prepare for the new alert. In vulnerability-centric alert correlation, alerts inherit the prepare-for relationship from the exploits that these alerts are mapped to. The prepare-for relationship is repetitively evaluated between a new alert and each received alert; this process is repeated for each new alert. Apparently, this procedure involves two nested loops, and is thus usually called the *nested loop* approach.

Figure 6 illustrates the nested loop approach. The left side of the figure shows a sequence of alerts with ascending timestamps, $a_0, a_1, \ldots, a_n$. For $i = 1, 2, \ldots, n$, the approach searches $a_0, a_1, \ldots, a_{i-1}$ for those a_j's that satisfy $Exp(a_j) \rightarrow Exp(a_i)$. However, this does not imply that a_i must be compared to every $a_j (0 \leq j \leq i-1)$, although it comprises a simple implementation of the search. The search for the alerts that prepare for a_i can be optimized with an index on $a_0, a_1, \ldots, a_{i-1}$. After a_i is processed, an entry corresponding to a_i is inserted into the index. By maintaining such an index in memory, the nested loop approach can have a relatively good performance (for example, 65k alerts can be processed in less than one second [22]).

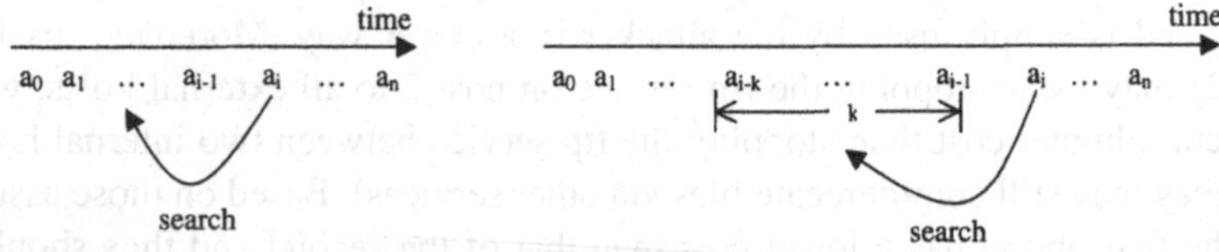

Fig. 6 The Nested Loop Approach With or Without a Sliding Window

Clearly, any finite amount of available memory will eventually be insufficient to hold the index as the number of received alerts keeps increasing. A *sliding window* approach comes to the rescue. That is, only the alerts close enough to the new alert are considered for correlation. As illustrated in the right side of Figure 6, for the alert a_i the search is only performed on $a_{i-k}, a_{i-k+1}, \ldots, a_{i-1}$, where k is a given window size determined by available memory. However, this sliding window approach leads to an unavoidable tradeoff between the performance and the completeness of correlation. On one hand, the performance requires k to be small enough so the index fits in memory. On the other hand, a smaller k means less alerts will be considered for correlation with the new alert, and thus the result may be incomplete as two related alerts may in fact be separated by more than k others.

In contrast to off-line applications, such as computer forensics, the situation is exacerbated in real-time correlation, where performance is critical and attackers are *alive*. Attackers may be aware of the ongoing detection and correlation effort, and they can employ a *slow attack* to defeat such efforts. Specifically, given an arbitrarily large window size k, for any two attacks that trigger the correlated alerts a_i and a_j, the attacker can delay the second attack until at least k other alerts have been raised since a_i, so $j - i > k$ meaning a_i and a_j will not be correlated. Instead of passively awaiting, a smarter attacker can actively launch bogus attacks between the two real attack steps, so the condition $j - i > k$ can be satisfied in a shorter time. The attacker can even script bogus attack sequences between the real attack steps, such that a deceived correlation engine will be kept busy in producing bogus attack scenarios, while the real intrusion will be advanced in peace of mind.

5.2 *Queue Graph-Based Alert Correlation*

Section 5.1 motivates us to propose a Queue Graph (QG) data structure to remove the limitation of the nested loop approach. The key observation is that the correlation between alerts does not always need to be explicitly recorded. Note that the correlation between two alerts actually mean two things. First, the prepare-for relationship exists between the exploits to which the two alerts are mapped. Second, the alert preparing for the other must occur before it. Knowing these facts, a new alert only needs to be explicitly correlated with the *last* alert matching each exploit. Its correlation with other earlier alerts matching the same exploit can be kept implicit through the temporal order and with the matching between alerts and exploits. This is illustrated in Example 0.7.

Example 0.7. In Figure 7, suppose the first three alerts a_i, a_j, and a_k all match the same exploit $Exp(a_k)$ (that is, their event types match the same vulnerability and they involve the same source and destination hosts). The alert a_h matches another exploit $Exp(a_h)$, and $Exp(a_k)$ prepares for $Exp(a_h)$. Hence, a_i, a_j, and a_k should all be correlated with a_h. However, if the correlation between a_k and a_h is explicitly recorded (shown as a solid line in the figure), then the correlation between a_j and a_h can be kept implicit (shown as a dotted-line). More precisely, the facts $Exp(a_j) = Exp(a_k)$ and $Exp(a_k) \rightarrow Exp(a_h)$ jointly imply $Exp(a_j) \rightarrow Exp(a_h)$, and the facts that a_j occurs before a_k and a_k occurs before a_h jointly imply that a_j must also occur before a_h. Similar arguments apply to the correlation between a_i and a_h.

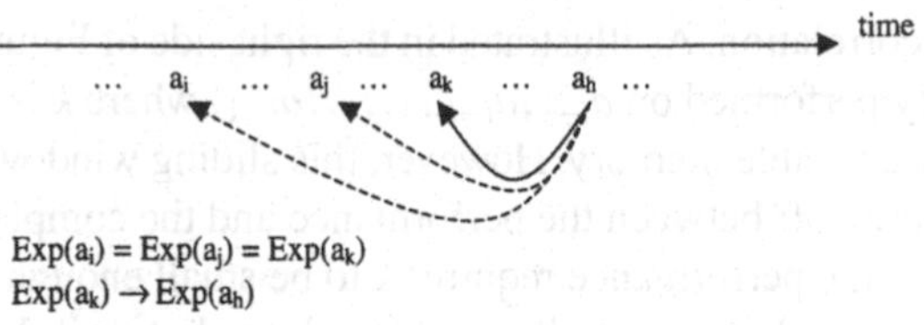

Fig. 7 Implicit and Explicit Correlation

This observation is important because keeping correlations implicit can significantly reduce the complexity and memory requirement. Intuitively, for each exploit the correlation algorithm only needs to search backward for the first (a_k in the above case) alert matching that exploit. For the nested loop approach, however, the correlation is always explicit. Hence, the approach must unnecessarily search all the received alerts, as discussed in Section 5.1. To take advantage of the above observation, we design an in-memory data structure, called *Queue Graph*. A queue graph is basically an in-memory materialization of the given attack graph with enhanced features (the purpose of the features will be clear in the following sections).

In a queue graph, each exploit is realized as a queue and each condition as a variable. The realization of edges is a little more complicated. Starting from each exploit e_i, a breadth-first search (BFS) is performed in the attack graph by following the directed edges. For each edge encountered during the search, a *forward* pointer is created to connect the corresponding queue and variable. Similarly, another search is performed by following the directed edges in their reversed direction, and a *backward* pointer is created for each encountered edge. Later we shall use the backward edges for correlation purposes and use the forward edges for prediction purposes.

The pointers are then placed at a separate *layer* tailored to the queue corresponding to the exploit e_i. The reason for separating pointers into layers is as follows. A BFS always creates a tree (namely, the BFS tree), and hence later another BFS starting from the same queue can follow only the pointers at that layer. This later BFS will then be performed within a *tree* instead of a *graph*, reducing the complexity from quadratic to linear. We first illustrate the concepts in Example 0.8, and then formalize the concepts in Definition 0.4. Example 0.9 rephrase Example 0.8 with the defined notations.

Example 0.8. In Figure 8, from left to right are a given attack graph, the corresponding queues (shown as buckets) and variables (shown as texts), and the (both forward and backward) pointers at different layers. Notice that the layer one pointers do not include those connecting v_2 and Q_3, because a BFS in the attack graph starting from e_1 will reach c_2 only once (either via e_2 or via e_3, but we assume e_2 in this example). The layer one pointers thus form a tree rooted at Q_1.

Definition 0.4. Let $G(E \cup C, R_r \cup R_i)$ be an attack graph, where $E = \{e_i \mid 1 \leq i \leq n\}$, $C = \{c_i \mid 1 \leq i \leq m\}$, $R_r \subseteq C \times E$, and $R_i \subseteq E \times C$.

- For $k = 1, 2, \ldots, n$,

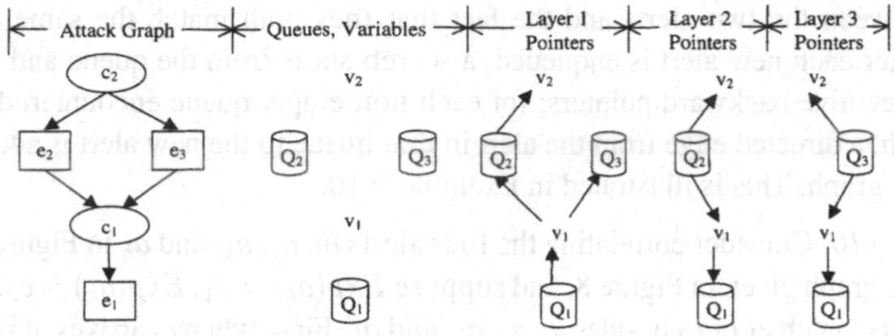

Fig. 8 An Example Queue Graph

- use $BFSR(k)$ to denote the set of edges visited by a breadth-first search in $G(E \cup C, R_r \cup R_i)$ starting from e_k, and
- use $BFS(k)$ for the set of edges visited by a breadth-first search in $G(E \cup C, R_r^{-1} \cup R_i^{-1})$ staring from e_k, where R_r^{-1} and R_i^{-1} are the inverse relations.

• The **queue graph** Q_g is a data structure with the following components:

- $\mathcal{Q} = \{Q_i \mid 1 \le i \le n\}$ are n queues of length one,
- $\mathcal{V} = \{v_i \mid 1 \le i \le m\}$ are m variables,
- for each $k = 1, 2, \ldots, n$,
  · $\mathcal{P}_k = \{\langle Q_j, v_i \rangle \mid (c_i, e_j) \in BFS(k)\} \cup \{\langle v_i, Q_j \rangle \mid (e_j, c_i) \in BFS(k)\}$ are the layer k backward pointers, and
  · $\mathcal{PR}_k = \{\langle v_i, Q_j \rangle \mid (c_i, e_j) \in BFSR(k)\} \cup \{\langle Q_j, v_i \rangle \mid (e_j, c_i) \in BFSR(k)\}$ are the layer k forward pointers.

Example 0.9. In Figure 8, the queue graph has three queues $\mathcal{Q} = \{Q_1, Q_2, Q_3\}$ and two variables $\mathcal{V} = \{v_1, v_2\}$. The layer-one forward pointers are $\mathcal{PR}_1 = \phi$, and the layer-one backward pointers are $\mathcal{P}_1 = \{\langle Q_1, v_1 \rangle, \langle v_1, Q_2 \rangle, \langle Q_2, v_2 \rangle, \langle v_1, Q_3 \rangle\}$ [1]. The layer two pointers include $\mathcal{P}_2 = \{\langle Q_2, v_2 \rangle\}$ and $\mathcal{PR}_2 = \{\langle Q_2, v_1 \rangle, \langle v_1, Q_1 \rangle\}$. The layer three pointers include $\mathcal{P}_3 = \{\langle Q_3, v_2 \rangle\}$ and $\mathcal{PR}_3 = \{\langle Q_3, v_1 \rangle, \langle v_1, Q_1 \rangle\}$.

We have discussed how a nested loop approach correlates alerts. As a comparison, we now perform the same correlation using a queue graph (we shall discuss other correlation requirements in Section 5.3). Intuitively, we let the stream of alerts flow through the queue graph, and at the same time we collect correlation results by searching the queue graph. Specifically, each incoming alert is first matched with an exploit and placed in the corresponding queue. Then, because the length of each queue is one, a non-empty queue must dequeue the current alert before it can enqueue a new alert.

The results of correlation are collected during this process as a directed graph, namely, the *result graph*. First, each new alert is recorded as a vertex in the result graph. Second, when a new alert forces an old alert to be dequeued, a directed edge between the two alerts is added into the result graph, which records the temporal

[1] We use the notation $\langle a, b \rangle$ for a pointer in a queue graph and (a, b) for an edge in a graph.

order between the two alerts and the fact that they both match the same exploit. Third, after each new alert is enqueued, a search starts from the queue and follows two consecutive backward pointers; for each non-empty queue encountered during the search, a directed edge from the alert in that queue to the new alert is added into the result graph. This is illustrated in Example 0.10.

Example 0.10. Consider correlating the four alerts a_i, a_j, a_k, and a_h in Figure 7 with the queue graph given in Figure 8, and suppose $Exp(a_h) = e_1$, $Exp(a_k) = e_2$, and no other alerts match e_1 or e_2 besides a_i, a_j, a_k, and a_h. First, when a_i arrives, it is placed in the empty queue Q_2. Then, a_j forces a_i to be dequeued from Q_2, and a directed edge (a_i, a_j) in the result graph records the facts that a_i is before a_j and they both match e_2. Similarly, a_k replaces a_j in Q_2, and a directed edge (a_j, a_k) is recorded. Finally, a_h arrives and occupies Q_1, a search starting from Q_1 and following two layer one backward pointers will find the alert a_k in Q_2. Hence, a directed edge (a_k, a_h) records the only explicit correlation.

The process for correlating alerts using a queue graph, as illustrated in Example 0.10, is more precisely stated as the procedure *QG_Alert_Correlation* in Figure 9. The result graph G_r has a set of vertices V and two separate sets of edges E_r and E_l. The edges in E_r correspond to the explicit correlations and those in E_l record the temporal order between alerts matching the same exploit. Initially, we set the queues in $\mathcal{Q}$, the sets V, E_r, and E_l as empty. The first step of the procedure inserts the new alert into the result graph. The second step dequeues a non-empty queue and updates the result graph by adding an edge between the old alert and the new alert. The third step enqueues the new alert into the queue graph. The fourth step does correlation by searching for the alerts that need to be explicitly correlated to the new alert.

Procedure *QG_Alert_Correlation*
Input: A queue graph Q_g with n queues and m variables, the initial result graph $G_r(V, E_r \cup E_l)$, and an alert a_{new} satisfying $Exp(a_{new}) = e_i$ $(1 \leq i \leq n)$
Output: The updated result graph $G_r(V, E_r \cup E_l)$
Method:
1. **Insert** a_{new} into V
2. **If** Q_i contains an alert a_{old}
   Insert edge (a_{old}, a_{new}) into E_l
   Dequeue a_{old} from Q_i
3. **Enqueue** a_{new} into Q_i
4. **For** each $Q_j (1 \leq j \leq n)$ satisfying $\langle Q_i, v_k \rangle \in \mathcal{P}_i \wedge \langle v_k, Q_j \rangle \in \mathcal{P}_i$ $(1 \leq k \leq m)$
   If Q_j contains an alert a_j
   Insert (a_j, a_{new}) into E_r
5. **Return** $G_r(V, E_r \cup E_l)$

Fig. 9 A Procedure for Correlating Alerts Using Queue Graphs

The procedure *QG_Alert_Correlation* is sufficient for demonstrating the advantages of the QG approach, although some of the features of the queue graph, such as the variables and the forward pointers, are not yet used and will be needed in the next section. First, the time for processing each new alert with the QG approach is linear in $(m+n)$, that is the number of vertices in the attack graph. In Procedure *QG_Alert_Correlation*, the fourth step visits at most $(m+n)$ edges, because it searches in a *tree* (that is, the BFS tree rooted at Q_i) by following the layered pointers in $\mathscr{P}_i$; the other steps of the procedure take almost constant time. Hence, the performance of the QG approach is independent of the number of received alerts, as n and m are relatively stable for a given network. In contrast, the nested loop approach (without using a sliding window) searches all alerts, and hence the performance keeps decreasing as more and more alerts are received.

Second, the memory usage of the QG approach is roughly $O(n(n+m))$ due to n layers of maximally $(n+m)$ pointers (the correlation only appends to the result graph but does not read from it, and hence the result graph needs not to reside in memory), which does not depend on the number of received alerts, either. In comparison, the nested loop approach without a sliding window needs memory for indexing on all the received alerts. Third, the QG approach is not vulnerable to slowed attacks, which can easily defeat the nested loop approach using a sliding window as described earlier. In the procedure *QG_Alert_Correlation*, an alert is no longer considered for correlation only if a new alert matching the same exploit arrives. Hence, if one alert prepares for another, then no matter how many unrelated alerts are injected, the earlier alert will always sit in the queue graph waiting for the second alert.

When an alert is dequeued from the queue graph, it will no longer be needed for correlation. This critically depends on the assumption that alerts arrive in the correct order. However, both the order suggested by timestamps and the actual order of arrivals can be wrong, since the temporal characteristics of alerts are typically imprecise. Instead, we adopt the following conservative approach. First, any two alerts whose timestamps have a difference no greater than a given threshold t_{con} are treated as *concurrent*; the *correct* order of concurrent alerts is always the one that allows the alerts to be correlated. Second, for non-concurrent alerts, the correct order is the one suggested by their timestamps, but alerts are allowed to arrive in a different (and incorrect) order.

This conservative approach enable us to tolerate varying delays in a network and small differences between the clocks of sensors (as discussed earlier, we assume the clocks of sensors are loosely synchronized). However, the basic QG approach does not work properly on alerts arriving in incorrect order. Consider an alert a_1 that prepares for another alert a_2 but arrives later then a_2. As described before, the procedure *QG_Alert_Correlation* will only look for those alerts that prepare for a_1, but not those that a_1 prepares for (a_2 in this case). Moreover, if another concurrent alert a'_2 matches the same exploit as a_2 does and arrives after a_2 but before a_1. Then, a_2 is already dequeued by the time a_1 arrives, and hence the correlation between a_1 and a_2 will not be discovered.

To prevent alerts from arriving the correlation engine in an incorrect order, we reorder them inside a time window before feeding them into the queue graph. Specifically, assume the varying delay is bound by a threshold t_{max}. We postpone the processing of an alert a_1 with a timestamp t_1 until t_{max} (the larger one between t_{max} and t_{con}, when concurrent alerts are also considered) time has passed since the time we receive a_1. We reorder the postponed alerts, so they arrive at the correlation engine in the correct order. Then after t_{max} time, any alert a_2 will have a timestamp t_2 satisfying $t_2 > t_1$. The worst case is when a_1 is not delayed but a_2 is delayed t_{max} time, and the fact a_2 is received t_{max} later than a_1 indicates $t_2 + t_{max} - t_{max} > t_1$, and hence $t_2 > t_1$. The above assumption about bound varying delays can be relaxed with a bound on the difference between the delay of any two alerts with t_{max}, while allowing the delay itself to be arbitrarily large (the worst case then becomes $t_2 + t_x + t_{max} > t_1 + t_x + t_{max}$, where t_x is an arbitrary delay).

Notice here a time window is used for reordering alerts, and no alert will be excluded from correlation. Unlike the time window used by the nested loop approach, this time window does not make the correlation vulnerable to slow attacks. The capability of dealing with concurrent alerts and varying delays comes at a cost. The additional delay introduced for reordering alerts causes an undesired decrease in the timeliness of alert correlation. However, if we choose to report results immediately as each alert arrives, then the imprecise temporal characteristics of alerts may cause incorrect and confusing results. Such results may diminish the value of the correlation effort. This reflects the inherent tradeoff between the capability of containing unavoidable uncertainties and the performance of processing alerts.

5.3 Hypothesizing Missing Alerts and Predicting Future Alerts

The queue graph approach introduced in previous section provides unique opportunities to hypothesize alerts missed by IDSs and to predict possible consequences of current attacks. Intuitively, missing alerts will cause *inconsistency* between the knowledge encoded in attack graphs and the facts represented by received alerts. By reasoning about such inconsistency, missing alerts can be plausibly hypothesized. On the other hand, by extending the facts in a consistent way with respect to the knowledge, possible consequences of an intrusion can be predicted. To elaborate on those ideas, we first define consistent sequences of alerts in Definition 0.5 and then illustrate the concept in an example.

Definition 0.5. We say an exploit is *ready* to be executed if all of its required intermediate conditions are satisfied by previous executions of exploits. We say a sequence of alerts is *consistent*, if every alert in the sequence matches an exploit ready to be executed by the time the alert is received.

Example 0.11. The sequence of alerts shown on the left hand side of Figure 10(that is, a_0, a_3) is inconsistent with respect to the attack graph, because the condition c_3 is not satisfied before the exploit e_3 is executed (as indicated by the alert a_3). On the other hand, the sequence a_0, a_1, a_3 is consistent, because executing the exploit e_1 (as indicated by the alert a_1) satisfies the only condition c_3 that is required by the execution of e_3 (as indicated by a_3). The sequence shown on the right hand side of Figure 10 is inconsistent, because the condition c_4 is not satisfied before the execution of e_3.

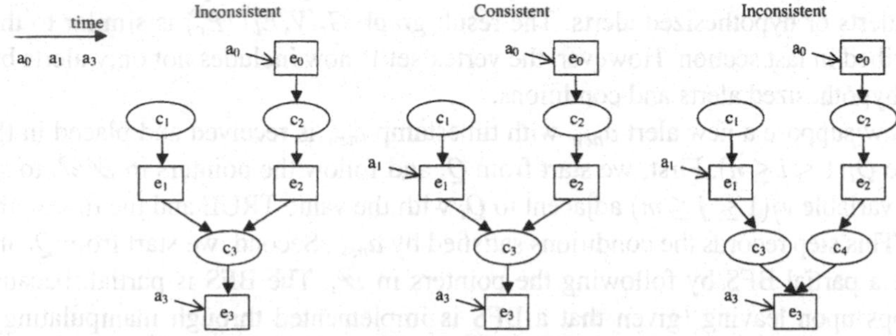

Fig. 10 Examples of Consistent and Inconsistent Alert Sequences

In the previous section, our correlation algorithm searches for alerts that prepare for the new alert by following two consecutive pointers. Such an approach only works for consistent alert sequences. For inconsistent sequences, such as those in Example 0.11, the search will stop at empty queues that correspond to missing alerts and the correlation result will be incomplete. A natural question is, *Can we continue to search and hypothesize missing alerts if necessary?* The question motivates us to extend the correlation method to hypothesize missing alerts. Intuitively, we want to *explain* the occurrence of a new alert by including it in a consistent sequence of alerts (by alert correlation) and missing alerts (by alert hypothesis).

Specifically, a search starts from the queue containing the new alert, and hypothesizes about missing alerts for encountered empty queues. It stops at each non-empty queue because it knows that the alert in that queue must have already been processed previously. The search expands its frontier in a breadth-first manner after each hypothesis is made, since the hypothesis itself may also need an explanation. Such attempts continue until a satisfactory explanation for the new alert and all the hypothesized ones has been obtained. The explanations of all received alerts collectively form the result graph, which is now composed of alerts, hypothesized alerts, and conditions that are either satisfied or hypothetically satisfied. This is illustrated in Example 0.12.

Example 0.12. Consider again the three cases, from left to right, in Figure 10 when the alert a_3 is received. For the first case, two missing alerts matching e_1 and e_2 need to be hypothesized and then a_3 can be correlated to a_0 (through one of the hypothesized alerts). For the second case, no alert needs to be hypothesized because the sequence is already consistent, and a_3 needs to be correlated to a_1. For the third case, a_0 needs to be correlated to a_1, and it also needs to be correlated to a_0 through a hypothesized alert matching e_2.

The correlation procedure described in Section 5.2 can be modified by replacing the step 4 with a new sub-procedure that correlates and hypothesizes alerts as follows. Given a queue graph Q_g with n queues $\mathscr{Q}$ and m variables $\mathscr{V}$. Each variable in $\mathscr{V}$ can now have one of the three values *TRUE*, *FALSE*, and *HYP*, together with a timestamp; those denote a satisfied condition, an unsatisfied one, a hypothetically satisfied one, and the time of the last update, respectively. Each queue in $\mathscr{Q}$ can contain alerts or hypothesized alerts. The result graph $G_r(V, E_l \cup E_r)$ is similar to that described in last section. However, the vertex set V now includes not only alerts but also hypothesized alerts and conditions.

Now suppose a new alert a_{new} with timestamp t_{new} is received and placed in the queue $Q_i (1 \leq i \leq n)$. First, we start from Q_i and follow the pointers in $\mathscr{PR}_i$ to set each variable $v_j (1 \leq j \leq m)$ adjacent to Q_i with the value TRUE and the timestamp t_{new}. This step records the conditions satisfied by a_{new}. Second, we start from Q_i and make a partial BFS by following the pointers in $\mathscr{P}_i$. The BFS is partial, because it stops upon leaving (given that a BFS is implemented through manipulating a separate queue as usual, we shall refer to the enqueues as *reaching* and the dequeues as *leaving* to avoid confusions) a variable with the value *TRUE* or the value *HYP* or a queue that contains a hypothesized alert. This step correlates a_{new} to previously received or hypothesized alerts.

The result graph G_r is updated during the above process as follows. First, after we enqueue a_{new} into Q_i and make changes to each v_j adjacent to Q_i, we add a_{new} and v_j (that is, the value and timestamp of v_j) as vertices, and an edge from a_{new} pointing to v_j into the result graph G_r. This step records the fact that the new alert a_{new} satisfies its implied conditions at time t_{new}. Second, during the partial BFS, we record each hypothesis. Whenever we change the value of a variable v_j from *FALSE* to *HYP*, we record this update in G_r; similarly, whenever we enqueue a hypothesized alert into an empty queue, we record this hypothesized alert in G_r. Third, whenever we leave a variable v and reach a queue Q, we insert into G_r a directed edge from each queue Q to v; similarly, we insert edges from a queue to its connected variables when we leave the queue. Example 0.13 illustrates the above procedure.

Example 0.13. Consider the left-most case of Figure 10. The first alert a_0 will only cause the condition c_2 to be changed from *FALSE* to *TRUE*. The result graph will be updated with the alert a_0 and the satisfied condition c_2 and the directed edge connecting them. When a_3 is received, a search starts from (the queue corresponding to) e_3; it changes c_3 from *FALSE* to *HYP*; it inserts a hypothesized alert a_1 into e_1 and a_2 into e_2, respectively; it stops at c_1 (which is initially set as *TRUE*) and c_2 (which has been set as *TRUE* when a_0 arrived). The result graph will be updated with the alert a_3, the hypothesized alerts a_1 and a_2, the hypothetically satisfied condition c_3, and the directed edges between them.

At first glance, the above procedure takes quadratic time, because a BFS takes time linear in the number of vertices $(n+m)$ and edges $(n+m)^2$, where n and m is the number of exploits and security conditions in the attack graph, respectively. However, this is not the case. As described in the last section, a queue graph organizes its pointers in separate layers, and each layer is a BFS tree rooted at a queue. Hence, a BFS that starts from a queue and follows the pointers in the corresponding layer will be equivalent to a tree traversal, which takes linear time $(n+m)$. This performance gain seems to be obtained at the price of more memory requirement, because a pointer may appear in more than one layer. However, the memory requirement is quadratic (that is, $O(n(n+m))$), which is indeed asymptotically the same as that of the original attack graph.

In the above discussions, we explain the occurrence of a new alert by searching backwards (that is, in the reversed direction of the edges in attack graphs) for correlated (or hypothesized) alerts. Conversely, we can also predict possible consequences of each new alert by searching forwards. A BFS is also preferred in this case, because the predicted conditions will be discovered in the order of their (shortest) distances to the new alert. This distance roughly indicates how imminent a predicted attack is, based on the alerts received so far (although not pursued in this chapter, probability-based prediction techniques, such as [31], can be easily incorporated based on the QG data structure to more precisely measure how imminent each attack is).

The procedure of prediction is similar to that of correlation and hypothesis discussed in the previous section. The main differences between the two procedures are as follows. After the correlation and hypothesis completes, the prediction starts. It begins at the conditions satisfied by the new alert and makes a partial BFS in the queue graph by following the pointers in $\mathcal{PR}_i$ (suppose the new alert is enqueued by Q_i). The search stops at previously received (or hypothesized) alerts and their (hypothetically) satisfied conditions to avoid repeating the previous prediction.

The result of the prediction process is a sequence of non-empty sets Con_1, Con_2, ..., with $Con_i (1 \leq i \leq m)$ containing the conditions that can possibly be satisfied in i steps from now. Unlike in correlation and hypothesis, the prediction process does not reason about the disjunctive and conjunctive relationship between exploits. Instead, a condition c will appear in the set Con_i as long as there exists a path of length $2i$ (the path consists of both security conditions and exploits) from c to some previously satisfied condition. Hence, the number i provides a lower bound to the number of exploits that must be executed before c can be satisfied.

5.4 Compressing Result Graphs

This section studies how to compress result graph without losing any information. In previous sections, avoiding unnecessary searches enables the QG approach to have a performance independent of the number of received alerts. As a side-effect, this also reduces the size of result graphs by having less transitive edges. However, the QG approach does not completely remove transitive edges from result graphs, as illustrated in Example 0.14. In practice, brute force attempts of the same attack with different parameters usually lead to a large number of alerts in a short time (the treasure hunt data used in Section 5.5 is a good example for such brute force attempts). In Example 0.14, if the b_i's happen to be such an attack, then a large number of transitive edges will make the result graph less perceptible. It is thus desired to remove such transitive edges.

Example 0.14. The left side of Figure 11 shows the result graph of correlating a series of alerts using the QG approach. Transitive edges such as (a_1,b_1) and (a_2,b_1) are not present, since the QG approach immediately stops after it reaches a_3. However, the edges (a_3,b_2) and (a_3,b_3) are both transitive edges. When b_2 and b_3 arrive, the QG approach repeats the same search as it does for b_1 and thus the two transitive edges are inserted into the result graph. Similarly, the edge (c,a_3) is also transitive.

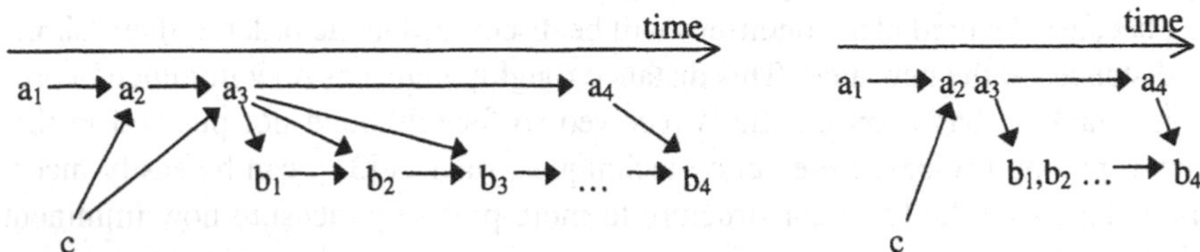

Exp(a_i) = Exp(a_j), Exp(b_i) = Exp(b_j), and Exp(c_i) = Exp(c_j) for $1 \leq i, j \leq 4$
Exp(a_i) → Exp(b_i) and Exp(c_i) → Exp(b_i)

Fig. 11 An Example of Compressing Result Graphs

The transitive edges also cause redundant information in alerts. Following the above example, b_1, b_2, and b_3 are *indistinguishable* in terms of alert correlation. That is, any other alert prepares for (or be prepared for by) either all or none of them. The three alerts can thus be *aggregated* as a single vertex in the result graph, with the edge connecting these alerts deleted. Similarly, a_2 and a_3 are also indistinguishable. On the other hand, a_1, a_2, a_3 are not indistinguishable, because c prepares for a_2 and a_3 but not a_1. The right side of Figure 11 shows a more compact version of result graph, with transitive edges deleted and indistinguishable alerts aggregated.

Existing alert correlation approaches usually take extra efforts in making the result graph more compact, such as aggregating alerts before correlating them [21]. The additional step increases the performance overhead of alert correlation. We show that our QG approach can be modified to directly produce a compact result graph. We also show that the modified QG approach may actually be more efficient. We first modify the QG approach to avoid inserting transitive edges into the result graph. For this purpose, we let each backward pointer in a queue graph to have one of the two states, *on* and *off*.

Initially, all the backward pointers are on. The backward pointers are then switched between the two states as follows. Whenever a directed edge (a_i,a_j) is inserted into E_r, we turn off the backward edges between the corresponding queues Q_i and Q_j. Whenever an alert is enqueued in a queue Q_i, all the backward pointers arriving at Q_i will be turned on. Finally, when we search for older alerts that prepare for a new alert, we follow a backward edge only if it is currently turned on. This process is illustrated in Example 0.15.

Example 0.15. In the left side of Figure 11 suppose the alerts a_i, b_i, c correspond to the queues Q_a, Q_b, and Q_c, respectively. When the alert b_1 arrives, it searches through the backward pointers from Q_b to Q_a and inserts an edge (a_3, b_1) into E_r. Then according to the above discussion, the backward pointers from Q_b to Q_a will be turned off. Consequently, the alerts b_2 and b_3 will not follow those pointers, and the transitive edges (a_3, b_2) and (a_3, b_3) are avoided. This remains true until the alert a_4 arrives, which turns on all the backward pointers arriving at the queue Q_a. Then later when b_4 arrives, it follows the backward pointers from Q_b to Q_a and inserts the edge (a_4, b_4).

Alerts are aggregated during the above process as follows. Suppose an alert a_i arrives and the corresponding queue Q_i already contains another alert a'_i. Then a_i is aggregated with a'_i if the following two conditions are true. First, all the backward pointers arriving at Q_i are on. Second, all the backward pointers leaving Q_i are off. The first condition ensures that a'_i does not prepare for any other alerts that arrive between a'_i and a_i, because otherwise a_i and a'_i would not be indistinguishable. The second condition ensures that a'_i and a_i are prepared for by the same collection of alerts, so they are indistinguishable with respect to those alerts. This process is illustrated in Example 0.16.

Example 0.16. Following the above example, a_3 is aggregated with a_2 because the backward pointers from Q_b to Q_a are on and those from Q_a to Q_c have been turned off by the alert a_2. Similarly, b_2 and b_3 are aggregated with b_1, because the backward pointers from Q_b to Q_a have been turned off by b_1. On the other hand, the alert b_4 will not be aggregated, because the backward pointers from Q_b to Q_a must have been turned on by a_4 by the time b_4 arrives.

This new procedure not only produces a more compact result graph, but is also more efficient than the original one in most cases. This is because unnecessary searches corresponding to transitive edges are avoided. In Figure 11, the alerts a_3, b_2, and b_3 will not lead to a search in the modified approach because the backward pointers have been turned off by earlier alerts. The performance gain can be significant in the case of brute force attempts where a large number of searches can be avoided.

5.5 Empirical Results

This section presents implementation and empirical results. The correlation engine is implemented in C++ and tested on a Pentium III 860MHz server with 1G RAM running RedHat Linux. We use Snort-2.3.0 [37] to generate isolated alerts, which are directly pipelined into the correlation engine for analyses. We use Tcpreplay 2.3.2 [43] to replay network traffic from a separate machine to the server running the correlation engine.

Two data sets are used for experiments, the Darpa 2000 intrusion detection LLDOS 1.0 by MIT Lincoln Labs [8], and the treasure hunt dataset by the University of California, Santa Barbara [42]. The attack scenario in the Darpa 2000 dataset has been extensively explored before (such as in [21]). Our experiments with the dataset show similar results, validating the correctness of our correlation algorithm. The treasure hunt dataset generates a large amount of alerts (about two million alerts taking about 1.4G of disk space, with most of them being brute force attempts of the same attacks), which may render a nested loop-based correlation method infeasible (we found that even running a simple database query over the data will paralyze the system). In contrast, our correlation engine processes alerts with negligible delays (Snort turns out to be the bottleneck).

5.6 Effectiveness

The objective of the first set of experiments is to demonstrate the effectiveness of the proposed algorithms in alert correlation, hypothesis, and prediction. We use the Darpa 2000 dataset for this purpose. The reason we use this dataset is that it has well known attack scenarios, which can be referenced in the included description or previous work, such as [21]. For correlation without hypothesis and prediction, we expect our method to produce exactly the same result as previous work do, with the redundant transitive edges removed in the result graph (given that the domain knowledge encoded in our attack graph exactly matches that used by previous work). Notice that the key contribution of this work is to improve the performance of previous approach and make them immune to slowed attacks. The correlation methodology itself is not different from that found in previous work, and similarly the accuracy of the correlation result also depends on the domain knowledge used for correlation. However, in contrast to the static result graph in previous work, our result *evolves* in time with the continuously arriving alerts, as illustrated in Figure 12 (due to space limitations, only two partial snapshots of the result graphs are shown). Such a result can more clearly reveal the actual progress of an intrusion.

Figure 13 shows two results on hypothesizing missing alerts during the correlation. On the left-side of the figure, two consecutive missing alerts (ICMP PING and ICMP Echo Reply) and the corresponding conditions are hypothesized (shown as shaded) when an alert (RPC portmap sadmind request UDP) is received but its required condition (Host 10 Alive) has not been satisfied. The right-hand side of the figure shows a conjunctive relationship between alerts, that is a DDoS mstream traffic between two hosts requires the mstream software to be installed on both hosts. We deliberately deleted the RSERVICES rsh alert on one of the host, which is successfully hypothesized (shown as shaded).

Figure 14 and Figure 15 shows the result of alert prediction. In the first figure, some conditions are predicted to be satisfied by possible upcoming alerts. The predicted conditions are shown as shaded, and the numbers are placeholders for alerts. The second figure shows a later snapshot of the result graph, in which some of the predicted conditions are indeed realized. Notice that here the attack graph exactly (and only) captures the necessary domain knowledge, and hence the prediction result is highly accurate. In practice, both false positives (predicted but not realized)

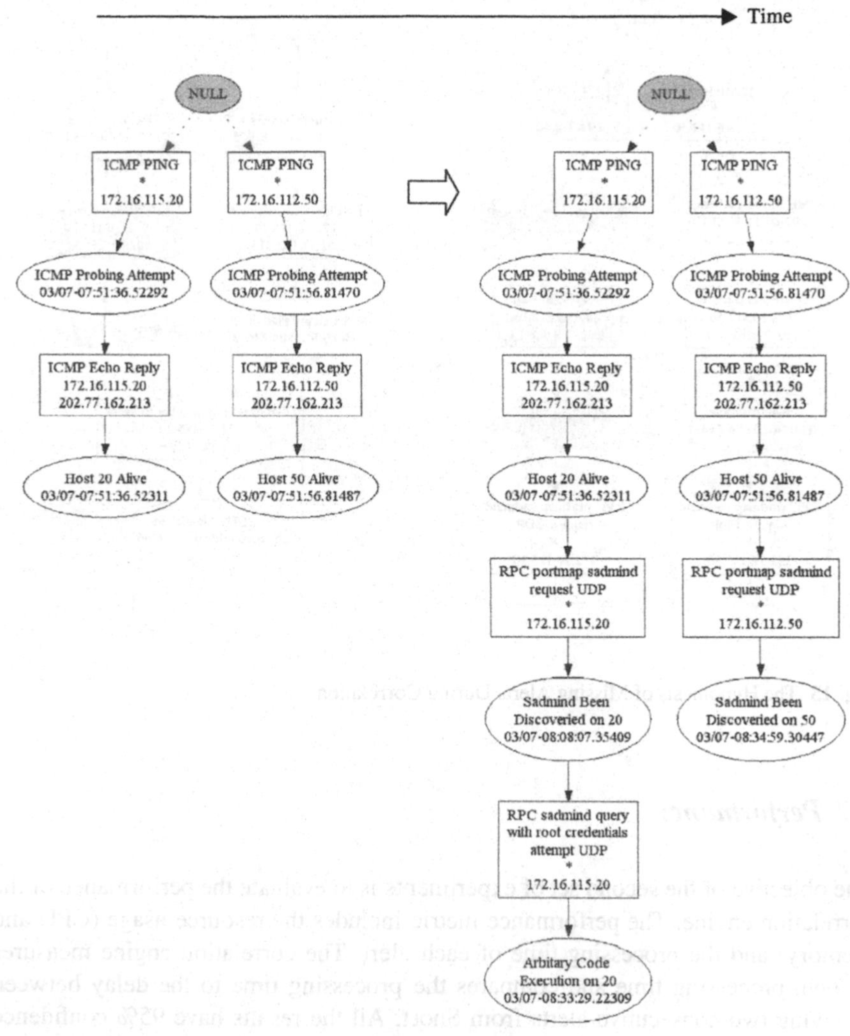

Fig. 12 The Evolving Result Graphs of Alert Correlation

and false negatives (realized but not predicted) may be introduced because of incomplete or inaccurate domain knowledge. Refining our prediction method to reduce such inaccuracy comprises an interesting future direction.

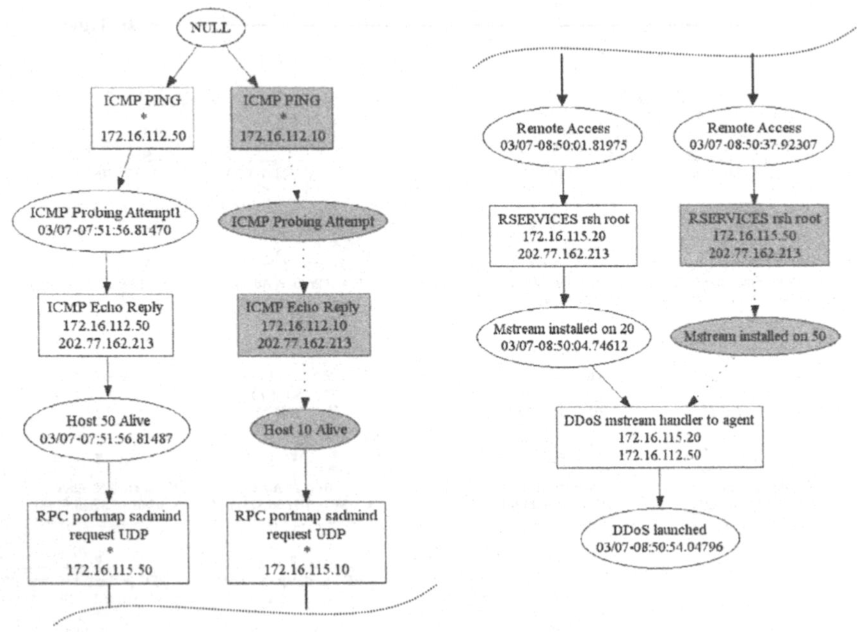

Fig. 13 The Hypothesis of Missing Alerts During Correlation

5.7 Performance

The objective of the second set of experiments is to evaluate the performance of the correlation engine. The performance metric includes the resource usage (CPU and memory) and the processing time of each alert. The correlation engine measures its own processing time and compares the processing time to the delay between receiving two consecutive alerts from Snort. All the results have 95% confidence intervals within about 5% of the reported values. Figure 16 shows the CPU usage (on the left-hand side) and memory usage (on the right-hand side) over time for the Darpa data set. The correlation engine clearly demands less resources than Snort (on average, the correlation engine's CPU usage and memory usage are both under 10% of Snort's).

The left chart in Figure 17 shows the processing time per alert (averaged per 22 alerts). Clearly, the correlation engine works faster than Snort in processing the entire data set. The result also proves that the performance does not decrease over time. Indeed, the processing time per alert remains fairly steady. We examine the scalability of the correlation engine in terms of the number of exploits and conditions. The treasure hunt data set is used for this purpose. The original attack graph only has about one hundred exploits. We increase the size of attack graphs by randomly inserting dummy exploits and conditions. The inserted exploits increase the complexity of correlation because the correlation engine must search through them.

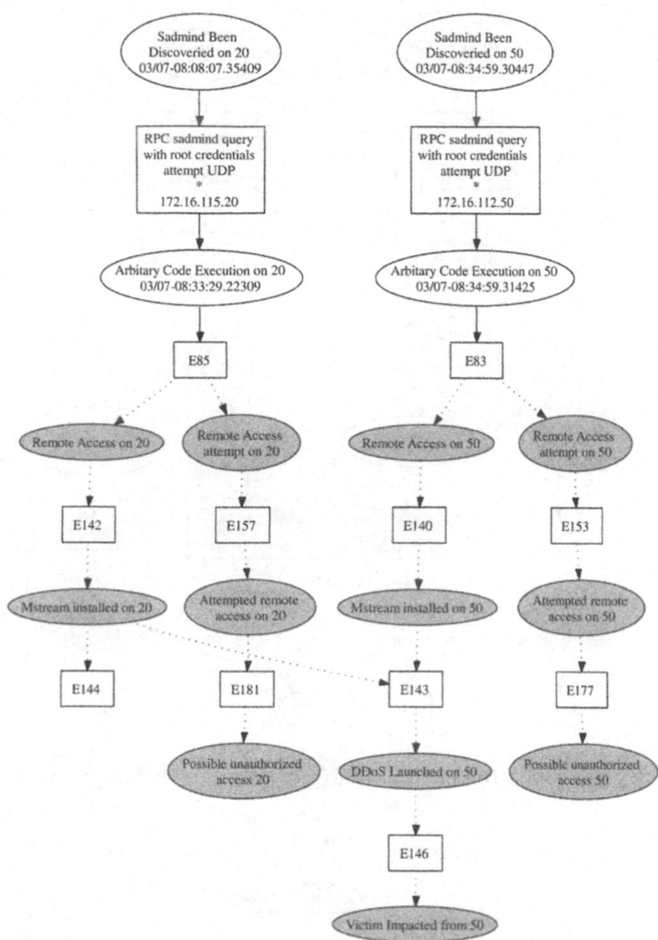

Fig. 14 The Prediction of Possible Consequences (Snapshot 1)

The right chart in Figure 17 shows that the average processing time scales with the size of attack graphs as expected.

We replay network traffic at relatively high speed (for example, the Darpa data set is replayed in about 26 seconds while the actual duration of the dataset is several hours). Real-world attacks are usually less intensive, and consequently our correlation engine will exhibit a better performance. However, we are aware that real-world traffic may bring up new challenges that are absent in synthesized data sets. For example, we currently set the time window used to reorder alerts (that is, t_{max} as discussed before as one second to deal with identical time stamps of alerts. In a real network, the windows size must be decided based on the actual placement of IDS

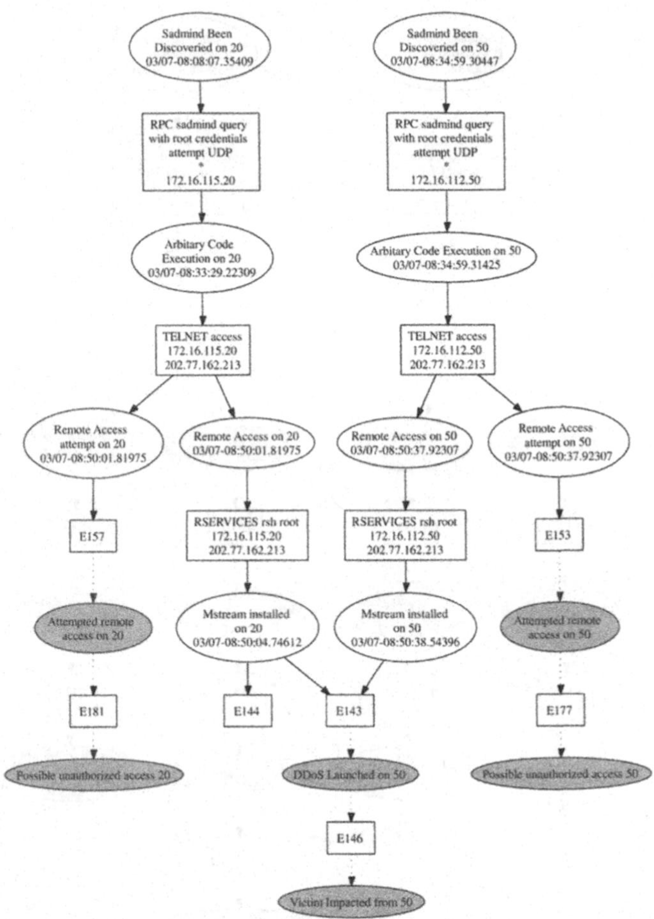

Fig. 15 The Prediction of Possible Consequences (Snapshot 2)

sensors and the typical network delays. In our future work, we plan to integrate our correlation engine in our TVA tool and test it in real-world network settings.

6 Conclusion

This chapter has studied defending against multi-step attacks. We described methods both for preventing such attacks from happening and for detecting and predicting the attacks. The network hardening method enables us to reduce the threat of multi-step attacks through removing vulnerabilities and reconfiguring our network. Unlike previous approaches, the network hardening solutions we derive are in terms of

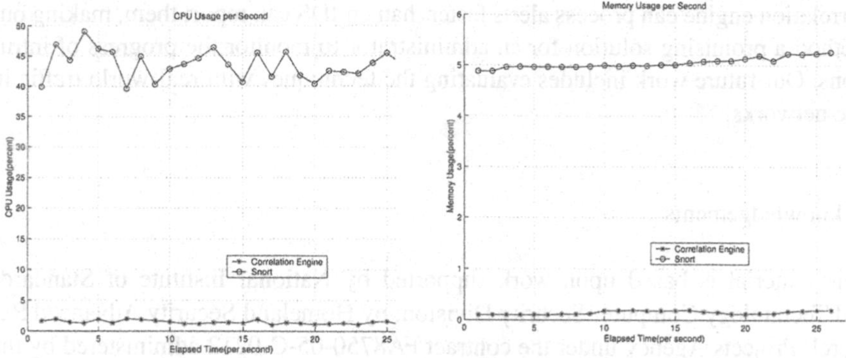

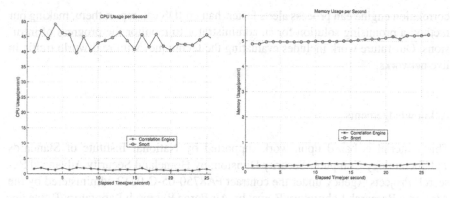

Fig. 16 The CPU and Memory Usage

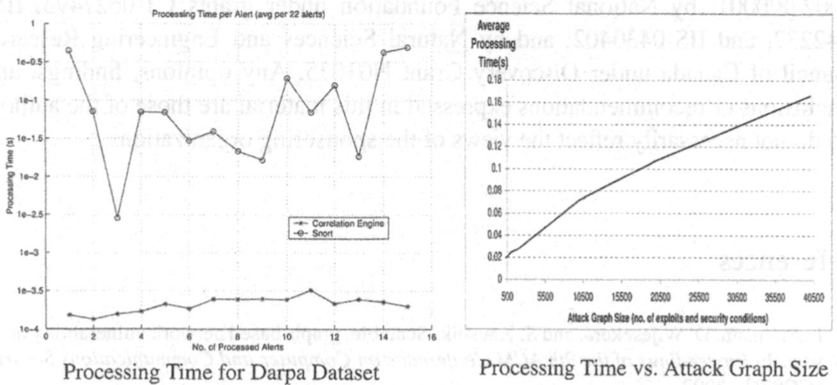

Processing Time for Darpa Dataset   Processing Time vs. Attack Graph Size

Fig. 17 The Processing Time and Its Relationship with the Size of Attack Graph

initial conditions, which can be independently disabled. Such solutions take into account the often complex relationships among exploits and conditions. In this way, our solution is readily enforceable. The new algorithm we have proposed can derive solutions with one-pass of search in the attack graph while avoiding logic loops. The current algorithm builds the logic proposition then simplifies it. In our future work, we shall pursue a solution that integrates the two steps into one single algorithm such that redundant clauses in the proposition can be avoided.

We have also described methods that can be used in situations where not all multi-step attacks can be avoided through network hardening. We identified limitations in applying the nested loop-based correlation methods and proposed a novel QG approach to remove this limitation. The method has a linear time complexity and a quadratic memory requirement and can correlate alerts arbitrarily far away. We further extended the QG approach to a unified method for the correlation, hypothesis, and prediction of alerts. We also extend the method to produce a compact version of result graphs with no transitive edges. Empirical results showed that our correlation engine can process alerts faster than an IDS can report them, making our method a promising solution for an administrator to monitor the progress of intrusions. Our future work includes evaluating the techniques with real-world traffic in live networks.

Acknowledgements

This material is based upon work supported by National Institute of Standards and Technology Computer Security Division; by Homeland Security Advanced Research Projects Agency under the contract FA8750-05-C-0212 administered by the Air Force Research Laboratory/Rome; by Air Force Research Laboratory/Rome under the contract FA8750-06-C-0246; by Army Research Office under grant W911NF-05-1-0374; by Federal Aviation Administration under the contract DTFAWA-04-P-00278/0001; by National Science Foundation under grants CT-0627493, IIS-0242237, and IIS-0430402; and by Natural Sciences and Engineering Research Council of Canada under Discovery Grant N01035. Any opinions, findings, and conclusions or recommendations expressed in this material are those of the authors and do not necessarily reflect the views of the sponsoring organizations.

References

1. P. Ammann, D. Wijesekera, and S. Kaushik. Scalable, graph-based network vulnerability analysis. In *Proceedings of the 9th ACM Conference on Computer and Communications Security (CCS'02)*, 2002.
2. F. Cuppens. Managing alerts in a multi-intrusion detection environment. In *Proceedings of the 17th Annual Computer Security Applications Conference (ACSAC'01)*, 2001.
3. F. Cuppens and A. Miege. Alert correlation in a cooperative intrusion detection framework. In *Proceedings of the 2002 IEEE Symposium on Security and Privacy (S&P'02)*, pages 187–200, 2002.
4. F. Cuppens and R. Ortalo. LAMBDA: A language to model a database for detection of attacks. In *Proceedings of the 3rd International Symposium on Recent Advances in Intrusion Detection (RAID'01)*, pages 197–216, 2001.
5. M. Dacier. Towards quantitative evaluation of computer security. Ph.D. Thesis, Institut National Polytechnique de Toulouse, 1994.
6. O. Dain and R.K. Cunningham. Building scenarios from a heterogeneous alert system. In *Proceedings of the 2001 IEEE Workshop on Information Assurance and Security*, 2001.
7. O. Dain and R.K. Cunningham. Fusing a heterogeneous alert stream into scenarios. In *Proceedings of the ACM Workshop on Data Mining for Security Applications*, pages 1–13, 2001.
8. 2000 darpa intrusion detection evaluation datasets. http://www.ll.mit.edu/IST/ideval/data/2000/ 2000_data_index.html, 2000.
9. H. Debar and A. Wespi. Aggregation and correlation of intrusion-detection alerts. In *Proceedings of the 3rd International Symposium on Recent Advances in Intrusion Detection (RAID'01)*, pages 85–103, 2001.
10. R. Deraison. Nessus scanner, 1999. Available at http://www.nessus.org.
11. S.T. Eckmann, G. Vigna, and R.A. Kemmerer. STATL: An attack language for state-based intrusion detection. *Journal of Computer Security*, 10(1/2):71–104, 2002.

12. D. Farmer and E.H. Spafford. The COPS security checker system. In *USENIX Summer*, pages 165–170, 1990.
13. N. Habra, Charlier B.L., A. Mounji, and I. Mathieu. ASAX: software architechture and rule-based language for universal audit trail analysis. In *Proceedings of the 2nd European Symposium on Research in Computer Security (ESORICS 1992)*, pages 430–450, 2004.
14. IBM. IBM tivoli risk manager. Available at http://www.ibm.com/software/tivoli/products/risk-mgr/.
15. SRI International. Event monitoring enabling responses to anomalous live disturbances (EMERALD). Available at http:// www.sdl.sri.com/projects/emerald/.
16. S. Jajodia, S. Noel, and B. O'Berry. Topological analysis of network attack vulnerability. In V. Kumar, J. Srivastava, and A. Lazarevic, editors, *Managing Cyber Threats: Issues, Approaches and Challenges*. Kluwer Academic Publisher, 2003.
17. S. Jha, O. Sheyner, and J.M. Wing. Two formal analysis of attack graph. In *Proceedings of the 15th Computer Security Foundation Workshop (CSFW'02)*, 2002.
18. Klaus Julisch and Marc Dacier. Mining intrusion detection alarms for actionable knowledge. In *Proceedings of the eighth ACM SIGKDD international conference on Knowledge discovery and data mining*, pages 366–375, 2002.
19. W. Lee, J.B.D. Cabrera, A. Thomas, N. Balwalli, S. Saluja, and Y. Zhang. Performance adaptation in real-time intrusion detection systems. In *Proceedings of The 5th International Symposium on Recent Advances in Intrusion Detection (RAID 2002)*, 2002.
20. E. Mendelson. *Introduction to Mathematical Logic, 4th ed.* Chapman & Hall, 1997.
21. P. Ning, Y. Cui, and D.S. Reeves. Constructing attack scenarios through correlation of intrusion alerts. In *Proceedings of the 9th ACM Conference on Computer and Communications Security (CCS'02)*, pages 245–254, 2002.
22. P. Ning and D. Xu. Adapting query optimization techniques for efficient intrusion alert correlation. Technical report, NCSU, Department of Computer Science, 2002.
23. P. Ning and D. Xu. Learning attack strategies from intrusion alerts. In *Proceedings of the 10th ACM Conference on Computer and Communications Security (CCS'03)*, 2003.
24. P. Ning, D. Xu, C.G. Healey, and R.S. Amant. Building attack scenarios through integration of complementary alert correlation methods. In *Proceedings of the 11th Annual Network and Distributed System Security Symposium (NDSS'04)*, pages 97–111, 2004.
25. S. Noel, S. Jajodia, B. O'Berry, and M. Jacobs. Efficient minimum-cost network hardening via exploit dependency grpahs. In *Proceedings of the 19th Annual Computer Security Applications Conference (ACSAC'03)*, 2003.
26. R. Ortalo, Y. Deswarte, and M. Kaaniche. Experimenting with quantitative evaluation tools for monitoring operational security. *IEEE Trans. Software Eng.*, 25(5):633–650, 1999.
27. OSSIM. Open source security information management. Available at http://www. ossim.net.
28. V. Paxson. Bro: A system for detecting network intruders in real-time. *Computer Networks*, 31(23-24):2435–2463, 12 1999.
29. C. Phillips and L. Swiler. A graph-based system for network-vulnerability analysis. In *Proceedings of the New Security Paradigms Workshop (NSPW'98)*, 1998.
30. X. Qin and W. Lee. Statistical causality analysis of INFOSEC alert data. In *Proceedings of the 6th International Symposium on Recent Advances in Intrusion Detection (RAID 2003)*, pages 591–627, 2003.
31. X. Qin and W. Lee. Discovering novel attack strategies from INFOSEC alerts. In *Proceedings of the 9th European Symposium on Research in Computer Security (ESORICS 2004)*, pages 439–456, 2004.
32. A. R. Chinchani andIyer, H. Ngo, and S. Upadhyay. Towards a theory of insider threat assessment. In *Proceedings of the IEEE International Conference on Dependable Systems and Networks (DSN'05)*, 2005.
33. C.R. Ramakrishnan and R. Sekar. Model-based analysis of configuration vulnerabilities. *Journal of Computer Security*, 10(1/2):189–209, 2002.
34. I. Ray and N. Poolsappasit. Using attack trees to identify malicious attacks from authorized insiders. In *Proceedings of the 10th European Symposium on Research in Computer Security (ESORICS'05)*, 2005.

35. R. Ritchey and P. Ammann. Using model checking to analyze network vulnerabilities. In *Proceedings of the 2000 IEEE Symposium on Research on Security and Privacy (S&P'00)*, pages 156–165, 2000.
36. R. Ritchey, B. O'Berry, and S. Noel. Representing TCP/IP connectivity for topological analysis of network security. In *Proceedings of the 18th Annual Computer Security Applications Conference (ACSAC'02)*, page 25, 2002.
37. M. Roesch. Snort - lightweight intrusion detection for networks. In *Proceedings of the 1999 USENIX LISA Conference*, pages 229–238, 1999.
38. O. Sheyner, J. Haines, S. Jha, R. Lippmann, and J.M. Wing. Automated generation and analysis of attack graphs. In *Proceedings of the 2002 IEEE Symposium on Security and Privacy (S&P'02)*, 2002.
39. S. Staniford, J.A. Hoagland, and J.M. McAlerney. Practical automated detection of stealthy portscans. *Journal of Computer Security*, 10(1/2):105–136, 2002.
40. L. Swiler, C. Phillips, D. Ellis, and S. Chakerian. Computer attack graph generation tool. In *Proceedings of the DARPA Information Survivability Conference & Exposition II (DISCEX'01)*, 2001.
41. S. Templeton and K. Levitt. A requires/provides model for computer attacks. In *Proceedings of the 2000 New Security Paradigms Workshop (NSPW'00)*, pages 31–38, 2000.
42. Treasure hunt datasets. http://www.cs.ucsb.edu/~vigna/treasurehunt/index.html, 2004.
43. A. Turner. Tcpreplay: Pcap editing and replay tools for *nix. Available at http: //tcpreplay. sourceforge. net/.
44. A. Valdes and K. Skinner. Probabilistic alert correlation. In *Proceedings of the 4th International Symposium on Recent Advances in Intrusion Detection*, pages 54–68, 2001.
45. L. Wang, A. Liu, and S. Jajodia. An efficient and unified approach to correlating, hypothesizing, and predicting intrusion alerts. In *Proceedings of the 10th European Symposium on Research in Computer Security (ESORICS 2005)*, pages 247–266, 2005.
46. L. Wang, A. Liu, and S. Jajodia. Using attack graphs for correlating, hypothesizing, and predicting intrusion alerts. *Computer Communications*, 29(15):2917–2933, 2006.
47. L. Wang, S. Noel, and S. Jajodia. Minimum-cost network hardening using attack graphs. *Computer Communications*, 29(18):3812–3824, 11 2006.
48. L. Wang, A. Singhal, and S. Jajodia. Measuring network security using attack graphs. In *Proceedings of the 3rd ACM workshop on Quality of protection (QoP'07)*, New York, NY, USA, 2007. ACM Press.
49. L. Wang, A. Singhal, and S. Jajodia. Measuring the overall security of network configurations using attack graphs. In *Proceedings of 21th IFIP WG 11.3 Working Conference on Data and Applications Security (DBSec 2007)*, 2007.
50. L. Wang, C. Yao, A. Singhal, and S. Jajodia. Interactive analysis of attack graphs using relational queries. In *Proceedings of 20th IFIP WG 11.3 Working Conference on Data and Applications Security (DBSec 2006)*, pages 119–132, 2006.
51. D. Xu and P. Ning. Alert correlation through triggering events and common resources. In *Proceedings of the 20th Annual Computer Security Applications Conference (ACSAC'04)*, pages 360–369, 2004.
52. D. Xu and P. Ning. Privacy-preserving alert correlation: A concept hierarchy based approach. In *Proceedings of the 21st Annual Computer Security Applications Conference (ACSAC'05)*, 2005.
53. D. Zerkle and K. Levitt. Netkuang - a multi-host configuration vulnerability checker. In *Proceedings of the 6th USENIX Unix Security Symposium (USENIX'96)*, 1996.

Response: bridging the link between intrusion detection alerts and security policies

Hervé Debar, Yohann Thomas, Frédéric Cuppens, and Nora Cuppens-Boulahia

Abstract With the deployment of intrusion detection systems has come the question of alert usage. The current trend of intrusion prevention systems provides mechanisms for isolated response, suffering from two important drawbacks. First, the response is applied on a single point of the information system. Second, its application is repeated every time an alert condition is raised. Both drawbacks result in a suboptimal response system, where security is improved at these particular network or host access control points, but where service dependancies are not taken into account. In this paper, we examine a new mechanism for adapting the security policy of an information system according to the threat it receives, and hence its behaviour and the services it offers. This mechanism takes into account not only threats, but also legal constraints and other objectives of the organization operating this information system, taking into account multiple security objectives and providing several trade-off options between security objectives, performance objectives, and other operational constraints. The proposed mechanism bridges the gap between preventive security technologies and intrusion detection, and builds upon existing technologies to facilitate formalization on one hand, and deployment on the other hand.

1 Introduction

Managing information systems requires to make a compromise between multiple parameters, one of them being security. Although security is of crucial interest, constraints such as performance and convenience are also to be strongly considered. In

Hervé Debar · Yohann Thomas
France Télécom R&D, 42 rue des Coutures - 14066 Caen, France, e-mail: {herve.debar, yohann.thomas}@orange-ftgroup.com

Frédéric Cuppens · Nora Cuppens-Boulahia
GET/ENST Bretagne, 2 rue de la Châtaigneraie - 35512 Cesson-Sévigné, France e-mail: {frederic.cuppens, nora.cuppens}@enst-bretagne.fr

particular, being able to serve large numbers of users concurrently or to maintain acceptable response times, while lightening the hardware budget, is a major issue, and sometimes results in conflicting choices with respect to security. Moreover, ease of use and automation are frequent requirements to provide better service to users.

Nowadays, this compromise between multiple adjustment variables is generally defined statically at design time. However, security is not static, since new vulnerabilities, new users and usages, and new attackers continually appear, and similarly for other variables. In particular, it is essential to reflect the evolution of the information system through an up-to-date view of hardware and software, which impact both performance and convenience, and thus maintain a better balance between the different requirements, as time goes by.

Consequently, the compromise between the considered system adjustement variables needs to change, and in particular to respond to threats. This paper describes a mechanism for threat management at the security policy level. The security policy is dynamically updated with respect to current threats. This update is performed in a global manner, ensuring that the whole security policy remains coherent and that threats are handled by order of importance, even when threats have conflicting impacts and may require conflicting countermeasures. Our policy update mechanism also enables countermeasures with safeguards, ensuring that the security officer has control over the most adverse operating conditions, and prevent self-inflicted denial of service. We also provide an architecture to deploy such policies, mostly by reusing already existing security and system management components and protocols.

2 Problem statement

2.1 Domain terminology

Previous chapters of this book have described alerts generated by intrusion-detection systems. In this chapter, we need to broaden the terminology used to introduce additional concepts, as shown by the question marks in figure 1.

We reuse definitions introduced by the MAFTIA project for dependability and security [1]. The central concept is the one of *fault*, that is defined as a breach of the security policy. A synonym in the litterature is *threat*, used for example by J. Anderson[2], E. Jonsson[15] or in RFC 2828[23]. We are particularly interested in the notion of *malicious fault*, when an *attacker* can exercise the fault to carry out an *attack*. When the attacker succeeds, such an attack becomes an *intrusion*; the advantage gained may be reused by the attacker to carry out further attacks. In this paper, we will use the terms *fault* and *threat* interchangeably to describe this same concept.

To prevent these faults from occuring, the MAFTIA project defines four categories of actions ([1], p 9) that can be undertaken in parallel. *Fault prevention* aims

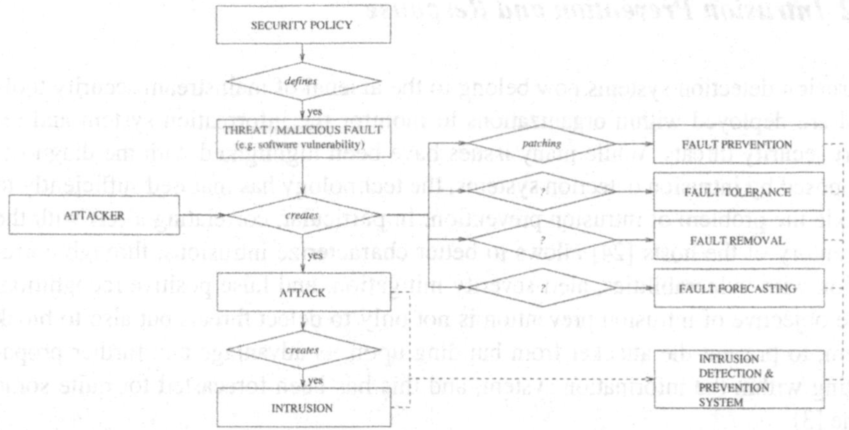

Fig. 1 Domain terminology

at preventing the existence of faults. *Fault tolerance* aims at continuing operations in the presence of faults. *Fault removal* aims at reducing the number or severity of faults. Finally, *fault forecasting* aims at estimating the number and severity of faults. Current intrusion detection and prevention systems are pertinent in the three later cases, aiming at alerting the security officer when attacks or intrusions manifest the existence of faults.

Fault prevention is outside the scope of our study, as we consider that patch management is an appropriate answer to the problem. If needed, we could incorporate patch deployment into the framework as a definitive and irreversible countermeasure, but that would be contrary to the philosophy of our approach, which promotes dynamicity (we do not want to "unpatch" systems automatically). We assume that some threats will not be removed, as their removal would have an adverse effect on the global system (for example adversely affecting cost), or because the security policy specifies contradicting objectives (e.g. the duality availability/confidentiality). Thus, system operation in the presence of these threats is a requirement. We are specifically interested in providing solutions for fault tolerance and fault removal, and handle fault forecasting as a possible side effect of our system, to be studied in future work. We further reduce the problem by observing that fault tolerance and removal assume the capability to first identify the fault and then act on it. We assume that fault detection will be handled by intrusion detection and security information management systems, and focus on actions to be carried out to the effect of tolerance or removal. We call these actions *response*.

Figure 1 also shows that response could be understood as *threat, attack or intrusion response*. With respect to intrusion detection, the most obvious term to define is attack response, i.e. responding to alerts that indicate an attack, a possible breach of security policy. Focusing on *intrusion response* would indicate that our system would only respond to successful attack. Threat response indicates that our system is specified from all latent faults, even though they may not materialize as attacks.

2.2 Intrusion Prevention and Response

Intrusion detection systems now belong to the arsenal of mainstream security tools and are deployed within organizations to monitor the information system and report security threats. While many issues have been highlighted with the diagnosis proposed by intrusion detection systems, the technology has matured sufficiently to tackle the problem of intrusion prevention. In particular, correlating alerts with the inventory of the hosts [24] allows to better characterize intrusions, through correlation with vulnerabilities, alert severity mitigation, and false positive recognition. The objective of intrusion prevention is not only to detect threats but also to block them, to prevent the attacker from building upon its advantage and further propagating within the information system, and this has been forecasted for quite some time [3].

Intrusion prevention currently means that when an alert is triggered, a mechanism is activated to terminate the network connection or the process associated with the event. Network-based intrusion prevention devices effectively act like classic firewalls, adding the capability to block traffic based on packet content in addition to headers and connection context. Response is statically associated with each alert, which leads to undesirable side effects [25]. Host-based intrusion prevention software has the capability to terminate a process that is trespassing or abusing its privileges, as shown by [21], but is limited to a single machine. In many cases, the time to react is so small that the threat response mechanism is implemented very close to the detection mechanism, to ensure that the response is effective in dealing with the threat. Previous network-based threat response mechanisms based on connection termination by TCP reset injection have shown that they have undesirable side effects in certain contexts, as shown in RFC 3360 [13] and that including response mechanisms online is a requirement for timely and successful response.

We argue that while threat response in itself is a desirable goal, the implementation of threat response at the intrusion prevention system level yields undesirable side effects. First of all, the response is based on an event analyzed by the intrusion prevention device. This means that for every malicious event, the threat response must be applied; unfortunately, this results in a *default permit* (or *open*) security policy, where only events that trigger an alert during the analysis process will be blocked. More generally, the decision on which the threat response is based is a local decision, which does not take into account other operating constraints. This has two undesirable side effects, 1. operators lacking the global vision of the behaviour of the information system will be reluctant to activate threat response mechanisms, and 2. local responses may interfere with global desired behaviour. The objective of the paper is to propose a more comprehensive approach to threat response.

2.3 Comprehensive Approach to Response

We observe that the deployment of modern information systems and networks is associated with access control technologies, located at critical points of the network. We therefore would like to link the threat detection performed by intrusion detection / prevention systems and the access control mechanisms, to provide an adaptive security policy capable of dynamically adjusting to threats. This comprehensive approach does not compete with the immediate application of threat response mechanisms by intrusion prevention systems, but should take over the application of threat response once the threat is properly characterized.

We assume in this approach that intrusion detection systems and alert correlation techniques allow a clear identification of the threat, including the threat type (typically represented by a set of signatures and references to vulnerability databases), the threat origin (represented in most cases by an IP address), and the threat victim (represented by a host under our control, a process, or any set of components of our information system), as in [8] for example. As shown in [24], it is indeed possible to use configuration information to adapt the detection mechanism to its environment, thus ensuring that contextual information in the alerts is exhaustive and correct. While this assumption may be considered strong given the history of false positives and negatives that has plagued intrusion detection research, we do believe that current intrusion detection systems, both commercial and research prototypes, allow a reasonable identification of the threat, and that they will make sufficient progress that the three parameters on which we rely will be filled with appropriate values.

3 Security Policy Formalism

In this section, we provide background on the security policy formalism and describe a use case.

3.1 Choice of a Security Policy Formalism

Most of current security models such as DAC [14] or RBAC [22] can only be used to specify *static* security policies. When an intrusion occurs, the security administrator has to manually update the policy by removing obsolete security rules or inserting new security rules. Unfortunately, the time required for such a manual update is generally too long to represent an effective way to react to an intrusion. The administrator has also to update the policy again once the intrusion is circumvented to restore the policy in a state corresponding to a non intrusive context. Note that in this paper, we will use the terms *policy rule* and *security rule* indifferently to specify security policy statements.

Our objective is to design a method to help the administrator in these tasks of updating the policy. For this purpose, we need a model to specify security policies that dynamically change when some intrusion is detected. In the absence of intrusion, the policy to be applied corresponds to a *nominal* context. Other contexts must be defined to specify additional security rules to be triggered when intrusions are detected. In fact, a parallel could be drawn with provisional authorizations [17]; contexts are linked to the history of reported intrusions, and activate provisional security rules. Some of these security rules may correspond to *permissions* (positive authorizations) but more often they will represent *prohibitions* (negative authorizations). The prohibitions will be automatically deployed over the information system as a reaction to the intrusion. For instance, this may correspond to automatically insert a new deny rule in a firewall.

Thus, the model to be used must provide means to manage conflicts between permissions and prohibitions. In particular, the policy associated with a nominal context can include *minimal* security requirements. These minimal requirements must not be overridden, even when an intrusion is detected. For instance, they may include minimal availability requirements. Of course, these minimal requirements may conflict with contextual rules associated with the detection of a given intrusion. In this case, simple strategies such as prohibition takes precedence or permission takes precedence will not be appropriate to solve the conflict. Instead, the model must include the possibility to specify high level conflict management strategies to find the best compromise between conflicting rules [6].

The model must also provide an abstract and global view of the security policy. This is the purpose of the Policy Instantiation Engine (PIE, see Section 5.1 below) to manage this global security policy. The PIE will have to clearly separate the global policy from its implementation in the PEPs (Policy Enforcement Points). In particular, the conflicts are to be solved at the abstract level before generating PEPs configurations. Unfortunately, most security models do not provide such a clear separation.

In this paper, we suggest using an approach based on the Or-BAC model [18]. In the following section, we briefly present the main concepts used in Or-BAC to specify a security policy and explain why this model is a good candidate to manage the kind of contextual security policies we need to support our proposal.

3.2 The Or-BAC Formalism

The concept of *organization* is central in the Or-BAC model [16]. Intuitively, an organization is any entity that is responsible for managing a security policy. Thus, a company is an organization, but concrete security components such as a firewall may be also viewed as an organization.

The objective of Or-BAC is to specify the security policy at the *organizational* level, that is abstractly from the implementation of this policy. Thus, instead of modeling the policy by using the concrete and implementation-related concepts of subject, action and object, the Or-BAC model suggests reasoning with the roles that subjects, actions or objects play in the organization. The role of a subject is simply called a *role* as in the RBAC model. On the other hand, the role of an action is called an *activity* whereas the role of an object is called a *view*.

Each organization can then define security rules which specify that some roles are permitted or prohibited to carry out some activities on some views. These security rules do not apply statically but their activation may depend on contextual conditions. For this purpose, the concept of *context* is explicitly introduced in Or-BAC. Thus, using a formalism based on first order logic, security rules are modeled using a 6-places predicate:

- *security_rule(type, org, role, activity, view, context)* where *type* belongs to {*permission, prohibition*}.

For instance, the following security rule:

- $security\_rule(prohibition, corp, pop\_user, read\_pop, mail\_server, pop\_threat)$.

means that, in organization *corp*, a pop user is forbidden to use the pop service to consult his or her mail in the context of pop threat.

All these concepts, organization, role, activity, view and context, may be structured hierarchically. Permissions and prohibitions are both inherited through these hierarchies (see [5] for more details).

Since a given security policy may include permissions and prohibitions, conflict management strategies have to be defined to solve the possible conflicts. In Or-BAC, such a strategy consists in assigning a priority to each security rule [6]. Priorities define a partial order on the set of security rules so that when a conflict occurs between two rules, preference is given to the rule with the higher priority. Priority assigned to security rules must be compatible with hierarchies defined on entities such as organization, role, activity, view and context. Thus, in case of conflict, if a given security rule is inherited by a given entity, this rule will have lower priority than another security rule explicitly assigned to this entity.

Once the organizational security policy is defined, it is possible to check if the conflict management strategy is *effective*, that is it will solve every conflict at the concrete level (see [18] for further details). Since the Or-BAC model abides to the Datalog restrictions [26], we can prove that it is possible to decide in polynomial time that a conflict management strategy is effective.

The organizational policy is then used to automatically derive concrete configurations of PEPs. For this purpose, we need to assign to subjects, actions and objects, the roles they play in the organization. In the Or-BAC model, this is modeled using the three following 3-places predicates:

- $empower(org, subject, role)$: means that in organization *org*, *subject* is empowered in *role*.
- $consider(org, action, activity)$: means that in organization *org*, *action* is considered an implementation of *activity*.
- $use(org, object, view)$: means that in organization *org*, *object* is used in *view*.

For instance, the fact *empower(corp, alice, pop_user)* means that organization *corp* empowers Alice in role *pop_user*.

Notice that, instead of enumerating facts corresponding to instances of predicate *empower*, it is also possible to specify role definitions which correspond to logical conditions that, when satisfied, are used to derive that some subjects are automatically empowered in the role associated with the role definition. Activity and view definitions are similarly used to automatically manage assignment of action to activity and object to view. For instance, in a network environment, we can use a role definition to specify that every host in the zone 111.222.1.0/24 are empowered in the role *DMZ*.

Notice that we shall use Prolog notation to specify Or-BAC security policies. For this purpose, the only important Prolog constructs to remember are that constant values start with a lowercase character, that variables start with an uppercase character, and that _ denotes any value.

3.3 Or-BAC Contexts

Regarding contexts, we have also to define logical conditions to characterize when contexts are active. In the Or-BAC model, this is represented by logical rules that derive the following predicate:

- *hold(org, subject, action, object, context)*: means that in organization *org*, *subject* performs *action* on *object* in context *context*.

We say that context *c* is active in organization *org* when it is possible to derive *hold(org, s, a, o, c)* for some subject *s*, action *a* and object *o*.

Using the model, one can then derive concrete authorizations that apply to subject, action and object from organizational security rules. This is modeled by the derivation rule shown in listing 1. In an organization *Org*, the security rule expresses a *permission* for a given *Role* to make a given *Activity* on a given *View* in a given *Context*. The predicates *empower*, *consider* and *use* indicate that *Role*, *Activity* and *View* are respectively abstractions of *Subject*, *Action* and *Object* in the considered organization. When the considered *Context* is being held for *Subject*, *Action* and *Object* through the *hold* predicate, we can thus derive the fact that it is permitted for *Subject* to make *Action* on *Object*.

Listing 1 Derivation of concrete authorizations

```
is_permitted(Subject, Action, Object) :-
    security_rule(permission, Org, Role, Activity, View, Context),
    empower(Org, Subject, Role),
    consider(Org, Action, Activity),
    use(Org, Object, View),
    hold(Org, Subject, Action, Object, Context).
```

This general principle of derivation of concrete authorizations from organizational authorizations is used to automatically generate concrete configurations (see [7] for further details in the case of network security policies).

3.4 *Presentation of a use case*

To illustrate the response mechanism, we present the following use case, access to mail. Users have access to their mail located on remote exchange servers. They can use three different mail clients, outlook, thunderbird and firefox, over four different transport mechanisms, the outlook mail client accessing the exchange server through native microsoft protocols, thunderbird accessing the POP and IMAP extensions of the same exchange servers, and Firefox accessing the OWA [1] extension of the same exchange servers. In normal operation, all these four modes are active and allow parallel access to the same information, the consistency being preserved by the backend exchange server.

3.4.1 Use case illustration

Figure 2 provides a description of the various entities involved in this use case. This description is layered to ease understanding of these entities, but a request for access will contain information belonging to all three layers. At the transport layer, a network packet contains information about IP addresses and ports in the headers, and commands and data for the programs in the packet payload according to the application-layer protocol specification. This is also true at the service layer, where commands and data are presented to the processes that obey and manipulate them.

In the case study, the ACE, PIE and PDP are implemented as Prolog predicates in SWI-Prolog, and the PEP as XSLT transformations. The components of the model (graphs of abstractions and instances) are modeled in a straightforward way using Prolog facts, *empower*, *consider* and *use*.

[1] Outlook Web Access

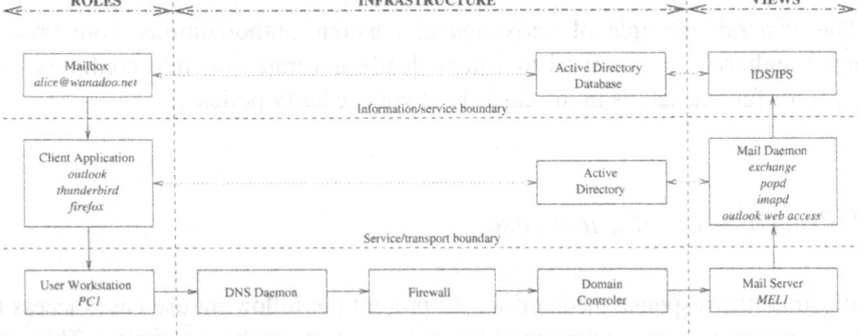

Fig. 2 Presentation of the use case

3.4.2 Horizontal layer segmentation

The information layer at the top models interactions between the humans and the information they wish to access. In our use case, users wish to access their mail messages. The middle layer represent the system intermediaries, typically programs, that make this mail reading possible. In our use case, mail clients such as Microsoft Outlook™, Mozilla Thunderbird or Mozilla Firefox[2] interact with mail servers such as Microsoft Exchange™. The bottom layer represents the communication channels, enabling communication between machines; in our case, this enables the exchange of TCP/IP packets between user workstations and servers.

3.4.3 Vertical segmentation

In addition to the layer segmentation, figure 2 also introduces a vertical separation. In addition to the classic Subject/Object duality, there are a large number of infrastructure functions that enable communication at one of the layers. Without these infrastructure functions, access is at best impaired and at worst impossible. Hence, they represent an attractive target for attackers and a possibility of countermeasure for the defender, and we wish to extend the classic policy model of subjects and objects by representing these components.

In our use case, user workstations rely on DNS to identify the target machine. User logins and access to information rely on ActiveDirectory to identify and au-

[2] used as support for webmail access

thenticate users, and associate user logins with mail boxes. They also need to traverse firewalls and intrusion detection/prevention systems. Note that it is not necessary to create new concepts to model these infrastructure entities; subjects and objects apply to them as well. Their presence in the model improves the understanding of the security policy and widens opportunities for threat response, since any combination of these elements can be leveraged.

3.4.4 Impact on policy enforcement

The vertical segmentation requires that our model for policy translation incorporate the ability to model reliably the infrastructure components and their interactions. We must incorporate contextual information, such as routing, that is not directly included in alerts (and rarely included in high-level security policies), that enables our system to infer the appropriate policy enforcement points where the policy is applicable and effective. Such a policy system also implies that there is a capability to collect and correlate state and contextual information (as is currently done in intrusion detection systems). With respect to state, the establishment of connectivity at the transport layer such as the three way TCP handshake will be required before users can present credentials such as user names, passwords and mailboxes. Higher up, we need to recognize service states (login in, logged in, etc.) and associations between sessions and users. With respect to information inference, we need to make use of configuration information, as in alert correlation. For example, while firefox will present its identity to OWA, Thunderbird and Exchange may not indicate themselves to the server. Furthermore, this identification information can be spoofed (it is for example very easy to fake the user agent of a web browser to another one). Our system will not be able to enforce the usage of firefox instead of opera or the usage of outlook instead of evolution if it only relies on transport level or view-side policy enforcement points. As long as the protocol exchanges are correct, we will not be able to model this at the abstract level or recognize it at the concrete level; this can only be enforced by a role-side, service-level policy enforcement point.

We are currently working on the representation of such models and are confident that the basic technologies, particularly state and correlation, can be provided by the intrusion detection and security information components available today.

3.5 Modelling of the use case

We now model the use case, define the appropriate abstract entities and describe their relationships with concrete entities. To do this, we will adopt whenever needed a simple tree representation, where properties defined at one node propagate to the nodes below. Abstract entities are represented as ovals and concrete entities are represented as square boxes. Note that we do not claim that the model is exhaustive; we will limit our description to the needed components.

3.5.1 Roles and views

Since roles and views have symetric behaviour with respect to the policy, we describe them together in figure 3. Both are segmented according to the three layers of 2; while this is not absolutely necessary and we could attach the various components that are in the layers to the *MailRole* or *MailViews* nodes, it provides additional segmentation that will prove useful for defining and analyzing countermeasures. Accordingly, the various concrete objects are attached to the appropriate abstract nodes.

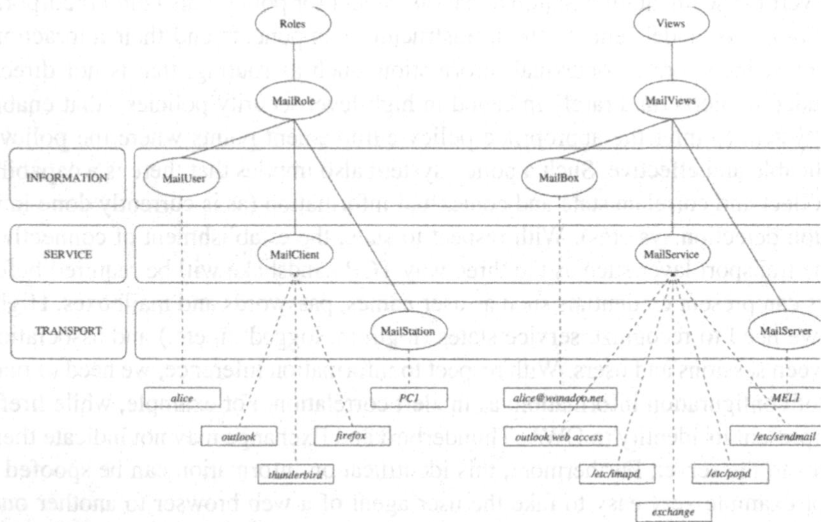

Fig. 3 Model of roles and views

This model presents a simplified view of the system. We model services by their startup/shutdown script names, mailboxes by the email address, mail clients by their names, and machines by their names. In a complete model, we would need more details on the various processes that intervene in the execution of a particular program, or relationships between machine names and IP addresses. These details could either be stated as additional facts or inserted as knowledge-gathering activities (e.g. using DNS to resolve host names into IP addresses).

We therefore obtain the appropriate role hierarchy, empower and use, as expressed in listing 2 (using the prolog formalism that we reuse in this chapter; the information is expressed as prolog facts).

Listing 2 Definition of roles and views

```
role(org,'MailRole').
role(org,'MailUser').
role(org,'MailClient').
role(org,'MailStation').
subrole(org,'MailUser','MailRole').
subrole(org,'MailClient','MailRole').
subrole(org,'MailStation','MailRole').

empower(org,'alice', 'MailUser').
empower(org,'Thunderbird', 'MailClient').
empower(org,'Outlook', 'MailClient').
empower(org,'Firefox', 'MailClient').
empower(org,'PC-Alice', 'MailStation').

view(org,'MailView').
view(org,'Mailbox').
view(org,'MailService')
view(org,'MailServer')
subview(org,'Mailbox', 'MailView').
subview(org,'MailService', 'MailView').
subview(org,'Mailserver', 'MailView').

use(org,'alice@wanadoo.net', 'Mailbox').
use(org,'OWA', 'MailService').
use(org,'/etc/imapd','MailService').
use(org,'/etc/popd', 'MailService').
use(org,'/etc/sendmail', 'MailService').
use(org,'Exchange', 'MailService').
use(org,'MEL1','MailServer').
```

The role and subrole (resp. view and subview) predicates construct the role (resp. view) hierarchy. Note that this listing is biased; in any realistic deployment, there should be many more concrete entities than abstract entities. The ratio of one to one in the listing is not representative of a realistic setting.

3.5.2 Activities

Activities are described in figure 4. The segmentation accross layers appears in this figure in the content of the square box, representing either ports or commands to the service. We have further segmented mail under three activities, connecting to the mailbox, reading mail and sending mail. This segmentation is introduced with respect to the response system, where options such as preventing new sessions but letting existing sessions continue, or letting users read but not send mail, are opening up additional opportunities for the response system to focus and limit the response on the area under attack.

Activities are modeled at the information level by retaining the various keywords used by the protocols to open the connection between the mail client and the mail server, and at the service and transport layer by the protocols and ports involved. Since protocols and ports are both found in IP packets and on machine (as bound ports), it is sufficient to model them with a single concrete object. For convenience, we are using a regular-expression-like notation for the microsoft protocols, since they need to be configured together to enable the activity to succeed. Protocol keywords for POP, IMAP and SMTP are taken from Request for Comments (RFC)

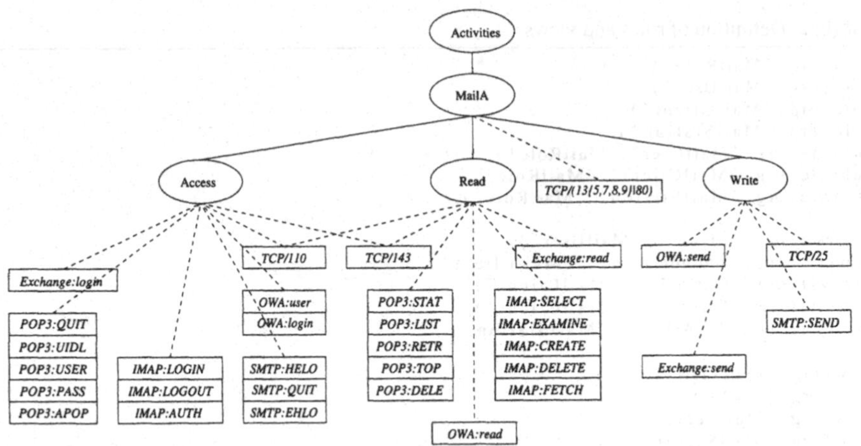

Fig. 4 Model of activities

1939, 2060 and 2821 respectively, although we have only introduced here a subset of these keywords. Keywords for OWA are inspired from the interface button names but should ideally associate URLs and AJAX commands. Since the Exchange/Outlook dialog is not a public standard, we have introduced meta-keywords that correspond to the various mail-related activities of Exchange.

In figure 4, we also have to acknowledge that this granularity does not apply to all possible activities. For example, the direct connection between the Microsoft Outlook mail reader and the Microsoft Exchange mail server limits our capability to separate get and send at the network layer, because all three sub-activities use the same set of ports. This is the same for the separation between login and read at the network layer. The login activity, however, is separable at the service layer, for example by manipulating the active directory server to prevent exchange login requests to succeed, or by filtering out IMAP and POP3 login requests.

Activities are described in listing 3. We have not listed all the consider facts, but the reader can easily construct them from figure 4.

Listing 3 Definition of activities

```
activity(org,'MailA').
activity(org,'Access').
activity(org,'Read').
activity(org,'Write').
subactivity(org,'Access','MailA').
subactivity(org,'Read','MailA').
subactivity(org,'Write','MailA').

consider(org,'TCP/(80|13[5,7,8,9])','MailA')
consider(org,'TCP/110',Access').
consider(org,'TCP/143',Access').
consider(org,'TCP/110','Read').
consider(org,'TCP/143','Read').
consider(org,'TCP/25',Write').
consider(org,'Exchange:login','Access').
consider(org,'POP3:APOP','Access').
```

```
consider(org,'IMAP:LOGIN','Access').
consider(org,'SMTP:HELO','Access').
consider(org,'OWA:user','Access').
consider(org,'POP3:STAT','Read').
consider(org,'IMAP:SELECT','Read').
consider(org,'SMTP:MAIL','Write').
consider(org,'Exchange:send','Write').
```

Note that the normal behaviour of certain protocols puts demands on the model. The rattachement of $TCP/(80|13[5,7,8,9])$ to 'MailA' is due to the fact that at the network level, all activities related to the Oulook-Exchange or Firefox-OWA connections cannot be differentiated easily. However, the service level does differenciate access, read and write activities.

3.5.3 Contexts

For the normal operation of our system, we only need one context, the 'MyMailbox' context, whose objective is to ensure that the user can only access his mailbox. This is necessary because access to the mailbox relies on access to the information system, and there is a need to link the authentication data (login,password) to the mailbox. The 'MyMailbox' context inherits from the 'Normal' context as shown in listing 4. We also define a partial order between contexts by indicating that the 'MyMailbox' context has priority over the 'Normal' context.

Listing 4 Definition of contexts

```
context(org,'Normal').
context(org,'MyMailbox').
subcontext(org,'MyMailbox','Normal').
context_priority_high_low(org,'MyMailbox','Normal').

hold(org, Subject, Action, Object, 'MyMailbox') :-
    empower(org, Subject, 'MailUser'),
    consider(org, Action, 'MailA'),
    use(org, Object,'Mailbox'),
    arelinkedinactivedirectory(Subject,Object).

hold(org, Subject, Action, Object, 'MyMailbox') :-
    empower(org, Subject, 'MailClient')),
    consider(org, Action, 'MailA'),
    use(org, Object, 'MailService')).

hold(org, Subject, Action, Object, 'MyMailbox') :-
    empower(org, Subject, 'MailStation')),
    consider(org, Action, 'MailA'),
    use(org, Object,'MailServer')).
```

The hold predicates are written in listing 4 using primitives to interrogate the Active Directory server. Since information about subjects and objects is separated in three layers, only the higher layer is pertinent for the assertion of the MyMailbox context, as described in the first hold statement. This hold statement verifies that the request is presented with a user name and a mailbox, and queries the active directory server for the connection between the two. However, if we only allow this, we will not succeed in deploying the security policy on policy enforcement points located below the information layer : the hold statement will never be satisfied, because this association only occurs at the information layer. Since servers and processes are shared by all users, the second and third hold statements satisfy the policy for lower-level policy enforcement points.

3.5.4 Security rules

Within the above model, the security policy is expressed by the two simple rules of listing 5.

Listing 5 Definition of contexts

```
security_rule(permission,org,MailRole,MailA,MailView,MyMailbox).
security_rule(prohibition,org,MailRole,MailA,MailView,Normal).
```

According to this policy, users are prevented from reading mailboxes in general. However, a potential conflict occurs when the MyMailbox context holds, and the higher priority of the MyMailbox context with respect to the Normal context enables access.

4 Applying Or-BAC for threat response

Or-BAC contexts provide a natural way to include threat response into Or-BAC policy rules, to create specific rules that apply during an attack. The central idea of our proposal is based on using contexts to model how to dynamically update the security policy when a threat is detected. Therefore, the core of our proposal is to manage contexts according to threat information. Note that we generically talk about *threat* contexts to refer to contexts used to characterize threats and to provide threat response. Thus, examples of threat contexts may in fact refer to attacks or intrusions (successful attacks). For instance, *syn_flooding* and *pop_attack* are two examples of threat contexts.

We present in this section how we define atomic and composed contexts, and how we aim at activating and deactivating these contexts according to threat level.

4.1 Examples of threat contexts

We propose here two examples of threats and explain how response is managed depending on the active *hold* predicates and the security rules describing the policy to apply in such cases. Listings follow the *prolog* syntax (SWI-Prolog is our implementation language), altough with a simplified representation of the alerts, as the IDMEF XML representation results in deeply imbricated lists that we have simplified to ease comprehension – alerts are abstracted as position dependant 4-tuples (timestamp, attack source, attack destination, attack identification), each of these 4-tuples being represented by a list of (IDMEF token, value) pairs.

4.1.1 Syn-flooding attack

Let us imagine a Syn-flooding attack towards a webserver. We use IDMEF messages (as explained in Section 4.4.1) to say that if a given alert message is received with (1) a classification reference equal to CVE-1999-0116 (corresponding to the CVE reference of a Syn-flooding attack) and (2) the target is attacked through a service whose name is *http* (or port is *tcp*/80) and (3) the target corresponds to a network node whose name is *ws*, then the *syn_flooding* context is active for *http* action on *ws* object. The corresponding translation in Prolog can be found in Listing 6.

Listing 6 syn_flooding context definition

```
% Simplification of alert information extraction
content(K,[[K,E]|_],E).
content(K,[[_,_]|L],E) :-
   content(K,L,E).

contentlist([],_,[]) :- !.
contentlist([K|LK],X,LER) :-
   findall(Es,content(K,X,Es),E),
   contentlist(LK,X,LE),
   flatten([E,LE],LER1),
   sort(LER1,LER).

% synflood context description
hold(corp, _, Action, Object, 'syn-flooding') :-
   alert(CreateTime, Source, Target, Classification),
   content('reference',Classification, 'CVE-1999-0116'),
   contentlist(['service'],Target, Action),
   contentlist(['hostname'],Target, Object).

% Arrival of an alert
alert('2001/01/01_01:01:01',
   [['hostaddress','1.2.3.4']],
   [['service','http'],['hostname','ws']],
   [['reference','CVE-1999-0116']]).

% The following now holds
?- hold(Org, Subject, Action, Object, Context).

Org = corp,
Action = [http],
Object = [ws],
Context = syn_flooding ;

?-
```

Notice that, since in a Syn-flooding attack, the intruder is spoofing its source address, the subject corresponding to the threat origin is not instantiated in the *hold* predicate which is represented by "_".

When an attack occurs and a new alert is launched by the intrusion detection process, (a) new fact(s) $hold(org,s,a,o,c)$ is (are) derived for some threat context c. So, c is now active and the security rules associated with this context are triggered to react to the intrusion.

Notice that our approach provides *fine-grained* reaction. For instance, let us consider a network where a given host *ws* is assigned to the role *web_server*. Let us assume that a Syn-flooding attack is detected against this host on port $tcp/80$, which corresponds to service *http*. In this case, we shall derive the following fact:

- $hold(org, \_, http, ws, syn\_flooding)$: means that host *ws* is now in the threat context $syn\_flooding$ through *http*.

Since the $syn\_flooding$ context is now active, security rules associated with this context are triggered. For instance, let us assume that there is the following security rule:

- $security\_rule(prohib, org, internet, tcp\_service, web\_server, syn\_flooding)$: means that, in the threat context $syn\_flooding$, *internet* is prohibited to perform $tcp\_service$ activity on the web_server.

This security rule is triggered once the $syn\_flooding$ context is active. However, only host *ws* (whose role is *web_server*) is in the context of $syn\_flooding$ through *http* (which is a tcp service). As a consequence, the reaction will not close every tcp service from the Internet to every web server. Instead, the reaction in this case will be limited to close *http* from the Internet to host *ws*.

4.1.2 Pop reconnaissance attack

Imagine now that an internal attacker is attempting a reconnaissance attack on a pop3 server in order to determine valid users. The reference CVE-2005-1133 is an instance of such an attack for a pop3 server in IBM iSeries AS/400.

The definition of the *pop_attack* context says that if a given alert message is received with (1) a classification reference equal to CVE-2005-1133 (corresponding to the CVE reference of a pop reconnaissance attack) and (2) the target is attacked through a service whose port is $tcp/110$ (or name is *pop*3) by (3) a source that corresponds to a mail user whose name is *charlie* and (4) the target corresponds to a network node whose name is *ms*, then the *pop_attack* context is active for *charlie* subject making $tcp/110$ action on *ms* object. Notice that we face here an internal attack and we consider that the diagnostic has revealed that the source is not a decoy, so we are able to instantiate the subject being the source in the *hold* predicate. The definition of the hold facts is more complex here, due to the need to maintain the coherence between the information, service and transport layers. The corresponding translation in Prolog can be found in Listing 7.

Listing 7 pop_attack context definition

```
% Simplification of alert information extraction
content(K,[[K,E]|_],E).
content(K,[[_,_]|L],E) :-
    content(K,L,E).

contentlist([],_,[]) :- !.
contentlist([K|LK],X,LER) :-
    findall(Es,content(K,X,Es),E),
    contentlist(LK,X,LE),
    flatten([E,LE],LER1),
    sort(LER1,LER).
% pop attack context description
hold(corp, Subject, Action, Object, 'pop_attack') :-
    alert(CreateTime, Source, Target, Classification),
    content('reference',Classification, 'CVE-2005-1133'),
    contentlist(['username'],Source, Subject),
    contentlist(['mailaddr','file'],Target, Object).
 hold(corp, Subject, Action, Object, 'pop_attack') :-
    alert(CreateTime, Source, Target, Classification),
    content('reference',Classification 'CVE-2005-1133'),
    contentlist(['hostaddr','hostname'], Source, Subject),
    contentlist(['service'],Target, Action),
    contentlist(['hostaddr','hostname','process'],Target, Object).
% Arrival of an alert
alert('2002/02/02_02:02:02',
        [['hostaddr','1.2.3.4'],['hostname','charliews'],
         ['username','charlie']],
        [['service','tcp/110'],['process','/etc/initd/pop'],
         ['file','/var/spool/mail/charlie'],
         ['hostname','ms'],['mailaddr','charlie@net.net']],
        [['reference','CVE-2005-1133']]).

% The following now holds
?- hold(Org,Subject,Action,Object,Context).

Org = corp,
Subject = [charlie],
Object = ['/var/spool/mail/charlie', 'charlie@net.net'],
Context = pop_attack ;

Org = corp,
Subject = ['1.2.3.4', charliews],
Action = ['tcp/110'],
Object = ['/etc/initd/pop', ms],
Context = pop_attack ;

?-
```

In this case, we shall derive the following *hold* facts:

- *hold(org,charlie,,['charlie@net.net','/var/spool/mail/charlie'],pop_attack)*: means that mailbox *charlie@net.net* (and its sibling representation *'/var/spool/–mail/charlie'* mail spool file) is now in the threat context *pop_attack*, the attacker being user *charlie*.
- *hold(org,['1.2.3.4',charliews],['tcp/110'],['/etc/initd/pop',ms],pop_attack)* means processes */etc/initd/pop* and server *ms* are now in the threat context *pop_attack*, the attack coming from workstation *charliews* with IP address 1.2.3.4

Since the *pop_attack* context is now active, security rules associated with this context are triggered. For instance, let us assume that there is the following security rule:

- *security_rule(prohib, org, mail_user, read_pop, mail_server, pop_attack)*: means that, in the threat context *pop_attack*, a *mail_user* is prohibited to perform *read_pop* activity on the *mail_server*.

This security rule is triggered once the *pop_attack* context is active. However, only host *ms* (whose role is *mail_server*) is in the context of *pop_attack* through port $tcp/110$ (or *pop*3 service, which are *read_pop* actions) for subject user *charlie* (which belongs to the *mail_user* role). Alike the previous example, the reaction in this case will be limited to forbid port $tcp/110$ to host *ms*, but for user *charlie* only.

These two examples illustrate the fact that, in our approach, we can associate threat contexts with *general* security rules. However, fine-grained instantiation of the intrusion can be used to limit the reaction to those entities that are involved in the attack (as an intruder or a victim). Notice that the presented listings could be generalized by replacing constants by variables. For instance, in listing 6, it is possible to replace the constant *ws* by a variable, and similarly for constants *charlie* and *ms* in listing 7.

4.2 Atomic contexts

We recon that this approach is likely to greatly increase the number of contexts. To facilitate context management, we consider that contexts may belong to three categories: *operational*, *threat* and *minimal*. Let C be a set of contexts. We consider a set $OC \subseteq C$ of *operational* contexts. For the sake of simplicity, we consider that, in the absence of characterized threat, that is in the absence of attack or intrusion, the organizational policy is defined using a single *nominal* context. Thus, we assume that $nominal \in OC$. However, in a more realistic setting, this policy may depend on other contexts, for instance temporal contexts. Thus, we assume that OC may contain additional sub-contexts, and that for example, $working\_hours \in OC$. Additional details about *operational* contexts may be found in [9]. Note that $c \in OC$ *is active* does not mean that there is no attack or intrusion, but that *it is possible that there is no attack or intrusion*. Indeed, *operational* contexts do not provide any information about threats. For example, *nominal* is always active, and *working_hours* only relies on time. We then consider a set $TC \subseteq C$ of *threat* contexts. A context $c \in TC$ is activated when a given threat is detected. This means that $c \in TC$ *is active* necessarily implies that *there is an attack or an intrusion.* It is associated to a set of new security rules that apply to fix the threat. Finally, we consider the set $MC \subseteq C$ of *minimal* contexts. Minimal contexts aim at defining high priority exceptions in the policy, allowing to describe minimal security requirements that must apply even when intrusions occur.

Contexts are organized hierarchically so that, when a conflict occurs, security rules associated with contexts higher in the hierarchy will override the ones associated with lower contexts. We assume that *operational* contexts are lower than *threat* contexts which are in turn lower than *minimal* contexts. However, potential conflicts may still remain between rules associated with contexts belonging to the same category. In such cases, a partial order has to be defined between concerned rules, in order to ensure conflict resolution at the policy evaluation level (see Section 5.3).

If c is a *threat* context, then subject s, action a and object o must be correctly mapped onto information available from threats, including threat source, threat classification and threat target. So, in that case, the context definition associated with c is a logical condition that matches the alert message generated by the intrusion detection process.

4.3 Composed contexts

Providing the possibility to express fine-grained contexts is of major interest, in particular to characterize threats. However, managing specific atomic contexts would rapidly become difficult since it would result in a huge number of definitions. We therefore define a context algebra to provide a way to combine atomic contexts through a boolean algebra. The algebra provides the following basic functions to manipulate composed contexts:

$$Negation: \; n(c) \leftrightarrow \textit{context } c \textit{ is } \textbf{not} \textit{ active}$$
$$Conjunction: \; \&(c1,c2) \leftrightarrow \textit{context } c1 \textbf{ and } \textit{context } c2 \textit{ are active}$$
$$Disjunction: \; v(c1,c2) \leftrightarrow \textit{context } c1 \textit{ is active } \textbf{or} \textit{ context } c2 \textit{ is active}$$

This algebra allows the expression of composed contexts based on the composition of atomic contexts, ensuring thus an easy way to define fine-grained security rules. Contexts entering in the composition of *composed* contexts are simply named *composing* contexts.

Managing security rules with composed contexts requires the ability to associate a property to the composed context, in relation with the priorities of the composing contexts. We now analyze the possible combinations, giving examples for a better understanding of composed context priorities.

Definition 1 *Since it is possible that there is no attack or intrusion in a negative context, the negation of a context, whatever its category, is an operational context.*

Property 1 *The priority of a negative context is equal to the priority of an operational context. Consequently, the priority of a negative context is lower than the priority of a threat context, and lower than the priority of a minimal context.*

Let us consider $c1 \in OC$, $c2 \in TC$ and $c3 \in MC$. According to definition 1, one can state that $n(c1) \in OC$, $n(c2) \in OC$ and $n(c3) \in OC$. Now, according, to property 1, one can state that $n(c1)$, $n(c2)$ and $n(c3)$ have a priority of an operational context. Thus, they have a lower priority than threat and minimal contexts.
Ex. *$n(working\_hours)$, like $working\_hours$, is an operational context; $n(pop\_attack)$, negation of pop_attack, is an operational context. Thus, $n(working\_hours)$ and $n(pop\_attack)$ have both a lower priority than pop_attack, which is a threat context.*

Definition 2 *The conjunction of two contexts belonging to the same category belongs to this category.*

Property 2 *The priority of the conjunction of two contexts belonging to the same category is the priority assigned to this category.*

Let us consider $c1 \in OC$ and $c2 \in OC$. According to definition 2, one can state that $\&(c1,c2) \in OC$. Now, according to property 2, one can state that $\&(c1,c2)$ has the priority of an operational context.
Ex. *$\&(working\_hours, in\_dmz)$ is the conjunction of a temporal (thus, operational) and a spatial (thus, operational) context. Consequently, $\&(working\_hours, in\_dmz)$ is an operational context.*

Now, let us consider $c3 \in TC$ and $c4 \in TC$. One can state that $\&(c3,c4) \in TC$ and that its priority is higher than operational, but lower than minimal.
Ex. *$\&(pop\_attack, syn\_flooding)$ is the conjunction of two threat contexts. Consequently, $\&(pop\_attack, syn\_flooding)$ is a threat context.*

Definition 3 *The conjunction of two contexts belonging to different categories belongs to the category of the composing context having the highest priority.*

Property 3 *The priority of the conjunction of two contexts belonging to different categories is the highest priority of the composing contexts.*

Let us consider $c1 \in TC$ and $c2 \in OC$. According to definition 3, one can state that $\&(c1,c2) \in TC$. Now, according to property 3, one can state that $\&(c1,c2)$ has the priority of a threat context.
Ex. *$\&(pop\_attack, working\_hours)$ is the conjunction of a threat context and an operational (temporal) context. Since a threat context has a higher priority than an operational context, $\&(pop\_attack, working\_hours)$ is a threat context, and thus it has the priority of a threat context.*

Dealing with the disjunction is not so trivial, in particular with two contexts belonging to different categories. Indeed, let us consider $c1 \in OC$ and $c2 \in TC$. Determining to which category $v(c1,c2)$ belongs requires to consider which composing context among $c1$ and $c2$ is activating $v(c1,c2)$, since $c1$ and $c2$ do not have the same priority. Indeed, if $v(c1,c2)$ is active because $c1$ is active, this means that $v(c1,c2)$ is an operational context, like $c1$. On the contrary, if $v(c1,c2)$ is active because $c2$

is active, this means that $v(c1,c2)$ is a threat context, like $c2$. Moreover, it is possible that $v(c1,c2)$ is active because $c1$ and $c2$ are both active. In this case, $v(c1,c2)$ belongs to the category of the composing context having the highest priority.

In order to avoid the issue of active context determination, we make the choice of automatically splitting the security rules defined with a disjunctive context into a set of equivalent rules, each one being defined for each composing context of the disjunction. For this purpose, we have simply to observe that a security rule defined with a disjunctive context $v(c1,c2)$ is logically equivalent to the conjunction of two security rules respectively defined with context $c1$ and with context $c2$. Therefore, we first convert contexts to Disjunctive Normal Form (DNF), that is as a disjunction of conjunctions, and then write the set of equivalent rules.

Composed contexts are not necessarily composed of atomic contexts. Based on the defined algebra, it is possible to envision not only the composition of atomic contexts, but also the composition of composed contexts, so that one can define rules triggered by fine-grained contexts expressing accurately the security requirements. For instance, one could express a prohibition for a role *user* to make the activity *read_pop* on the view *mail_server* in the context:

$$\&(v(remote\_access, \&(internal\_access, n(working\_hours)), pop\_attack)),$$

that is either in a context of pop attack **and** remote access, **or** in a context of pop attack **and** internal access on non-working hours.

4.4 Context activation

Activation of threat contexts raises two major points: (1) which information is available to characterize threats, and (2) what do we do with this information to characterize threats at the policy level. We should insist on the fact that when we talk about context activation, we deal in fact with the activation of complete *hold* facts, that is context, but also organization, subject, action and object. This allows a full characterization of the threat, that is not only which kind of threat (*e.g.* context *pop_threat*), but also which subject, action and object it deals with, and within which organization.

4.4.1 Information about threat

IDMEF (Intrusion Detection Message Exchange Format [12]) messages generated by intrusion detection sensors naturally carry threat information. Even outside intrusion detection, IDMEF provides an appropriate format for describing log events, as shown for example by the Prelude IDS framework[3]. Therefore, we use IDMEF messages to select contexts and policy rules to activate. Among the IDMEF message attributes, we particularly use:

CreateTime The CreateTime timestamp indicates the time at which the alert was created and is mostly relevant for context activation.

Assessment The Assessment attribute carries information related to the risk of the attacker's actions.

Classification The Classification provides information about the mechanism of the attack. This is important to relate the alert to the views and activities of the Or-BAC policy rules, and to activate contexts.

Target The Target attribute carries information about the victim. This is important to relate the alert to the views and activities of the Or-BAC policy rules, and to activate contexts.

Source The Source attribute carries information about the attacker. This may be relevant for roles in the Or-BAC policy rules if the attacker is an insider, and to activate contexts.

We use the two first attributes to compute a context lifetime, as shown in table 2. Attributes are also translated into contexts through the use of mapping functions, as shown in Section 4.4.2.

4.4.2 Mapping alert information on hold predicates

Mapping alert information to context requires creating transformations from alert content to instantiated triples $(Subject, Action, Object)$ by writing the appropriate *hold* predicates. Unfortunately, the naive mapping from *IDMEF.Source* to *Subject*, from *IDMEF.Classification* to *Action*, and from *IDMEF.Target* to *Object*, is far from sufficient, and this for three reasons:

1. We need a mapping that has variable granularity, to take into account the different scope of different attacks. For example, a distributed denial-of-service on all areas of the network needs to be handled differently than a targeted brute-force password-guessing attack.
2. Alert information is sometimes incomplete; sources can be inexistent, incomplete or wrong. Multiple classifications may provide inconsistent information, such as conflicting attack references, may cover multiple attacks, or may not be modeled in our system. We need to specify what happens when an alert is incomplete.
3. We also need to specify complex responses mechanisms, that take into account environmental information, expressing complex reaction scenarios. For example, a complete response system may require moving from HTTP to HTTPS, and hence opening and closing multiple network accesses, and starting and stopping multiple services.

		Subject	Action	Object	Context	Lifetime
Createtime	ntpstamp				X	
Source	Node.name	X				
	Node.Address.address	X				
	Node.Address.netmask	x				
	User.Userid.name	X				
	Process.name	x			x	
	Service.name	x			x	
	Service.port	x			x	
Target	Node.name			X		
	Node.Address.address			X		
	Node.Address.netmask			x		
	User.Userid.name			x		
	Process.name		X	x	x	
	Service.name		X	x	x	
	Service.port		X	x	x	
Classification	Reference.name		x		X	
Assessment	Impact.severity					X
	Impact.type					X

Table 1 Mapping IDMEF classes on Or-BAC parameters

Table 1 lists the elements which should be taken into account to provide relevant mappings. 'X' means that the considered information is very likely to be found in the IDMEF messages and thus to be used in the mappings. 'x' means that the information is less likely to be found, or that it is not yet used in the mappings. While table 1 does not take into account all IDMEF attributes, we are are using the most important ones with respect to the description of alert conditions. We are investigating the alerts produced by different systems to ensure that we are not leaving out important parameters, particularly with respect to information that is stored in the additional data blob.

The table reveals for instance that not only *Classification.Reference* can be considered to instantiate contexts, but also *Target.Process* and *Target.Service*. In fact, some information may be redundant. For instance, both the reference CVE-2005-1133 and the target service $tcp/110$ can be used to diagnose a *pop_attack* context. This kind of redundancy can help detecting conflicting attack references, and is also used to determine contexts even in case of missing information. For example, an alert with a missing reference but a target port could be managed considering only the target port. However, one has to note that such information are not necessarily rigorously equivalent, since one may look for more precise evidences. For example, CVE-2005-1133 not only inform that we face a pop threat, but also that it is a reconnaissance attack, which can be of interest in the mapping process. On the opposite, target port $tcp/110$ only provides means to derive that we are coping with pop threat.

This mapping also takes into account organization-related policies for response. For example, mappings may always ignore *IDMEF.Source* information, concentrating on blocking traffic that reaches *IDMEF.Target*. They may prefer system-related information (host names or network addresses) to user names, to ensure a global

[3] `http://www.prelude-ids.org/`

response to the threat, or prefer user names to deliver extremely targeted responses at the user account level.

4.5 Context deactivation

Deactivating threat contexts is used to revocate countermeasures once threats are no longer present. We currently manage static context lifetimes, which are computed thanks to IDMEF alerts assessment attributes. Indeed, IDMEF alerts provide an *IDMEF.Assessment.Impact* attribute with three sub-attributes, severity, completion and type. If completion is set to failed, no context will be activated. Otherwise, based on the impact severity, and type, we derive the duration of the context activity, according to the matrix defined in table 2. This is a basic example that relies purely on risk analysis done by the alert providers, but better analysis can be adapted using finer threat analysis, as shown in section 7.1.

Impact severity Impact type	info	low	medium	high	Comment
admin	1	2	4	8	This is the most severe case.
dos	0	0	0	0	We are not currently handling DoS attacks.
file	0	1	2	3	
recon	0	0	0	0	We are not currently handling scans, as they do not result in compromise.
user	0	1	2	4	
other	0	0	1	2	

Table 2 Intrusive context lifetime according to IDMEF impact severity and type, in minutes

When an alert occurs, it is asserted for a certain duration. Thus, the corresponding context is activated with the expiration date set according to the table. While this alert remains stored in the system, the context remains active. When the lifetime expires, the alert is removed from the database, and the context is deactivated, unless another instance of the alert has been received in the meantime. Both asserts and retracts trigger a re-evaluation of the security policy.

The values of table 2 have been defined through expert knowledge of the risks incurred by each protocol. We currently use the same matrix for evaluating the risk incurred by each access mechanism; the variation in risk associated with each individual protocol is handled by the proper setting of the impact severity attribute.

4.6 Influence of Mapping on the Response Strategy

The mapping from alerts to contexts (or more generally to Or-BAC *hold* facts) also influences the response strategy. Depending on the information available, one may provide a network-oriented response by retaining only network-based information such as IP addresses and port numbers and discarding user-based information such as user names, or conversely provide a user-oriented response. One may also combine both for a very specific response. In a number of cases, network-oriented response may be the only practical option, as network information is available in the alerts and network security devices such as firewalls are capable of blocking the undesired traffic.

Also, mapping influences the response to be either victim-centric or attacker-centric. A victim-centric response aims at blocking traffic towards the attack target, assuming that other attackers may attempt to exploit the same attack mechanisms. An attacker-centric response aims at blocking traffic from the attack source, ensuring that the attacker is prevented from accessing other servers that may offer the same service or vulnerability. This is often the case in large environments – indeed, our own case study shows three mail servers with identical characteristics; an attack on one of them is equally dangerous for the two others, even though the attacker may not have yet stricken.

Finally, one may degrade the mapping, for example by authorizing a mapping from IP addresses to subnet masks only. Hence, the response would apply to all machines in the subnet, instead of the single victim machine.

5 The Threat Response System

5.1 System Architecture

The architecture of the threat response system is presented in figure 6. Software or hardware modules are depicted by circles and messages and configuration information associated with our components by diamonds. We assume that any organization will deploy sensors and a security information management framework, from which we will collect alert information. This is depicted by the *sensor* block. The policy changes will be applied to *PEPs*, for example mail servers, firewalls or intrusion detection systems. It is therefore likely that some PEPs will also act as sensors. The function of our software modules is described further in table 3.

5.2 Alert Correlation Engine (ACE)

Generally, information produced by sensors cannot be considered on their own. Indeed, this information actually comes from many sources (sensors), and with different formats (ex: a Snort alert, a Netfilter firewall log, etc.). Moreover, there is a strong need for alerts volume reduction and semantics improvement. Alert correlation aims at realizing this task, thus permitting false positives reduction and pro-

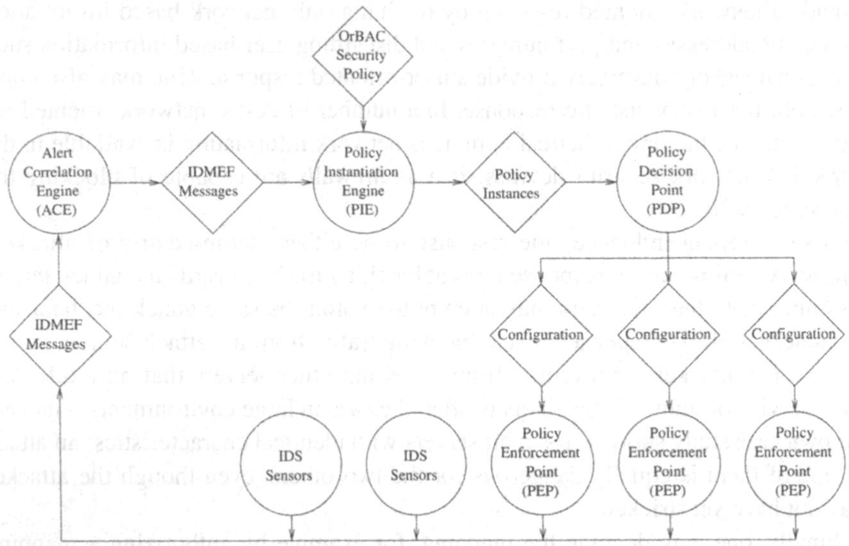

Fig. 5 Threat response system architecture

Module	Input	Output	Configuration	Function
ACE	IDMEF messages	IDMEF messages	External security reference databases	Verify and update information in IDMEF messages for threat assessment.
PIE	IDMEF messages	Or-BAC concrete rules	Or-BAC policy and context definitions	Activate threat contexts. Extract a new security policy from the active contexts.
PDP	Or-BAC concrete rules	Config scripts	Policy to script translation rules	Segment the policy according to PEP realms and capabilities, and translate the policy rules to PEP-specific scripted commands.
PEP	Config scripts	IDMEF messages		Apply the configuration script that implements the security policy.

Table 3 Function of the software modules

ducing meta-alerts offering a better semantics and severity levels for more efficient analysis. This is mainly done by merging redundant information and similarities in order to obtain global alerts with a fusion process [4]. We define an ACE as an entity receiving as input every possible event produced by sensors and giving as output high-level IDMEF-compliant alerts (meta-alerts).

Note that the exact definition of this module is considered out of the scope of this paper, since we consider the existence of valuable works on the subject [11, 19, 4, 20] and of a SIM commercial market as a proof of feasibility. Our current ACE prototype only verifies and modifies impact information in the IDMEF message, and validate sources and targets with respect to contexts.

5.3 Policy Instantiation Engine (PIE)

The security policy description corresponds to a set of Or-BAC rules. The possibility to express contextual policies offered by Or-BAC is used in order to trigger rules considering high-level and fine-grained information. Thus, a policy instantiation engine (PIE) has two major functions: (1) activate contexts (through Or-BAC *hold* facts) which (2) trigger re-evaluation of the security policy (through activation of abstract Or-BAC rules). Intrusive contexts activation is addressed in Section 4.4. For operational contexts, such as temporal ones, one can refer to [9] for further information. Note that the PIE also deals with context deactivation, according to Section 4.5. Generic policy rules triggering is explained in Section 3, and examples are given in Section 4.1.

Note that the PIE manages conflict resolution at the policy evaluation level to produce a coherent set of policy instances (concrete Or-BAC rules) to deploy. Conflict resolution is managed at the abstract level, by deciding which rule takes precedence when two or more rules present intersections of roles, activities, views and/or contexts. On this purpose, we consider Or-BAC abstract entities inheritances and priorities depending on contexts categories to define a partial order relationship between conflicting rules, which is sufficient to ensure the proper evaluation of the security policy, as shown in [10].

5.4 Policy Decision Point (PDP)

Policies instantiated in response to threat contexts are transmitted to one or more PDP(s). A PDP is in charge of local policy decisions. Whenever it receives a new policy instance, that is an Or-BAC concrete rule (permission or prohibition), a PDP has to map this information onto concrete actions to be performed on PEPs to enforce the new policy. A PDP thus have to be aware of its PEPs abilities, so that it can translate first the rules into generic configurations, considering the kind of PEP (*e.g.* a firewall), and then the generic configurations into specific configurations, considering the implementation of the PEP (*e.g.* a "Netfilter" firewall) [7]. Note that part of the decisional capability of the PDP relies on the fact that a given Or-BAC concrete policy rule may provide different actions on the PEPs. For instance, depending on the architecture of the information system, reconfiguring access to mail user accounts may be realized on the service itself, (*e.g.* pop3 service native configuration files) in the case of dedicated services, or at the infrastructure level (*e.g.* reconfiguration of Active Directory) in the case of federated services environment. One may also imagine advanced deployment scenarios, taking into account network or application sessions continuity. For example, an advanced scenario could be to first alert users on an imminent service disruption, but let them a definite time to terminate their immediate action.

5.5 Policy Enforcement Point (PEP)

PEPs receive new policies (or policy elements), which have been translated by the PDP [7]. Expressing a new policy may have implications on multiple PEPs. For example, it can involve both a server (stopping a service) and a firewall (blocking a port). Each PEP dealing with a policy instance is sent a configuration script, considering its type (ex: firewall), but also its implementation (ex: Netfilter). Note that a PEP can also be considered a sensor, which possesses specific functionalities of policy enforcement. This characteristic can provide information allowing validation of new policies effective application.

6 From alerts to new policies

We present here the workflow allowing the mapping from alerts to new policy instances. The PIE is divided into two subparts allowing (1) to map alerts reported as IDMEF messages into Or-BAC hold facts characterizing threats and allowing adequate countermeasures, and (2) to derive new policy instances thanks to hold facts and to the abstract policy definition. Figure 6 presents a global view of these two PIE functions. Mapping threats to hold facts is managed through the Threat Characterization Engine (TCE), whereas concrete policy instantiation is realized thanks to the Policy Core Engine (PCE). Note that conflict resolution is managed at PCE level since it is ensured at the policy evaluation step.

Figure 6 also presents in details the components of the Threat Characterization Engine. Threat characterization does not actually consist in a trivial and static mapping, since (1) IDMEF messages may contain various information which can be translated in different Or-BAC triples (subject, action, object), (2) some information may lack in IDMEF messages, and (3) generated hold facts must be relevant to current threat in order to provide the best adequate response. On this purpose, the TCE process is divided into three steps: (1) syntactic mapping, (2) enrichment, and (3) strategy application.

6.1 Syntactic mapping

The first stage consists in realizing a quite trivial syntactic mapping, that is extracting as many triples $(subject, action, object)$ as possible from a given IDMEF message, to ensure that all subjects, actions and objects known to be participating in the attack process are included in the response. The obtained information is called *raw Or-BAC instances*, since they are not usable to respond to threat. Such mappings are statically defined, a $subject$ being for instance the IP address of the source host given by the IDMEF message. An example of an *action* is the target port (service) and an example of an $object$ is the DNS name of the target.

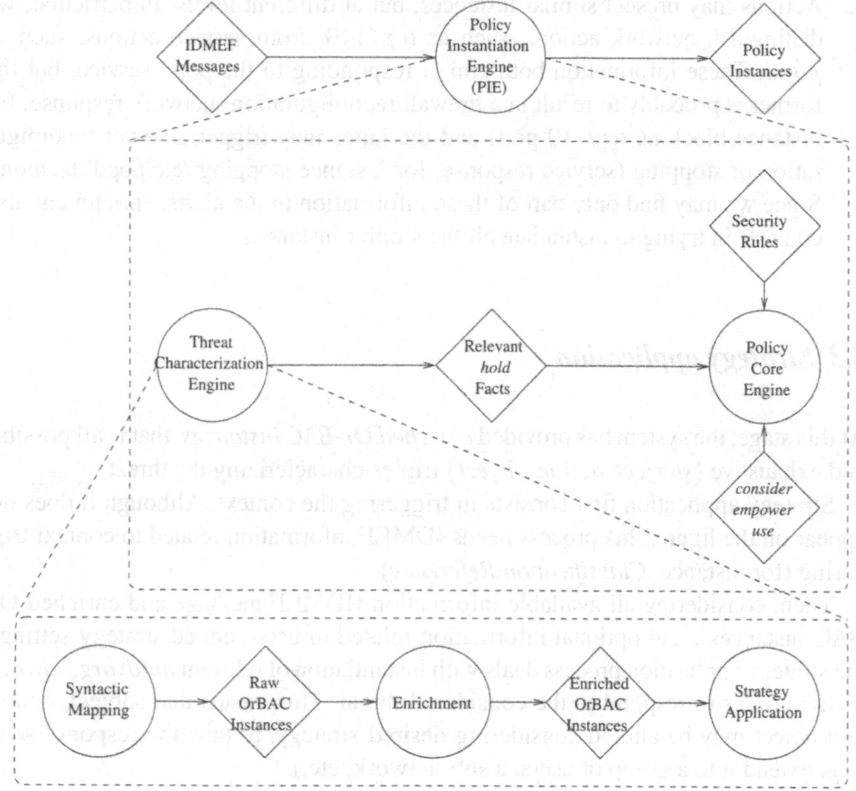

Fig. 6 Information workflow, from alerts to new policy instances

6.2 Enrichment

Once syntactic mapping has been realized, we face two issues related to the fact that alerts are sometimes incomplete, or that some optional parameters are not necessarily defined. Thus, two enrichment steps are provided: (1) enrich subjects, actions and objects which are only partially instantiated, and (2) find similar actions to instantiated ones, but at different levels (*e.g.* network and service levels, as aforementioned in Section 5.4).

1. Subjects, actions and objects are in fact data structures sometimes regrouping equivalent information. For instance, IP addresses and DNS names are considered equivalent since they qualify the same subject. Another example is the equivalence between a service port (tcp/110) and a service name (pop3). Consequently, and because we may sometimes find in IDMEF messages only part of these information, a first enrichment step consists in finding all equivalences and thus provide exhaustive subjects, actions and objects.

2. Actions may present similar instances, but at different levels. In particular, we distinguish network actions, such as $tcp/110$, from service actions, such as $popd$. These information both aim at responding to the pop3 service, but the former is probably to result in a firewall reconfiguration (network response, for instance blocking tcp/110 port) and the latter may trigger a server reconfiguration or stopping (service response, for instance stopping /etc/popd daemon). Since we may find only part of these information in the alerts, enrichment also consists in trying to instantiate all the similar instances.

6.3 Strategy application

At this stage, the system has provided *enriched Or-BAC instances*, that is all possible and exhaustive $(subject, action, object)$ triples characterizing the threat.

Strategy application first consists in triggering the context. Although it does not appear on the figure, this process needs IDMEF information related to context triggering (for instance, *Classification.Reference*).

Then, considering all available information (IDMEF message and enriched Or-BAC instances), and optional information related to user-defined strategy settings, the strategy application process deals with instantiation of relevant $hold(org, s, a, o, c)$ facts in order to respond to the considered threat. This means that subject, action, and object may be altered considering desired strategy, to tune the response scale (*e.g.* extend it to a group of users, a sub-network, etc.).

Finally, given the obtained *hold* fact(s), the PIE is able to find the associated *security_rule*(s), which allow(s) then to derive concrete authorizations as explained in listing 1. Concrete examples of these processes are given in the case study of section 7.

7 Case Study: e-mail Server

We now come back to the case study. As shown in section 3.4, users are able to access their mailboxes through several communication ptotocols. However, each protocol is vulnerable to attacks, either because of software vulnerabilities or inherent design. Our response system aims at protecting them by disabling usage of the particular component under attack. IDS sensors and other logging systems will detect malicious attempts. When a malicious attempt is detected, we will react by blocking access to the mechanisms (servers, services or mailboxes) under attack.

We use SWI-Prolog to implement first-order logic based reasoning required by Or-BAC.

7.1 Threats related to the use case

As shown in section 4, and particularly 4.1, the first requirement in our threat response system is to understand the threats that are relevant to the environment of the use case, and derive the appropriate contexts. This means that the security officer needs to carry out a risk analysis on this environment, as already mentioned in section 2.3

We have carried out a software vulnerability search using the National Vulnerability Database[4] (NVD) using the keywords "exchange" and "pop3". A partial result of this search is illustrated in table 4. In the table, column 1 gives the CVE reference of the vulnerability. Column 2 evaluates the relevance of this vulnerability to the use case ; the vulnerability is highly relevant if the vulnerable software is clearly present in the use case, low if the vulnerability is clearly absent from the use case, and medium if we could not determine it clearly. Column 3 contains the Common Vulnerability Scoring System[5] (CVSS) score for the vulnerability, computed from the CVSS vector. The CVSS vector itself is partially explicited in the impact column, where the (C) indicates complete impact and the (P) indicates partial impact of the vulnerability on either availability, confidentiality or integrity. Finally, columns 5, 6 and 7 analyze the model abstract or concrete entities that are impacted by the vulnerability.

The table contains only cursory information about each vulnerability. The reader is refered to the NVD for a detailed description of the vulnerabilities associated with each CVE reference, and in particular a textual description and the complete CVSS vector. Table 4 only shows partial results from our search, and the search term themselves are not exhaustive ; a thorough examination should include all installed software (we only included 2). It should take into account the detection capability, i.e. the fact that an attempt to use the vulnerability will result in an alert provided by one of the sensors ; if an attack using one of these vulnerabilities cannot be detected, then no response can be included in the threat response system. Also, in the specific case of software vulnerabilities, patching applications will change the relevance of the vulnerability for the threat response system, and thus may change the associated response. We do consider though that there will be some time between vulnerability discovery and patching where such response will be important, and that non-software vulnerabilities (e.g. password guessing) are relevant to the threat response system. The proposed analysis merely illustrates the technology, but must of course be updated when new vulnerabilities are discovered.

We derive the hold facts of the case study from table 4. At least one hold fact is created for each CVE reference. The activity, view and role columns are analyzed to determine where this information is present in the IDMEF alert, under which keyword and form. The reader can refer to the example of CVE-1133 in section 4.1.2 for an example of a definition of a hold fact. Finally, the impact, relevance and

[4] nvd.nist.gov

[5] http://www.first.org/cvss/cvss-guide.html

CVE Reference	Relevance	CVSS Severity	Impact	Activity *(Action)*	View *(Object)*	Role *(Subject)*
Passwd guessing	High	-	User access	Access	*any*	*any*
CVE-2006-7040	Low	3,3	DoS	*TOP*	*POP3*	*any*
CVE-2006-6940	Low	10	Admin access, Confidentiality (C), Integrity (C), Availability (C), DoS	Write, Read, Transfer	*OWA*, *POP3*	*any*
CVE-2006-1193	High	1,9	Unauthorized modification	Read	*OWA*	Mail user
CVE-2006-0027	High	7	User access, Confidentiality (P), Integrity (P), Availability (P), DoS	Write, Transfer	*Exchange*	*any*
CVE-2006-0002	High	7	User access, Confidentiality (P), Integrity (P), Availability (P), DoS	Write, Transfer	*Exchange*	*any*
				Read	*any*	*Outlook*
CVE-2005-1987	High	7	User access, Confidentiality (P), Integrity (P), Availability (P), DoS	Write, Transfer	*Exchange*	*any*
CVE-2005-1133	Low	3,3	Allows unauthorized disclosure of information	*USER*	*POP3*	*any*
CVE-2005-0738	High	3,3	DoS	Read	*Exchange*	Mail user
CVE-2005-0563	High	3,3	Allows unauthorized modification	Read	*OWA*	*any*
CVE-2005-0560	High	7	Unauthorized access, Confidentiality (P), Integrity (P), Availability (P), DoS	Write Transfer	*Exchange*	*any*
CVE-2005-0420	High	7	Unauthorized access, Confidentiality (P), Integrity (P), Availability (P), DoS	Access	*OWA*	*any*
CVE-2005-0044	High	7	User access, Confidentiality (P), Integrity (P), Availability (P), DoS	Write, Transfer	*Exchange*	*any*
				Read	*any*	*any*
CVE-2004-0840	High	10	Admin access, Confidentiality (C), Integrity (C), Availability (C), DoS	Write, Transfer	*Exchange*	*any*
CVE-2004-0203	High	10	Unauthorized access, Confidentiality (P), Integrity (P), Availability (P), DoS	Read	*OWA*	*any*
CVE-2003-0904	High	5,6	Unauthorized access, Confidentiality (P), Integrity (P), Availability (P), DoS	Access	*OWA*	*any*
CVE-2003-0714	High	8	Unauthorized access, Confidentiality (P), Integrity (P), Availability (P), DoS	Write Transfer	*Exchange*	*any*
CVE-2003-0712	High	7	User access, Confidentiality (P), Integrity (P), Availability (P), DoS	Read	*OWA*	*any*
CVE-2003-0007	High	3,3	Allows unauthorized disclosure of information	Write	*any*	*Outlook*
CVE-2002-1876	High	2,3	DoS	Read	*Exchange*	*any*
CVE-1999-0116	Medium	3,3	DoS	*any*	*any*	*any*

Table 4 Example of threats considered relevant for the use case

CVSS score are used to adapt the context lifetime values from the defaults sown in table 2.

7.2 Threat analysis

Table 4 lists the $(role, activity, view)$ or $(subject, action, object)$ triples potentially impacted by the vulnerability. This definition corresponds to our understanding of the information available in the description of each vulnerability. We use the *any* keyword to denote that any entity can participate in the vulnerability (the value of this field is not important in exploiting the vulnerability directly), italics to denote concrete entities, and plaintext to denote abstract entities. In the table, we observe the following:

Prevalence of any for roles and subjects There are only three exceptions to this in table 4. There are two explanations to this phenomenon:

1. the query term were oriented towards server vulnerabilities. A search for client-side vulnerabilities would likely yield many results where the role would be a specific server side software. Searching the NVD for "Microsoft Outlook" yields 102 responses, 244 for "Mozilla Firefox", and 124 for "Mozilla Thunderbird". While these are the immediate query terms, we could also imagine searching for Microsoft Office vulnerabilities (as Outlook is part of the Office suite) or for specific components such as images, OLE or COM. Limiting ourselves to server-side vulnerabilities helps in ensuring that we will indeed have signature and thus alerts that represent usage of these vulnerabilities. Furthermore, e-mail servers are also a gateway to the outside world (as we will see later in this section), and thus carry more risk.
2. the faulty component has been identified, but the table does not take into account natural dependencies. For example, all the table entries listing *OWA* as the object should list firefox as the subject, since it is the email client (web browser) used to connect to OWA. Taking these dependencies into account in the table is complicated because we then need to determine whether the client software is impacted by the flaw and how ; for all the cross-site scripting vulnerabilities, it is unclear to us whether firefox would effectively be vulnerable and whether the user making the final decision would interact in a dangerous way with the server. We consider that this information should not be part of the decision process, because it is not reliable.

Prevalence of abstract entities as activities Many vulnerability descriptions do not refer to a specific action from the user. We have only two exceptions in the table, *TOP* and *USER*, which refer to specific commands of the *POP3* protocol. In the other cases, we can identify a general activity that the user is performing, but not the exact action ; this would probably be possible if we analyzed attack code, but it is unlikely that a security administrator will have the time to do this from a security report highlighting security risks. He will have to base his decision on the vulnerability description, and we have done so as well.

Prevalence of concrete entities as objects As already noted, our search terms were server-oriented, hence it is quite natural that we obtain concrete software vulnerabilities in this column, attached to concrete software objects. As views and roles are symetric, the same queries we mentioned for roles would yield *any* for the relevant view. The exceptions appear in only two cases, *CVE-2006-0002* and *CVE-2005-0044*. *CVE-2006-0002* impacts separately both exchange and outlook, as noted in the vulnerability description ; however, in the use case, outlook will be the client that connects to exchange, so the two lines are really identical.

Apparition of a "Transfer" activity Many vulnerability descriptions indicate that the vulnerability can be exploited by sending a message from a remote location. The *Write* activity does not fully reflect this, as mail servers also exchange mail with other outside servers. In our use case, we had not originally taken this dimension into account, and considered a closed email system. A better analysis of table 4 has led to the creation of the *Transfer* activity. With respect to server-side threats, *Write* and *Transfer* activities are very close ; client-side threats (as shown for example in *CVE-2003-0007* do imply that the dialog is between a registered user and an internal server, and do not implicate the Transfer activity. This "Transfer" activity would enable us to move from a closed mail system to a more realistic open one, although this is left for future work.

Specific handling of low level threats It seems likely that transport-level threats have a much broader impact than the ones at the higher layers. The only example of low level threat in the table, synflood (CVE-1999-0116), can be carried out regardless of the role, activity or view, provided that all roles can inject traffic at the transport layer. We believe that all threats related to traffic injection (land, ping-of-death, ...) are likely to be difficult to include in the model unless specific network-level access-control policies are in place (such as authentication of DHCP requests or network level policy enforcement such as DHCP switching as practiced by ungoliant[6].

We have also included a line about information level threats with the password guessing activity. This attack can occur against the *Access* activity, but can occur through any of the mail clients against any of the mail servers. This is likely due to the synchronization mechanism that replicate the same user/password information throughout all channels.

7.3 Revised description of the Policy Components

As explained in section 3, we use contexts to formulate additional policies for threat response. We will derive our threat contexts in a tree fashion, according to the information provided in table 4. The key issue is to create the appropriate contexts and the associated hold facts. As shown in figure 7, we re-use the *nominal* and the *my_mailbox* contexts introduced in section 3.5.3. We introduce the *minimal* and *minimal_mail* contexts to support the minimal security requirements introduced in section 3. We also introduce the threat contexts, that correspond to the threats identified in figure 7.

[6] http://ungoliant.sourceforge.net/

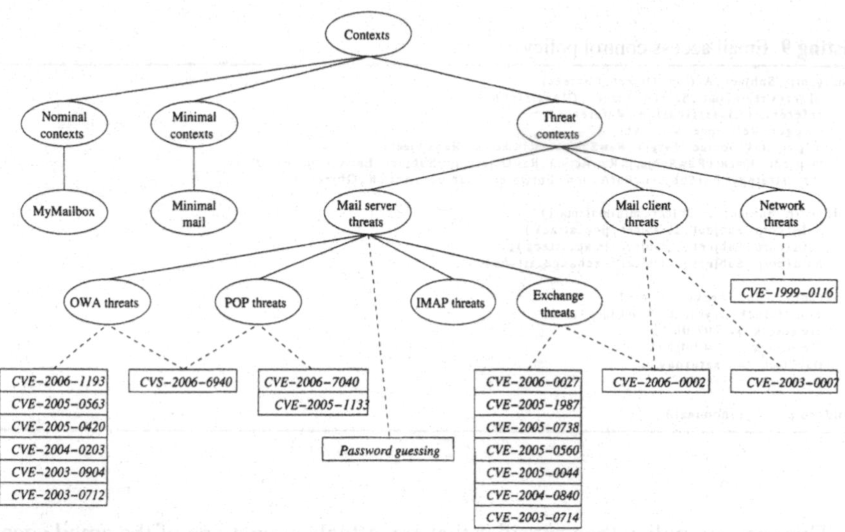

Fig. 7 Model of threat contexts

In this case, we separate between network-level threats (where enforcement will occur through filtering devices on the network only), and application (mail)-level threats, where we have more options for enforcement. We further refine mail threats into server-side threats and client-side threats. As a result of our analysis, some of the identified threats are relevant to several contexts.

7.4 Definition of the Security Policy

Listing 8 Email access control policy

```
sr(perm,corp,mail_user,read_exchange,mail_server,&(minimal_mail,working_hours)).
sr(prohib,corp,pop_user,read_pop,mail_server,pop_attack).
sr(prohib,corp,imap_user,read_imap,mail_server,imap_attack).
sr(prohib,corp,outlook_user,read_exchange,mail_server,exchange_attack).
sr(perm,corp,mail_user,read_mail,mail_server,nominal).
```

Following the definitions of Section 3, we define the security policy as shown in listing 8. In this policy, we consider that it should always exist a way to read mail during working hours, but not necessarily on non-working hours. Indeed, although availability is of crucial interest during working hours, it may not be so important during non-working hours, and the priority could be higher for confidentiality and integrity. A solution to this availability issue is to define an exception with a rule permitting for example exchange via outlook access with a high level priority (*minimal* context), as shown in the first rule of listing 8. Thus, we avoid the case for which the system would close all possible paths to mail, which would lead to self-inflicted denial-of-service.

Listing 9 Email access control policy

```
hold(corp,Subject,Action,Object,Context) :-
    alert(CreateTime,Source,Target,Classification),
    reference(Classification,Reference),
    trigger(Reference,Context),
    map_syntax(Source,Target,RawSubject,RawAction,RawObject),
    map_enrichment(RawSubject,RawAction,RawObject,EnrSubject,EnrAction,EnrObject),
    map_strategy(EnrSubject,EnrAction,EnrObject,Subject,Action,Object).

hold(corp,Subject,_,Object,minimal_mail) :-
    hold(corp,Subject,_,Object,pop_attack),
    hold(corp,Subject,_,Object,imap_attack),
    hold(corp,Subject,_,Object,exchange_attack).

hold(corp,_,_,_,working_hours) :-
    globalclock(DayClock,TimeClock),
    TimeClock >= '07:00:00',
    TimeClock < '20:00:00',
    DayClock != 'saturday',
    DayClock != 'sunday'.

hold(corp,_,_,_,nominal).
```

This security policy then specifies that any attack against one of the email access mechanisms invalidates the access mechanism being attacked, and that by default, mail users have access to all mechanisms to read mail. This simple expression is obtained by taking into account that each rule also applies to children in the graphs.

Note that this concise expression is generic and adaptable to multiple physical architectures. If we had multiple mail servers spread per location instead of a centralized mail server farm, we would express the same policy. However, we would change the deployment strategy at the PDP level and have a different list of PEPs.

Once we have modeled the environment and the security policy, we need to express the *hold* predicates as shown in listing 9. The *working_hours* context is modeled in a straightforward way, as is the *nominal* context. We define the *minimal_mail* context as a sub-context of the *minimal* context. The context *minimal_mail* is active when all three email access mechanisms are attacked. Hence, during working hours, when the $\&(minimal\_mail, working\_hours)$ context is active, the policy expresses that the exchange access is re-opened ensuring continued availability of email information.

Note that we do not necessarily consider only availability in such a case. Indeed, confidentiality and integrity guarantees can also be provided by defining additional constraints. For instance, one could define security rules ensuring that resources are accessed only via a secured protocol. For example, one may choose to switch from *pop* to *pops* in the case of pop3, or from *imap* to *imaps* in the case of imap, etc. Moreover, it is possible to elevate authentication requirements. For example, users could be forced to use certificates or biometric means to authenticate. Thus, availability requirement is still fulfilled, but provided that additional conditions related to confidentiality and integrity are ensured.

7.5 The Mapping Predicates

The core of the *hold* predicate related to threats (the first one in listing 9) is represented by the four mapping functions, *trigger*, *map_syntax*, *map_enrichment* and *map_strategy*. The *trigger* function aims at mapping an alert reference on its corresponding context, as explained in Section 4.1. References are thus grouped considering attack classes, which represent threat contexts. The *map_syntax*, *map_enrichment* and *map_strategy* functions are implemented with respect to requirements explained in Section 6. An example of mapping in this case study is given by listing 10.

Listing 10 Possible mapping in the case study

```
subject = IDMEF.Target.User.Userid.name
action  = IDMEF.Classification.Reference.name or IDMEF.Target.Service.{name, port}
object  = IDMEF.Target.Node.{name, Address}
```

Note that concerning response strategy, we have chosen here to protect user accounts rather than eliminate attackers. It is thus different from the example given in Section 4.1. For example, if Charlie performs a brute-force attack on Alice's email password, the *Source.User.Userid.name* will be charlie and the *Target.User.Userid.name* will be alice. According to our mapping, we will block access to Alice's account, not from Charlie's account. This stems from the fact that *Source.User* is rarely instantiated in our alerts, and is often unreliable. Another solution may consist in blocking the source, but at the host level rather than at the user level. However, although this may apply to the case of an internal attack, as explained in Section 4.1, where the actual attacker is reported by the alert, it is not clear whether it would be efficient for an external attack. Indeed, the proxy is seen as the source of the attack from the internal network, and this may lead to the blocking of the proxy, instead of the real source. Such a response would mean that all external hosts are blocked instead of attacker only. Moreover, another issue deals with spoofing, that is react on the source is impossible when the alert reports a spoofed source, since it is not the actual attacker. Such considerations are typical information entering into the process of response strategy. The exact implementation of the mappings predicates is still an area of research; while our case study shows that it is possible to define such mappings, the evaluation of what constitutes the "best" mapping remains to be done.

8 Issues with the Approach

While this approach is still under development, the current work has brought up a number of interesting issues, especially concerning service continuity and dynamicity of policy changes.

Service Continuity

The first question raised by this approach is service continuity. If connectivity is cut at the network level, clients receive error messages but are not informed automatically about other opportunities to access the information they need. We therefore need to interact with clients to inform them that they should change their access mechanism.

Server-side-only automated redirection is possible only in a limited number of protocols. For example, in a web environment where clients have the opportunity to use both HTTP and HTTPS, we would be able to automatically redirect clients from HTTP to HTTPS by changing the URLs embedded in the web pages returned by the server. When the client clicks on a particular link (assuming that the security policy has not changed in the meantime), he is redirected to the appropriate service. Unfortunately, this opportunity does not seem to exist for email protocols; therefore, we are studying the possibility to configure multiple email accounts on a mail client, and change configurations when needed.

Dynamicity of Policy Changes

System and network administrators are quite conservative when it comes to policy changes. Therefore, we need to discourage rapid changes in policies and oscillations between policies, that would perturb the clients and force them to change their access mechanisms several times during their sessions. Experiments with the matrix shown in table 2 should clarify this problem and in particular allow us to verify if the proposed timings converge towards the *working_hours* policy or leave enough room for multiple simultaneous access methods. Implementing dynamic context deactivation should also prevent from such issues. Indeed, defining static context lifetimes is a first step towards context deactivation, but it requires a strong expertise, and it may not provide the best results, since the threat could be shorter than the resulting countermeasure lifetime, or on the contrary, longer than the resulting countermeasure. Future work shall in part consist in improving the context deactivation process, by making use of information reported by policy enforcement points, acting as sensors, in order to dynamically characterize the state of a considered threat.

9 Conclusion

In this paper, we have proposed a systematic approach to threat response. The approach builds upon Or-BAC, an advanced security policy formalism, to define a contextual security policy that will be applied to the information system. This enables the definition of multiple equilibrium points between security, performance, convenience and compliance objectives. These equilibrium points are expressed as contexts or context combinations of the security policy. The Or-BAC framework includes tools for formally verifying the security policy and for translating the formal security policy into practical configuration scripts that can be applied to policy enforcement points to change the security policy. The expression of the security policy allows the definition of simple responses to each threat, a global and efficient response in the face of multiple threats being computed during the instantiation of the security policy.

The threat contexts vary according to alerts collected by various sensors. These alerts received as IDMEF messages are mapped onto policy subjects, actions and objects and are used to activate specific contexts. The mapping from IDMEF messages to policy entities is complex and has implications on the choice of response that will be available to handle the threat. When a particular context is activated, the new set of policy rules is validated and translated to the enforcement points. These mechanisms have been implemented and validated on a case study environment. The organization-based approach shows encouraging results and we are confident that deployment at a larger scale will be possible.

Future work includes modeling service continuity, ensuring that clients get continuous access to information seamlessly, defining and evaluating mapping functions to formalize the impact these mapping functions have on threat response choices, and evaluating the performances of the prototype approach with respect to performance and efficiency in threat response.

References

1. A. Adelsbach, D. Alessandri, C. Cachin, S. Creese, Y. Deswarte, K. Kursawe, J.-C. Laprie, D. Powell, B. Randell, J. Riodan, P. Ryan, R. J. Stroud, P. Verssimo, M. Waidner, and A. Wespi. Conceptual model and architecture of MAFTIA. MAFTIA deliverable d21, Malicious- and Accidental-Fault Tolerance for Internet Applications, Project IST-1999-11583, january 2003. http://www.maftia.org, last accessed 2007-03-01.
2. J.P. Anderson. Computer Security Threat Monitoring and Surveillance. Technical report, Fort Washington - Technical Report Contract 79F26400, 1980.
3. Richard Brackney. Cyber-intrusion response. In *Proceedings of the 17th IEEE Symposium on Reliable Distributed Systems*, pages 413–415, West Lafayette, IN, USA, October 1998. IEEE Computer Society Press.
4. F. Cuppens and A. Miège. Alert Correlation in a Cooperative Intrusion Detection Framework. In *Proceedings of the IEEE Symposium on Security and Privacy*, 2002.
5. Frédéric Cuppens, Cuppens-Boulahia, and Alexandre Miège. Inheritance hierarchies in the orbac model and application in a network environment. In A. Sabelfeld, editor, *Proceedings of the 2004 Foundations of Computer Security Workshop (FCS04)*, pages 41–60, Turku,Finland, July 2004. Turku Center for Computer Science. Report G-31.
6. Frédéric Cuppens, Nora Cuppens-Boulahia, and Meriam Ben Ghorbel. High-level conflict management strategies in advanced access control models. In *Workshop on Information and Computer Security (ICS)*, Timisoara, Roumania, November 2006.
7. Frédéric Cuppens, Nora Cuppens-Boulahia, Thierry Sans, and Alexandre Miège. A formal approach to specify and deploy a network security policy. In *Proceedings of the Second Workshop on Formal Aspects of Security and Trust (FAST'04)*, Toulouse, France, August 2004. IFIP WCC 2004.
8. Frédéric Cuppens, Sylvain Gombault, and Thierry Sans. Selecting appropriate countermeasures in an intrusion detection framework. In *17th IEEE Computer Security Foundations*

Workshop (CSFW'04), page 78, Pacific Grove, CA, USA, June 2004. IEEE Computer Society Press.
9. Frédéric Cuppens and Alexandre Miège. Modelling contexts in the or-bac model. In *Proceedings of the 19th Annual Computer Security Applications Conference (ACSAC 2003*, pages 416–427, Miami Beach, Florida, USA, December 2003. IEEE Computer Society Press.
10. Frédéric Cuppens and Alexandre Miège. Administration Model for Or-BAC. *Computer Systems Science and Engineering (CSSE'04)*, 19(3), May 2004.
11. O. Dain and R. Cunningham. Fusing a Heterogeneous Alert Stream into Scenarios. In *Proceedings of the 2001 ACM Workshop on Data Mining for Security Applications*, pages 1–13, November 2001.
12. Hervé Debar, David Curry, and Ben Fenstein. The intrusion detection message exchange format. RFC 4765, November 2006. http://www.ietf.org/rfc/rfc4765.txt.
13. S. Floyd. Inappropriate tcp resets considered harmful. RFC 3360, August 2002. http://www.ietf.org/rfc/rfc3360.txt.
14. M.A. Harrison, W.L. Ruzzo, and J.D. Ullman. Protection in operating systems. *cacm*, 19(8):461–471, August 1976.
15. Erland Jonsson. Towards an integrated conceptual model of security and dependability. In *Proceedings of the First International Conference on Availability, Reliability and Security (ARES 2006)*, pages 646–653, Vienna, Austria, April 2006. IEEE Computer Society Press.
16. Anas Abou El Kalam, Salem Benferhat, Alexandre Miege andRania El Baida, Frédéric Cuppens, Claire Saurel, Philippe Balbiani, Yves Deswarte, and Gilles Trouessin. Organization based access control. In *Proceedings of the Fourth IEEE International Workshop on Policies for Distributed Systems and Networks (POLICY'03)*, pages 120–134, Lake Como, Italy, June 2003. IEEE Computer Society Press.
17. Michiharu Kudo and Satoshi Hada. Xml document security based on provisional authorization. In *Proceedings of the 7th ACM conference on Computer and communications security (CCS '00)*, pages 87–96, Athens, Greece, November 2000. ACM Press.
18. Alexandre Miège. *Definition of a formal framework for specifying security policies. The Or-BAC model and extensions*. PhD thesis, Ecole Nationale Supèrieure des Télécommunications, 2005.
19. Benjamin Morin, Ludovic Mé, Hervé Debar, and Mireille Ducassé. M2D2 : A Formal Data Model for IDS Alert Correlation. In *Proceedings of the Fifth International Symposium on Recent Advances in Intrusion Detection (RAID)*, October 2002.
20. P. Ning, Y. Cui, and D. S. Reeves. Constructing Attack Scenarios Through Correlation of Intrusion Alerts. In *Proceedings of the 9th Conference on Computer and Communication Security*, 2002.
21. M. Petkac and L. Badger. Security agility in response to intrusion detection. In *Proceedings of the 16th Annual Computer Security Applications Conference (ACSAC'00)*, page 11, New Orleans, Louisiana, USA, December 2000. IEEE Computer Society Press.
22. Ravi S. Sandhu, Edward J. Coyne, Hal L. Feinstein, and Charles E. Youman. Role-based access control models. *ieeec*, 29(2):38–47, 1996.
23. R. Shirey. Internet Security Glossary. RFC 2828, 2000.
24. Yohann Thomas, Hervé Debar, and Benjamin Morin. Improving security management through passive network observation. In *Proceedings of the First International Conference on Availability, Reliability and Security (ARES'06)*, pages 382–389, Vienna, Austria, April 2006. IEEE Computer Society Press.
25. Thomas Toth and Christopher Kruegel. Evaluating the impact of automated intrusion response mechanisms. In *Proceedings of the 18th Annual Computer Security Applications Conference (ACSAC'02)*, pages 301–310, Las Vegas, Nevada, USA, December 2002. IEEE Computer Society Press.
26. Jeffrey D. Ullman. *Principles of database and knowledge-base systems, Vol. I*. Computer Science Press, Inc., 1988.

Intrusion Detection and Reaction: an Integrated Approach to Network Security

M. Esposito, C. Mazzariello, F. Oliviero, L. Peluso, S. P. Romano, and C. Sansone

Abstract Denial of Service (DoS) attacks represent, in todays Internet, one of the most serious security threats. A session is under a DoS attack if it cannot achieve its intended throughput due to the misbehavior of other sessions. Many research studies have dealt with DoS, proposing models and/or architectures mostly based on an attack prevention approach. Prevention techniques lead to different models, each suitable for a specific type of misbehavior, but they do not guarantee the protection of a system from a more general DoS attack.

In this work we analyze the fundamental requirements to be satisfied in order to protect hosts and routers from any form of Distributed DoS (DDoS). Then we propose a framework which satisfies most of the identified requirements. It appropriately combines Intrusion Detection and Reaction techniques and comprises a number of components actively cooperating in order to effectively react to a wide range of attacks. Functional to our approach is a network signaling protocol, named Active Security Protocol,which allows a set of active routers to interact in order to isolate the sources of a DDoS attack even in the case of address spoofing.

As to Intrusion Detection, which plays a major role in the framework, we present a reference model for a real-time network Intrusion Detection System (IDS) based on Pattern Recognition techniques. First, we describe how network traffic can be effectively represented through the definition of an appropriate set of traffic features. Issues arising when building-up a database for training an IDS will be highlighted, by also taking into account anonymization requirements. The feasibility of the proposed approach will be experimentally demonstrated in terms of both packet loss and detection capability in the presence of real traffic data. Finally, a distributed version of the proposed IDS will be presented.

M. Esposito
Università Campus Bio-Medico di Roma, via Alvaro del Portillo 21, 00155 - Roma, Italy, e-mail: `marcello.esposito@unicampus.it`

C. Mazzariello, F. Oliviero, L. Peluso, S. P. Romano, and C. Sansone
Dipartimento di Informatica e Sistemistica, via Claudio 21, 80125 Napoli, Italy e-mail: `{cmazzari,folivier,lorenzo.peluso,spromano,carlosan}@unina.it`

1 Introduction

The term *Denial of Service (DoS)* indicates an attack explicitly designed to prevent a system from performing its regular operations, or at least to produce a degradation in its performance. A more formal definition of the term has been proposed by the CERT/CC (Computer Emergency Response Team/Coordination Center) [1]: "intentional degradation or blocking of computer or network resources". DoS attacks on the Internet can be directed toward two types of targets: networks and hosts. Attacks against networks aim at collapsing them; this is achieved either through data-flooding techniques or by corrupting routing tables inside routers. On the other hand, attacks against hosts aim at preventing authorized users from accessing a server, by directly attacking it and making it unable to provide one or more services [2]. A further attack classification is based on the involved hosts number. Two attack classes can be identified: indexsingle-source attacks *single-source attacks*, launched by a single source, which most likely is a previously compromised host, with enough available resources (especially in terms of bandwidth); *distributed attacks*, simultaneously originated from many systems, against one or more targets.

In this paper we present a general framework specifically conceived with the aim of mitigating as far as possible the effects of a DDoS attack. Such a framework exploits both detection and reaction techniques in order to increase the level of availability of network resources, in the presence of a variable number of attack sources spread throughout the network. More precisely, the architecture we propose is composed of two major building blocks: (*i*) an Intrusion Detection module, in charge of detecting in real-time the occurrence of a potential attack; (*ii*) an Intrusion Reaction module, enabling the orchestrated operation of network routers with the aim of tracing back (i.e. determining the sequence of routers crossed by the attack traffic) detected attacks. Intrusions identified by the detection module thus represent the events triggering the subsequent reaction phase, during which all of the network routers cooperate in order to go upstream as close as possible to the attack sources and put into place the most appropriate countermeasures (e.g. filter out malicious traffic entering the network).

The paper is organized in 6 sections. Section 2 illustrates some background on both intrusion detection and traceback techniques, by reporting related research activities ongoing in the international scientific community. In the light of the provided background, Section 3 describes our framework, which combines detection and reaction approaches to perform the envisaged defense activities. Section 4 provides some more insights about issues and proposed solutions concerning the detection phase. In such section, we also address some important side issues regarding the need for ensuring privacy when dealing with network data. Section 5 explains how we designed and implemented an effective solution for cooperative reaction to detected attacks. Finally, Section 6 provides some concluding remarks, together with information about our future work.

2 Related Work

Two are the key factors to be taken into account when designing a system capable of reacting to DoS attacks: *Intrusion Detection* and *Traceback*. In the following of this section, we discuss related work in both areas.

2.1 Intrusion Detection Systems

On the basis of the information sources analyzed to detect an intrusive activity, the Intrusion Detection Systems (IDS) are typically grouped into two main categories: Network-based Intrusion Detection Systems (N-IDS) [3] and Host-based Intrusion Detection Systems (H-IDS) [4]. N-IDS analyze packets captured directly from the network. By setting network cards in promiscuous mode, an IDS can monitor traffic in order to protect all of the hosts connected to a specified network segment. On the other hand, H-IDS focus on a single host's activity: the system protects such a host by directly analyzing the audit trails or system logs produced by the host's operating system. In addition, in [5] two other categories are introduced: Application-based Intrusion Detection Systems (A-IDS) and Stack based Intrusion Detection Systems (S-IDS). Indeed, A-IDS are a subset of H-IDS. In fact, application audit logs are the source of information for these systems. Finally, S-IDS work directly on the TCP/IP stack, by monitoring packets during their transport through OSI layers. Note that they monitor not only incoming traffic, but also outgoing traffic. In the following we will concentrate our attention on N-IDS, since the other categories are outside the scope of the present paper.

Depending on the detection technique employed, IDS can be roughly classified as belonging to two main groups as well [6]. The first one, that exploits signatures of known attacks for detecting when an attack occurs, is known as misuse, or signature, detection based. IDS's that fall in this category are based on a model of all the possible misuses of the network resources. The completeness requirement is actually their major limit [7]; this notwithstanding in the literature there are some very recent proposals that follow this approach [8, 9, 10]. A dual approach tries to characterize the normal usage of the resources under monitoring. An intrusion is then suspected when a significant difference from the resource's normal usage is revealed. IDS's following this approach, known as anomaly detection based, seem to be more promising because of their potential ability to detect unknown intrusions. However, in this case, a major problem is the need of acquiring a model of the normal use general enough to allow authorized users to work without raising false alarms, but specific enough to recognize unauthorized usage [11, 12].

The difficulty of acquiring a purely normal set of data has given rise, more recently, to a third category of detection techniques, based on the unsupervised anomaly detection approach [13]. In unsupervised anomaly detection, there is a set of data for which neither normal nor anomalous elements are known. Unsupervised anomaly detection can be seen as a variant of the classical outlier detection problem [14]. The main advantage is that unsupervised anomaly detection algorithms can be performed over an unlabeled set of data that can be obtained by simply collecting raw audit data from a network.

Most unsupervised anomaly detection systems [15, 16] use information extracted from the packet headers. On the contrary, some more recent approaches also consider the payload content. In particular, in [17] a payload-based anomaly detector for intrusion detection is proposed. It models the normal application payload of network traffic in a fully automatic and unsupervised way. During the detection phase, the Mahalanobis distance is used to calculate the similarity of new data against the pre-computed profiles. In [18], a two-stage architecture is presented: the first stage is made-up of an unsupervised clustering algorithm that classifies the payload of the packets, observing one packet at a time and compressing it into a single byte of information. The second stage is a traditional anomaly detection algorithm, whose efficiency is improved by the availability of data on the packet payload content.

Finally, it is worth mentioning that, in order to keep as low as possible the number of false alarms, alert correlation techniques have been also proposed in the last years [19, 20]. Alert correlation is a process that mainly tries to give a high-level description of occurring or attempted intrusions by using the sequence of alerts provided by one or more IDS [20].

2.1.1 A Pattern Recognition approach

Different attack types can occur in a real network. The most used attack taxonomy in the IDS field is the one proposed by Kendall in [21]. Here attacks are grouped into four major categories: Probes, Denial of service (DoS), Remote to local (R2L) and User to root (U2R). The first category is made up of attacks that test a potential target for collecting information about a possible intrusion. Therefore, they are usually harmless, unless vulnerability is discovered and later exploited. DoS attacks, as previously seen, prevent normal operations, but do not violate the target host. On the contrary, the last two categories group attacks that permit the attacker to compromise the target host. In particular, in R2L attacks, an unauthorized user is able to bypass normal authentication and to execute commands on the target host, while in U2R attacks, a user with login access is able to bypass normal authentication to gain the privileges of another user, typically the root user.

Using this taxonomy, network intrusion detection can be also seen as a typical Pattern Recognition problem [22] : given information about network connections between pairs of hosts, the task is to assign each connection to one out of five classes, respectively representing normal traffic conditions and the four different attack categories described above. Here the term "connection" refers to a sequence of data packets related to a particular service, as a file transfer via the ftp protocol. Since an IDS must detect connections related to malicious activities, each network connection can be viewed as a "pattern" to be classified.

As regards the features used for describing network connections, it has to be noted that malicious activity cannot be detected by examining just a single packet:

some types of attacks generate in a certain time interval a great amount of packets belonging to different sessions. Hence, an effective detection needs statistical parameters taking into account the temporal relation between sessions. Starting from this observation, Lee and Stolfo [23] defined a set of connection features which summarize the temporal and statistical relations of the connections with reference to each other. Such features have been used for generating the 1999 KDD Cup Data[1], that is the most well-known database in the pattern recognition and machine learning fields.

The above described formulation of the network intrusion detection problem implies the use of an IDS based on a misuse detection approach. However, the main advantage of the pattern recognition approach is the ability to generalize which is peculiar to pattern recognition systems. They are able to detect some novel attacks, without the need of a complete description of all the possible attack signatures, so overcoming one of the main drawbacks of the misuse detection approach. In fact, signature based systems may fail in detecting attacks that underwent even slight modifications with respect to a known pattern. On the other hand, the difficulty in collecting a representative labeled set of data for training a pattern recognition-based system could be overcome, for example, by following the approach proposed in [13]. Here, the authors suggest using an unsupervised algorithm for recovering the anomalous elements from an unlabeled set of data. After anomalies or intrusions are detected and removed, it is then possible to train a misuse detection algorithm over the polished data.

The feasibility of the pattern recognition approach for the intrusion detection problem has been addressed in [22]. Different pattern recognition systems have been proposed in the recent past for realizing an IDS, mainly based on neural network architectures [11, 24, 25]. In order to maximize performance, approaches based on multiple classifier systems have been also proposed [22, 26].

An objection against most of the papers reviewed in this subsection is that the authors only test their approaches off-line, so disregarding the problems arising when a real-time intrusion detection has to be performed. Traffic model definition based on an off-line analysis, in fact, does not consider the unavoidable problems of real-time computation of connection features. In real-time intrusion detection, instead, the incoming packets do not contain all of the information needed to compute the connection features, but an appropriate system has to be implemented in order to compute relations among the existing connections. Moreover, off-line analysis does not consider the problem of potential packet losses in the IDS, which has to be taken into account in the case of real-time analysis.

On the contrary, in this paper we present an architecture for real-time intrusion detection. It is capable to effectively detect intrusions and to operate under a variety of traffic conditions, thus providing a solution to the issue of real-time analysis. As it will be better described later, our intrusion detection system uses a set of connection features, derived by those proposed by Lee and Stolfo, in order to fully exploit the advantages of a pattern recognition approach. In the following we will also present

[1] `http://kdd.ics.uci.edu/`

an implementation of this architecture within the proposed framework for intrusion detection and reaction, and evaluate its performance in a real network scenario, by focusing on the evaluation of the packet loss increase due to the computation of the connection features.

2.2 Traceback

IP Traceback [27] is concerned with detecting the source(s) of a DoS attack, as a fundamental step to allow the adoption of an effective defense strategy. The most complex issue to be faced when performing traceback, is related to the fact that attackers often use spoofed IP addresses, thus preventing effective detection via a simple analysis of the IP header of the received packets. To avoid this problem, packet marking techniques are often employed [28].

Node Append is the easiest form of marking currently available: routers add to each packet their own IP address. This clearly facilitates the traceback process, at the cost of a substantial overhead. *Node Sampling* and *Edge Sampling* try mitigating such a problem by relying on probabilistic packet marking techniques, thus reducing the overhead. The drawback of these two approaches resides in the need for more complex path reconstruction algorithms.

Our approach to traceback, does not alter regular IP packets at all, but it is based on an *ad-hoc* defined signaling protocol among routers. By means of recursive hop-by-hop message exchanges, it is possible to go upstream until reaching the actual attack source, without relying on possibly deceptive information carried by hostile IP packets. This approach has the major advantage to clearly separate the forwarding and the control planes, thus allowing a better control over the induced overhead.

Many works addressed the problems related to possible approaches to reaction. In particular, in [29] a defense strategy against DoS attacks is described. It is based on a packet marking technique located at the edge of the considered domain. The labels associated with each packet are used to identify attacks. This approach presents two major drawbacks: (*i*) it is not that efficient to mark and check labels for all packets, since it requires a significant router CPU time; (*ii*) the attacker could intercept true labels and use them to pass off as a benign sender.

In [30] the authors address the need of designing a network protocol for defining the set of information that different routers must send each other. They only describe the main ideas of such a protocol, by emphasizing authentication issues.

Again, our approach is based on a different perspective. It defines an overlay architecture which does not influence the regular forwarding mechanisms during normal network operation, thus leaving unchanged overall network performance. Only upon detection of an intrusion, our infrastructure instantiates its own data structures and triggers a distributed signaling process in order to properly react. This aspect fosters an incremental deployment of the system within the network. In other words, density of routers inside the network just affects overall attained performance, without compromising system operation.

Another interesting work on this topic is represented by [31]. Their approach has many similarities with ours: as the authors themselves highlight, DDoS threat cannot be addressed through isolated action of sparsely deployed defense nodes. Instead, various defense systems must organize into a framework and interoperate, exchanging information and service, and acting together against the threat.

3 The Proposed Framework

The reference framework is depicted in Fig. 1. It shows the three main components which will be described in more detail in the following sections of this work:

Intrusion Detection System: based on models for anomalous traffic classification, it uses traffic summarization algorithms (feature computation) and pattern recognition techniques in order to classify anomalous traffic; traffic probes, placed in one or more strategic points of a network architecture, act as input units; computation results are presented in the form of alert signals, which feed the reaction components; our implementation of this component, is based on the *Snort*™ [37] IDS, which has been appropriately modified in order to be integrated in the proposed architecture;
Anonymizer: a module useful to strip and/or scramble sensitive data (MAC- and IP-level addresses, application-level information, etc.) from real traffic traces; such traces are required to train pattern-recognition algorithms used for intrusion detection, and their anonymity is needed in order to preserve users' privacy;
Intrusion Reaction System: alert signals coming from the intrusion detection module, act as triggers for processes of information exchange among network routers, aimed at tracing back the attack sources, and thus limiting their range of action as much as possible.

Such an architecture is designed to rely on a classic network IP infrastructure. Data flowing through the network are copied and distilled, before feeding the network security system.

From the transport network point of view, the framework can be definitely seen as a parallel information extraction and processing system which, in absence of any anomalies, does not interfere at all with regular network operation. Only in case anomalies are detected, the security system is enabled to engage appropriate countermeasures, by following a policy based configuration paradigm. Policies activate onto the network actions belonging to two main different classes:

- policies for altering normal traffic forwarding schemes (e.g. shaping, dropping); this is useful to mitigate the effects of an attack by means of a fine grained intervention on single packets; such policies configure the behavior of traffic classifiers and traffic scheduler modules embedded in the routers forwarding plane;

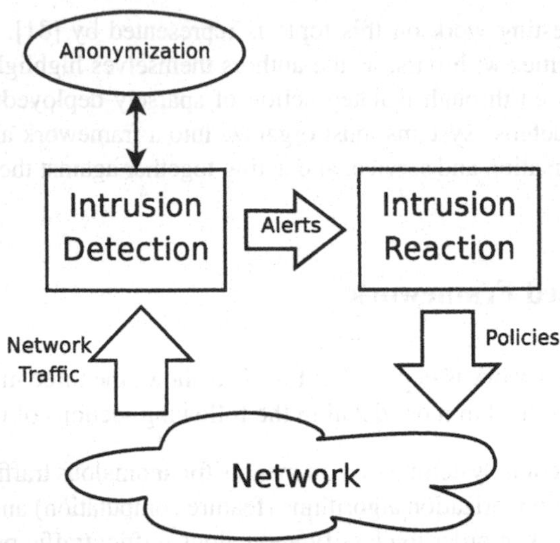

Fig. 1 Macro-components positioning within the security system framework

- policies for logging traffic packets belonging to well-identified flows; this is aimed at both archiving anomaly-related data and collecting information useful for a better system tuning after an offline analysis.

The main architecture building blocks have been implemented as distributed components, although they are represented as logically centralized blocks in the picture. Since attacks might be originated from multiple sources, physical distribution of components plays a fundamental role to improve overall system performance. This is especially true for intrusion reaction components, which in our architecture are fully embedded in the network routers, enabling at network level security-oriented packet classification and scheduling algorithms.

This also means that the logical security framework depicted in the top part of Fig. 1 is actually deeply deployed in the network infrastructure. More precisely, it belongs to the control plane of each router, and affects the forwarding plane only in case of need for facing attacks.

In the following, these three main components will be described in greater detail, by highlighting both the internals and the communication paradigms which enable them to cooperate in order to achieve in an orchestrated fashion a full network protection against DDoS attacks.

4 An Architecture for Intrusion Detection

As stated in Section 3, an IDS is one of the crucial components in order that the proposed system could effectively work. In this section we will describe the issues related to building a real-time IDS, all the components such a system needs, their role in the whole architecture, and the impact of each of them on the overall performance. We will present a framework which implements such a general model employing computational intelligence techniques, proper of the pattern recognition field, aimed at improving the capability of the system to detect novel attacks [33, 14]. We will individuate some bottlenecks of the proposed framework and, based on the concept of distribution of concerns, we will also introduce a distributed version of the architecture. We will show how it helps improving the scalability of the system, thus enabling a more in-depth analysis of the scanned traffic without affecting too much the real-time requirement; hence, more complex and elaborate detection techniques can be used. The timeliness requirement for the intrusion detection operation is strictly needed as the overall goal of the project is the definition and the implementation of an intrusion detection and reaction framework: the quicker and prompter the reaction to an attack is, the more it results in an effective defense of the monitored environment. Some privacy issues, related to the need to prevent users' sensible information to be accessible without explicit consent or permission, will also be discussed and an approach to traffic *anonymization* will be presented.

4.1 An Approach to Intrusion Detection

The work of an IDS consists in analyzing some input data. Input data might range from audit trails and operating system or application logs to raw network traffic. According to the selected class of input data, the used system can be ascribed to one of the classes of IDS described in Section 1.

Despite the inherent differences among IDS classes, some common building blocks can be identified, with respect to the high level functionalities needed for fulfilling the task of detecting intrusions. Such components, depicted in Fig. 2, are:

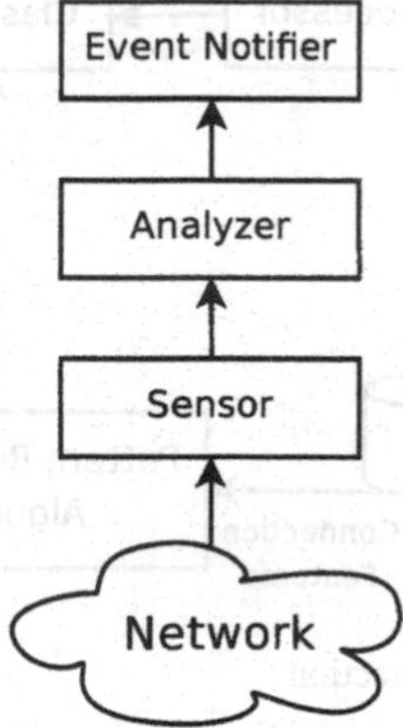

Fig. 2 Canonical IDS structure

- **Sensor**: whatever the used input data is, a component is needed which can read such data and convert it to a format which is compatible with the one required from the analyzer. The conversion into such a format sometimes involves the extraction of some parameters of interest aimed at synthesizing the properties of the data which are of greater interest for the problem at hand. In the case of the proposed intrusion detection system, network packets are usually decoded, all the header fields are evaluated, and a set of traffic features are computed, related to some statistical properties of the traffic.
- **Analyzer**: once the data is modeled into a common format, it needs to be analyzed. In principle, the analyzer component of such an IDS could be independent of the type of data. It needs to be aware of a set of criteria aimed at detecting some particular properties in the analyzed data and, when at least one out of such criteria is matched, notify an entity about the occurrence of such an event. If each criteria is associated to the most likely cause which might have generated the event it's related to, the analyzer not only is able to notify in case of the occurrence of some particular events, but is also able to ascribe such events to a generating cause, thus enabling the *classification* of each reported event.
- **Event Notifier**: any time the analyzer reports the occurrence of some events, it is necessary to enable the whole system to communicate with the external world, in order to allow the notification of such occurrences. The *event notifier* is in charge of interpreting the results of the analysis and correctly formatting the messages required for communicating with the system users.

According with such canonical architecture, we proposed a framework for intrusion detection exploiting pattern recognition techniques so as novel attacks can be identify. The reference framework is depicted in Fig. 3.

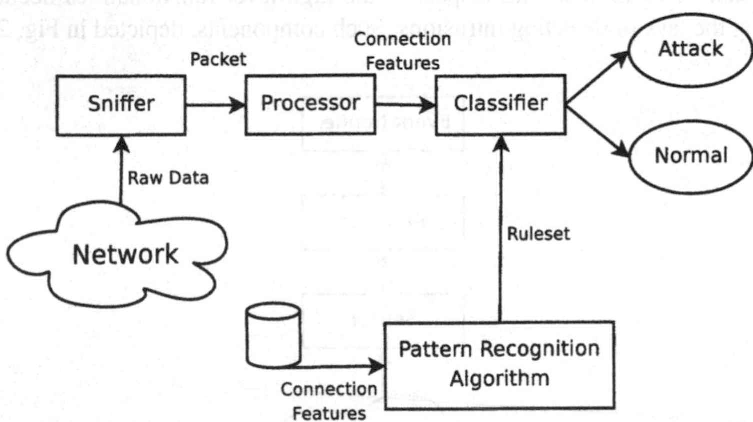

Fig. 3 A Framework for Intrusion Detection

The overall model is composed of two parts: the former is a real-time intrusion detection system which analyzes and classifies network traffic based on well-known user behavioral models; the latter is a pattern recognition process, which extract such behavioral models from pre-elaborated network traffic, and consists of a database of labeled network traffic features and a pattern recognition algorithm.

In particular, as discussed in more detail later, we execute an off-line algorithm on a suitably chosen data set in order to extract a set of behavioral rules; such a set is then used in the real-time classification process deployed by the IDS.

4.1.1 Real-Time Intrusion Detection

The on-line system presents some operational blocks which perform the functionalities described for a canonical IDS architecture. The lowest block is the *processor* module, which essentially implement the sensor's functionalities. Connected directly on the network infrastructure, the processor firstly performs the sniffing task, capturing and decoding in a human-readable data all the packet on the wire. Then, it elaborates the packet captured in order to extract a the set of information; such information, called *connection features*, are needed to improve the behavioral classification process. The connection features represent a summarization of the network user behavior. The greater the capability of the set of features to discriminate among different categories, the better the classifier.

There are three levels at which feature sets may be defined:

- The features may be referred to the single packet captured from the network: although this set is easy to compute, it is not able to detect all the potential attack types.
- A set of features related to the entire session which the packet belongs to may be defined:
  this is due to the fact that some intrusions may be realized by means of a sequence of packets belonging to either the same connection or different connections.
- The computed set of features may perform a statistical analysis of the relation between the current session and the other ones:
  this is needed in order to capture intrusions which affect the interrelation among different sessions.

To cope with the aforementioned requirements, we have adopted a model descending from the one proposed by Lee and Stolfo [34]. Such model characterizes the user behavior by means of a set of connection properties, the connection features; the features can be classified in three main groups: *intrinsic* features, *traffic* features and *content* features. Intrinsic features specify general information on the current session, like the duration in seconds of the connection, the protocol type, the port number (i.e. the service), the number of bytes from the source to the destination, etc. (see Table 1).

The traffic features can be divided in two groups: the *same host* and the *same service* features. The same host features examine all the connections in the last two

duration	connection duration (s)
protocol_type	type of transport protocol
service	port number on the server side
src_bytes	bytes from source to destination
dst_bytes	bytes from destination to source
flag	status of the connection
land	land attack
urgent	number of urgent packets

Table 1 Intrinsic Features

seconds to the same destination host of the current connection, in particular the number of such connections, or the rate of connections that have a "SYN" error. Instead, the same service features examine all the connections in the last two seconds to the same destination service of the current one. These two features set are defined *time–based* traffic features because they analyze all the event occurred in a time interval of two seconds (Table 2); some types of attacks, instead, as the slow probing, may occur every few minutes. Therefore these features could not be proper able to detect all the attack types. To this aim a new set of traffic features, called *host-based*, have been defined; the same host and the same service traffic features are also computed on a window of one hundred connections rather that on a time interval of two seconds. Finally, the content features are related to the semantic content of connection payload. In our framework, however, we will adopt only the intrinsic and the traffic features. Our purpose is to realize network-based intrusion detection system, while the the content features are more adapted in a host-based scenario. In fact, payload content inspection can be easily evaded when using ciphered communication or tunneled flows, so as to make the content feature useless. Thanks to the access to the operating system's audit trails or system logs, an H-IDS is instead more efficient in the analysis of the dangerous commands execution on a single host. It is also worth noting that content features were originally proposed for trying to detect R2L and U2R attacks, while our framework is focused on the detection of DoS attacks.

Same Host	
count	number of connections to the same host
serror_rate	% of connections with SYN errors
rerror_rate	% of connections with REJ errors
same_srv_rate	% of connections to the same service
diff_srv_rate	% of connections to different services
Same Service	
srv_count	number of connections to the same service
srv_serror_rate	% of connections with SYN errors
srv_rerror_rate	% of connections with REJ errors
srv_diff_host_rate	% of connections to different services

Table 2 Time-Based Traffic Features

The main issue of the features computation process is related to the need of keeping up-to-date information about the current connection, as well as on the other active sessions. We have to keep in memory a representation of the current network state in order to evaluate the statistical relations among the active connections. Data in memory have to be properly organized in order to reduce feature computation time.

The classifier is the core of the proposed architecture; this component analyzes the current connection features and classifies them. Based on of a misuse detection approach, the classification process uses a set of rules extracted by means of pattern recognition algorithms. The features are compared against all the rules in the set; when the examined vector of features matches at least one rule, an intrusive action is detected. As to the connection data in the processor component, the rules may be organized in memory in a suitable way in order to reduce the time of analysis.

In the following we will introduce the main issues related the implementation of the real-time component of our framework.

The implemented architecture addresses the main requirements of a real-time detection system: monitoring the network traffic in order to extract a set of features from it, as well as behavior classification based on the extracted features. Monitoring, in particular, is the most challenging issue to face from the point of view of a real-time analysis. In our architecture, the monitoring system can be divided into two components: the sniffer that captures traffic from the network, and the processor that computes both the *intrinsic* and the *traffic* features. While in an off-line analysis features computation is simpler, since all the information about connections are stored in a database, in a real-time analysis statistic measures have to be be computed every time a new packet is captured from network [35].

In order to extract features from the traffic, an effective processor must ensure two requirements:

- it holds information about the state of the connection which the analyzed packet belongs to;
- it holds comprehensive information about the traffic flows that already have been seen across the network.

According to the definition proposed in the previous section, every packet can be considered as a single unit that is inserted in a more complex structure, namely the *connection*, and on which the features are computed. While neither UDP nor ICMP traffic requires a heavy load of computation, TCP traffic requires to emulate the TCP state diagram both on the client and the server sides and for every active connection. In particular, when a new packet is captured, the system retrieves information about the connection to which such a packet belongs and updates the connection state of both the client and the server based on the TCP protocol specifications.

In order to compute the statistical relations, information on the past TCP, UDP and ICMP flows is required, including those connections which have been closed. Traffic features, in fact, are computed by analyzing all the connections (either active or expired) having similar characteristics — besides the destination IP address and/or the destination port — to the current one. Every connection has to be kept in memory until it is not needed anymore for other computations.

Our architecture is implemented by means of the open-source N-IDS *Snort*™; we have used this system as the base framework on top of which we have built our components. *Snort*™ is a lightweight network IDS created by Marty Roesch. Its architecture is made up of four main blocks: a *sniffer*, a *preprocessor engine* that realizes a pre-computation of captured packets, a *rules-based detection engine*, and a set of *user output tools*. Thanks to *Snort*™'s modular design approach, it is possible to add new functionality to the system by means of *program plugins*. Moreover, *Snort*™ provides an efficient preprocessor plugin that reassembles TCP streams and can thus be used to recover the TCP connections status.

We have implemented a new preprocessor plugin which computes the connection features and a new detection plugin which implements the classification process of the feature vectors.

4.1.2 A Preprocessor Plugin for *Snort*™

The main issue we tackled has been the computation of the traffic features, which requires that a proper logical organization of the data is put into place in order to recover information on the past network traffic. Moreover, to assure that the real-time requirement of the system is met, a fast access to stored data is mandatory.

As to the data structures, we have adopted a binary search tree. In the worst case this structure guarantees a performance comparable with a linked list from the point of view of search time; performance further improves in case the tree is a static and well-balanced one. Unfortunately, our structure is not a static tree because the connections are not known in advance; though, a self-adjusting binary tree can be adopted in this case in order to balance a dynamic tree.

We have used a *Snort*™ library of functions to manage the so-called *Splay Trees*. A Splay Tree is an elegant self-organizing data structure created by Sleator and Tarjan [36]: it actually is an ordered binary tree, in which an item is moved up to the entry point — i. e. the tree root — whenever it is accessed, by means of a number of rotations of the item with the parent nodes. This makes it faster to access the most frequently used elements than the least frequently used ones, without sacrificing the efficiency of operations such as *insert* and *search*. It can be shown, in fact, that the amortized complexity of the *search*, *insert* and *delete* operations on a splay tree is $O(\log n)$[36].

With the above mentioned tree structure, we have implemented two trees, a *Same Host Tree* and a *Same Service Tree* to compute the same host and the same service traffic features, respectively. Every node in the tree is identified by the destination IP address in the first tree, or by the destination service in the second one. In this way, we want to store in the same node information about all the connections that share the same characteristics. In order to compute both the time-based and the host-based traffic features, for every node in the tree we have implemented two linked lists, one for each set. The linked lists contain information like source IP address and/or source port for all the connections that have been identified and that have the same destination IP address and/or the same destination service (Fig. 4). The elements of the list, one for every connection, are ordered in time: the first element is the oldest one, the last is the most recent.

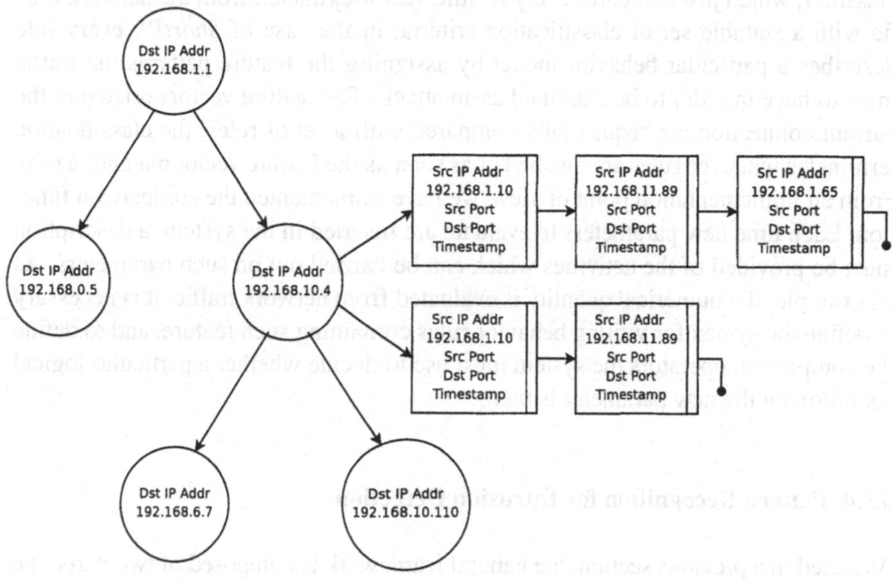

Fig. 4 Same-Host Tree Structure

When a new packet is captured from the network, our preprocessor plugin first analyzes the protocol of the packet in order to identify the most appropriate procedure to compute the intrinsic features. If the packet belongs to either a UDP or an ICMP traffic, the information required to compute the intrinsic features is entirely contained in the packet. In case of TCP traffic, the procedure recovers the session which the packet belongs to in order to determine some crucial information, like the duration of the connection or the number of bytes sent along both directions of the stream, that cannot be directly inferred from the packet. Then, the procedure analyzes the destination IP address and the destination port to compute the traffic features. The searches in the two trees are performed: if no node has been found, a new one is created, and the traffic features relative to the current connection are set to zero. If a node is already in the tree, the procedure analyzes the two linked lists to compute the statistics for both time-based and host-based traffic features. Every element in the list is analyzed and the statistics are updated. During this process the elements that do not belong neither to a time interval of two seconds, nor to a window of the latest one hundred connections, are pruned.

4.1.3 A Detection Plugin for *Snort*™

While the preprocessor is not straightforward to implement, as it has many commitments to pursue within the packet interarrival time, the detection plugin conversely requires lower implementation efforts. Such a plugin is the implementation of a classifier, which just compares every feature vector extracted from the network traffic with a suitable set of classification criteria; in the case of *Snort*™, every rule describes a particular behavior model by assigning the feature patterns the traffic must to have in order to be classified as an attack. The feature vectors related to the current connection are sequentially compared with a set of rules; the classification terminates when the rules are finished or as soon as the feature vector matches a rule. From an implementation point of view, we have implemented the comparison function. Each time new parameters to evaluate are inserted in the system, a description must be provided of the activities which can be carried out on such parameters. As an example, if a numerical quantity is evaluated from network traffic, it is necessary to define the syntax for writing behavior rules containing such feature, and to define the comparison operators the system must use to decide whether a particular logical condition on the new parameter is met.

4.1.4 Pattern Recognition for Intrusion Detection

As stated in a previous section, the general framework is composed of two parts: the on-line process of real-time monitoring and classification, and the off-line process of classification behavior model extraction. In this section we present a different contribution, dealing with an approach to the off-line extraction of models.

In particular we will illustrate the computational intelligence techniques used for extracting behavioral model, techniques that can be profitably exploited in a real-time system.

One of the main issues related to pattern recognition in intrusion detection is the use of a proper data set, containing user profiles on which the data mining processes work in order to extract the patterns. In principle, an efficient set of patterns for the detection has to contain all of the possible user behaviors. Moreover, the data set has to properly label the behavior profile items with either "normal" or "attack". Although this might look like an easy task, labeling the data imposes a pre-classification process: you have to know exactly which profile is "normal" and which is not.

In order to solve the issue related to data set building, two main approaches are possible: the former relies on simulating a real-world network scenario, the latter builds the set using actual traffic.

The first approach is usually adopted when applying pattern recognition techniques to intrusion detection. As stated in Section 2.1.1, the most well-known dataset is the KDD Cup 1999 Data, which was created for the Third International

Knowledge Discovery and Data Mining Tools Competition[2], held within KDD-99, the Fifth International Conference on Knowledge Discovery and Data Mining. Such a set was created by the Lincoln Laboratory at MIT in order to conduct a comparative evaluation of intrusion detection systems, developed under DARPA (Defense Advanced Research Projects Agency) and AFRL (Air Force Research Laboratory) sponsorship[3].

Although widely employed, several criticisms have been raised against the 1999 KDD Cup Data [15, 37]. Indeed, numerous research works analyze the difficulties arising when trying to reproduce actual network traffic patterns by means of simulation [38]. Actually, the major issue resides in effectively reproducing the behavior of network traffic sources.

Based on the considerations above, it appears evident that the KDD Cup 1999 Data can just be used to evaluate the effectiveness of the pattern recognition algorithms under study, rather than in the real application of intrusion detection.

Collecting real traffic can be considered as a viable alternative approach for the construction of the traffic data set [39]. Although it can prove effective in real-time intrusion detection, it still presents some concerns. In particular, collecting the data set by means of real traffic needs a data pre-classification process. In fact, as stated before, the pattern recognition process needs a data set in which packets are labeled as either "normal" or "attack". Indeed, no information is available in the real traffic to distinguish the normal activities from the malicious ones in order to label the data set. So we have a paradox: *we need pre-classified traffic in order to extract the models able to classify the traffic*. Last but not least, the issue of privacy of the information contained in the real network data has to be considered: payload anonymizers and IP address spoofing tools are needed in order to preserve sensitive information (see Section 4.4).

This notwithstanding, we preferred to adopt the real traffic collection approach for extracting the network behavior models. This approach needs to define a suitable method to: (*i*) collect real data from a network; (*ii*) elaborate such information in order to build and appropriately label the associated data set.

Our data set has been built by collecting real traffic on the local network at Genova National Research Council (CNR). The *raw traffic* data set contains about one million packets, equivalent to 1*GByte* of data. The network traffic has been captured by means of the TCPdump tool and logged to a file. In order to solve the pre-classification problem (which, as already stated, requires labeling the items in the data set), we have used a previous work of Genova's research team. By using different intrusion detection systems, researchers in Genova have analyzed the generated alert files and manually identified, in the logged traffic, a set of known intrusions. We have leveraged the results of this research in order to extract the connection features record and properly label it with either a *normal* or an *attack* tag, as it will be clarified in Section 4.2.

---

[2] http://kdd.ics.uci.edu/databases/kddcup99/kddcup99.html

[3] http://www.ll.mit.edu/IST/ideval

After building the data set, we have focused on the management of the data in order to realize the pattern recognition process. Every record in the data set is composed of the 26 connection features described in Section 4.1.1. Indeed, just few features can be used to tell apart normal from anomalous traffic in the analyzed network scenario. In fact, some attacks can be classified only with a small set of connection features. This can be considered as an advantage: we can reduce the dimensional space of the data set, letting the pattern recognition process become simpler. Common to pattern recognition and data mining processes, the issue of feature subset selection is known as *feature selection problem.* In feature selection, the objective is to select the smallest subset of features that meets the classification performance requirements, at the same time reducing computational complexity. This technique is based on the notions of relevance and irrelevance of the features with respect to the specific classification process [40]. In our context, we have adopted ToolDiag[4], a pattern recognition toolbox, in order to realize the feature selection.

The last step in our work has concerned the extraction of network behavior patterns from the data set. By using the connection features defined in 4.1.1 for representing network traffic, we chose to characterize attacks by using a set of rules, in order to utilize the above described Detection Plugin for Snort as classifier. Among the various techniques proposed so far for extracting a set of rules from a data set, we have adopted the SLIPPER[5] [41] tool. SLIPPER is a rule-learning system exploiting the Boosting technique [42].

4.2 Performance evaluation

In this section we present some experimental results concerning both the attack detection capabilities attained by using the proposed approach and the feasibility of the proposed system. We will mainly focus on the missed detection rate and, more important, on the false alarm rate, which is a critical requirement for an effective intrusion detection system [43]; furthermore, we will evaluate the overhead on the performance of Snort caused by the operation of the preprocessor plugin.

Besides the measurements regarding the effectiveness of the employed detection techniques, our purpose is to show the affordability of real-time intrusion detection, by evaluating, in particular, the increase in packet loss ratio using a general purpose machine. Such tests are deployed in two scenarios: in the first case, we built a testbed to emulate network traffic in a controlled environment; in the second, we sniffed traffic flowing on the Genova CNR local network. We evaluated *Snort*™alone, version 2.1.0, and *Snort*™plus our plugins. In both cases we observed a very low increase in packet loss ratio, showing the affordability of such a technique (Table 3).

Though in other pattern recognition applications a false positive rate below 5% may be a very satisfactory value, in intrusion detection such a rate may not be ac-

[4] http://www.inf.ufes.br/ thomas/home/tooldiag.html

[5] http://www-2.cs.cmu.edu/w̃cohen/slipper/

	Snort-2.1.0	Snort + Plugins
Emulated Traffic	0.39%	0.42%
Real LAN Traffic (Genova CNR)	0.14%	0.16%

Table 3 Packet Loss

Train Error Rate	Test Error Rate	Hypothesis Size	Learning Time
0.20%	0.36%	10 Rules, 37 Conditions	217.33s

Table 4 Detection accuracy after feature selection – Average values

Training Set	Test Set	Missed Detections	False Alarms
1st Half	**2nd Half**	33.59%	0.06%
2nd Half	**1st Half**	50.41%	0.03%

Table 5 Detection accuracy after filtering and feature selection

Training Set	Test Set	Missed Detections	False Alarms
1st Half	**2nd Half**	13.57%	0.16%
2nd Half	**1st Half**	55.32%	0.07%

Table 6 Detection accuracy without feature selection

ceptable. For example, if we imagine to work on a network with a packet rate of 1000000 packets per hour, a false alarm rate of 0.1% would lead to 1000 annoying alert messages sent to the administrator every hour: though characterized by a very low false alarm rate, the number of unjustified alerts would be too high and would lead the administrator to ignore or eventually switch the intrusion detection system off.

We ran different tests on some previously collected data (see Section 4.1.4). First of all, we decided to subsample the data by a factor of $1/10$ in order to reduce the computation time of the results; as stated before, we use ToolDiag for the feature selection step and SLIPPER for the classification. In the first experiment we subsample the data-set by choosing one connection record out of ten, then we split the subsets in two parts. On each of the half-subset obtained we perform feature selection and, by examining the discriminating power and the number of occurrences over the whole data set of the selected features, we choose an "optimum" set of 8 features out of the 26 features available. By "optimum" feature, we mean a feature whose ability to discriminate between attacks and normal traffic, within the training data, is the highest with respect to the discriminating power of all the examined features. We consider then, in turn and for each subset, the first half as the training set, and the second half as the test set; then we swap training and test sets, using the second half of each subset as the training set and the first half as the test set. All these experiments are useful to understand which is the best data set we have, as we suppose to have no prior knowledge about the discriminating power of the connection records included in each one of them. In table 4 we point out the average values emerging from the analysis of the presented results.

Training Set	Test Set	Missed Detections	False Alarms
1st Half	2nd Half	13.79%	0.16%
2nd Half	1st Half	62.19%	0.05%

Table 7 Detection accuracy after filtering without feature selection

Training Set	Test Set	Missed Detections	False Alarms
1st Half	2nd Half	4%	0%
2nd Half	1st Half	0%	0%

Table 8 Detection accuracy without feature selection – Trin00 attack

Training Set	Test Set	Missed Detections	False Alarms
1st Half	2nd Half	0%	0%
2nd Half	1st Half	0%	0%

Table 9 Detection accuracy after filtering and without feature selection – Trin00 attack

It is worth pointing out that the data we are working on contain some connection records tagged as *uncertain*. During the data preparation, we decided to label as attacks the connection records corresponding to the packets classified as attacks by both the IDS used at Genova CNR; in case only one of the used tools raised an alert, in this first experiment we decided to label the corresponding packet as normal. It is straightforward, indeed, to have a doubt about this approach: what if the *uncertain* packets were attack packets? Would this affect in a meaningful way the detection capability of the system? We had two chances: we could consider the *uncertain* packets as attacks as well, though this would have led us to a complementary mistake with respect to the one committed so far; we could, as well, simply discard such packets, considering them as belonging to an unknown class of traffic. Thus we built and processed a "filtered out" data set, made up by all the connection records corresponding to packets whose classification was clear enough, obtained by deleting from the set the *uncertain* connection records.

Again we proceeded with feature selection and obtained, in the same way as before, the best set of eight features. On the filtered data we decided to deploy a test by using the whole dataset, with no subsampling. We divided the dataset in two halves and, in Test 1 we considered the first half as the training set, and the second half as the test set; in Test 2, instead, we consider the second half of the data set as the training set and the first half as the test set.

Furthermore, to test the effect of feature selection on the detection capability of the system, we decided not to apply subsampling, and to test the classifier on the datasets before and after the filtering process described above (tables 6, 7). We notice a very low false alarm rate, which is good, and a missed detection rate sometimes around 60%. This might seem a not so good result, but it is not; missing an attack packet does not mean to miss the whole attack itself; in fact, an attack pattern may consist of a burst of packets thus, not detecting a few of such packets doesn't mean to lose the attack. Stressing again the false alarm rate problem, we notice that the rate obtained within our experiments is very low, and encouraging for the development of this kind of detection techniques.

In order to strengthen these observations, we also sketch, in Table 8 the detection capabilities tested over a particular DoS attack, Trin00, which is always correctly detected by our IDS without rising any false alarm. This confirms the applicability of the realized IDS within the proposed framework for intrusion detection and reaction.

Finally, as we have a little lower missed detection rate when not using feature selection, we noticed an increase of one order of magnitude in rule calculation time and number of rules. This is due to the fact that we have to strike the balance between detection accuracy, number of adopted criteria and computation time.

4.3 A Distributed Intrusion Detection System

In this section we want to deal with the design of a distributed architecture for IDS based on the previous implementation. Our idea starts from the assumption that it is possible to divide the monitoring and user behavior extraction process, performed by the preprocessor engine in the "monolithic" architecture, from the classification process. In fact, the two processes are sequential and substantially independent: they could be realized by two different programs, just realizing the suitable interface between them. The classification process, in fact, require just the set of connection features and other few information to realize its detection process. According with this assumption, it is possible to realize two separate process, in case running on different machines, that communicate between them by means of a network. As we will see in the following, such an approach introduces a lot of advantages in the IDS efficiency.

Our architecture is based on previous experiences in the field of the "collaborative" systems; an example of these systems is the well known project *seti@home* [6], proposed by the University of California at Berkeley. In spite of previous distributed intrusion detection systems [44, 45], which mainly realize the "distribution" of the monitoring process by means of a set of probes locate within the network, but having usually a "centralize" classification process, our architecture realizes also the "distribution" of the classification process. In particular, we have a set of elements that first separately realize the classification of the user behavior and then collaborate in order to compute a final result on the detection process. The proposed architecture is shown in the Figure 5.

Such architecture allows us to improve the IDS efficiency with regard to several aspects. First, a distributed system allows the separation of concerns among a well-defined set of entities, each suited to deal with a particular aspect of the problem. This on one side simplifies the task of each involved entity, and on the other side allows a deeper specialization of each module, which can thus be modified without necessarily affecting the performance of the overall system.

[6] http://setiathome.ssl.berkeley.edu/

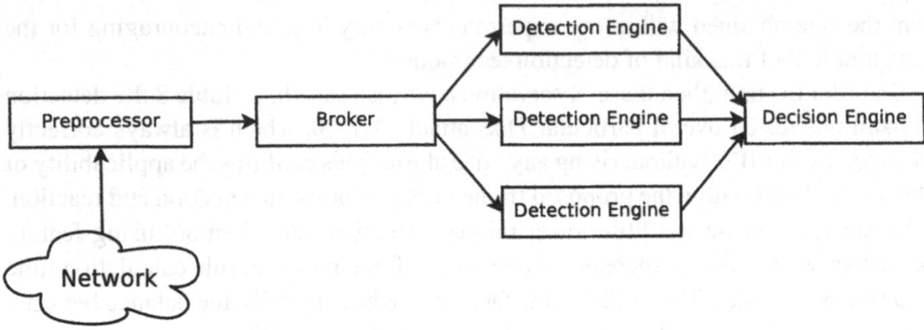

Fig. 5 Distributed IDS Architecture

As for the effectiveness of the IDS classification process, our architecture introduce two important advantages. First, one of the main problem related to the classification problem of IDS is the packet loss; if some packets are lost, the information contained in the user behavior features could be compromised, so several traffic patterns could be misclassified, and a great amount of false alarms or missed detections could be generated. In order to improve the effectiveness of the classification process, we need to reduce the packets loss; this can be performed by a distribution of the task: a process that realize exclusively the traffic sniffing and the summarization of the user behavior, and a process that classifies them. Some preliminary experimental results have shown the effectiveness of such a solution [47]. Moreover, the distributed system can improve the capability of the classification process: it is possible to adopt different methodologies, for example the anomaly detection or the misuse detection, adding just a new detection module for each new methodologies. Adopting several detection techniques to analyze the same network traffic, we can improve the detection capability exploiting the advantages of each techniques. Such approach could reduce the number of false alarms or missed detections.

Finally, adopting a distributed systems, we could improve also the intrinsic security of the overall system. In a monolithic IDS architecture the system itself could be victim of several threats: a direct attack to the IDS can compromise the security of overall network. Distributing the functionalities among different components allows us to improve the security because an attack must compromise all the components to gain the same effect then in a monolithic architecture. Moreover, a distributed system improves the efficiency by means of a reconfiguration system policy in case of attack to one or more components of the architecture. Then, it is possible to expose to risk of an attack just the behavior summarization modules, protecting other components of the architecture by a secure network zone.

Such architecture falls in a new "autonomic" approach [48] to network security; in particular, if we assume that the network be aware of itself, security assurance might be regarded as a *service* inherently provided by network infrastructures. In such a scenario, a framework capable to deploy, both proactively and reactively, on-demand security services is well suited. The distributed IDS can fit such approach:

all the components could deploy on demand in response to anomalous situations that require network security services.

In the following we will briefly describe all the elements of the proposed architecture. The first element is the *preprocessor*. It has the function of monitoring user behavior, summarizing it by means of a set of parameters – in our case the previously described connection features. In particular, the preprocessor captures the packets directly from the network and computes the parameters related to the user behavior. This behavior is based on the well-known Behavioral Network Engineering approach [49]. According with a distributed solution, also the preprocessor can be realize by means of a distributed architecture, as proposed in [50].

The connection features computed by each preprocessor are then sent to another element of the architecture, the *broker*; the main functionality of the broker is to gather information coming from the preprocessors and sent it to a new set of elements of the architecture, namely *detection engines*. The forwarding policy can be base on different algorithms, depending on the strategy adopted for classification process and the set of detection engine connected with broker.

The detection engines are the core of the classification process. Such modules can be added and removed on demand from the architecture in order to perform a specific classification strategy by means of a suitable protocol. As stated before, each detection engine could adopt a different detection technique in order to improve the effectiveness of the detection process. All the results provided by detection engines are sent to the last component of the architecture, the *decision engine*.

The decision engine collects the information coming from the detection engines and extracts a final result exploiting a well-known decision algorithm. Several decision techniques can be implemented such as majority voting, weighted voting [51], or more complex solutions [52, 53].

4.4 Privacy Issues in Intrusion Detection

Pattern recognition approaches to intrusion detection, as presented in Section 4.1.4, sometimes need a training phase to accomplish their detection task. In order for the classification to be reliable and effective, a suitable training set must be chosen, which is representative enough of the protected scenario. The samples used in training, in fact, are the base which the knowledge of the system is built on: if such samples don't cover a broad enough range of the properties of the traffic the system is bound to operate on, it won't be able to recognize correctly some classes of traffic. On the other hand, if the training samples are not general enough, they might lead the system to a bias, making it too specialized for the characteristics of the training samples alone, thus almost canceling the effects of the generalization capabilities of computational intelligence based systems. Hence, the best choice would be to carefully project and implement the collection of the training samples. For research purposes, the demand for traffic traces is impelling in many research fields, both in the networking and artificial intelligence scientific communities. Network traffic always contains private information, thus not allowing to freely collect and distribute any logged trace as is. Hence, as the proposed framework aims at aiding a user to deploy a fully functional security system, it also includes some research activities related to effective traffic anonymization [54].

Many anonymization tools are already available at production level, but most of them are somewhat incomplete for our purposes. Such tools, in fact, only tackle physical, network and transport layer header anonymization: by suitably scrambling the addressing fields of such headers, they make the actors of the communication unrecognizable by the header point of view; yet, they completely disregard the above layers, by simply cutting off the payloads from the transport layer up. In the context of network monitoring for security purposes, packet inspection techniques are used, which need well-formed packets, thus including the whole payload. Indeed, when cutting the payload off, two choices are possible: the packet dimension reported in the header can be left unchanged, thus resulting in a malformed packet, or it can be changed, thus altering the nature of the packet itself, together with the resulting traffic profile. Our aim is to develop a software capable of effectively anonymizing the header, and also replacing the private information contained in the payload with random symbols [55]. Such an operation requires the recomputation of checksums, in order to output well-formed packets.

For source and destination port anonymization, we simply built a function which makes a random association between the original port and the anonymized one. For IP address anonymization, two techniques will be described in the following, both aiming at preserving some specific properties of the header fields.

4.4.1 Class Preserving IP Anonymization

The first issue to cope with regards the structure of an IP address. Due to the existence of different address classes, we want an anonymization tool to preserve the class an IP address belongs to, in order to leave the relative distribution of IP addresses over the five possible classes unchanged. Thus, we keep the four most significant bits of the IP address untouched, so that the transform of an address belonging to class X, where $X \in \{A,B,C,D,E\}$, will still belong to the same class. Private addresses within each class will be translated into private addresses as well. By taking into account the different proportions between the number of available networks and hosts within each class, we adopted different encoding and implementation techniques for each of them, resulting in an overall complexity equal to $O(\log n)$, where n represents the number of anonymized addresses.

4.4.2 Prefix Preserving IP Anonymization

In order to preserve more of the statistical properties of the original network traffic, it might be useful to introduce a new constraint to the anonymization operation. The prefix preserving technique for IP addresses anonymization not only leaves unchanged the class of the original address, but also transforms addresses sharing a common prefix of p bits into addresses still sharing a common prefix of the same length. Furthermore, a random inversion of the $p+1-th$ bit is performed after anonymization, in order to not introduce a longer common prefix. As an IP address consists of a constant number of bits, each time a constant number of comparisons with the other addresses must be performed, thus resulting in a constant complexity of this algorithm. No matter what the number of anonymized addresses is, as an IP address consists of 32 bits, 32 comparisons must be made at each occurrence of a packet to be anonymized. Thus, the complexity is $O(1)$.

5 Intrusion Reaction: a System for Attack Source Detection

Active Security SYSTem (ASSYST) has been designed to provide a mechanism for reacting to DDoS attacks. It is a router level architecture, being its components located inside network routers, without involving end-systems. The system is fed by the output coming from an external IDS performing a real-time traffic analysis, which is aimed at detecting potential attack attempts; when an intrusion is detected, the involved router sends to adjacent routers a message carrying the attacking traffic specification, in order to identify those located on the path to the attack. If one or more routers realized to belong to the attack path, they would recursively apply the same algorithm and, at the same time, would begin to mitigate the effect of anomalous traffic, according to the parameters specified by the downstream router. This approach guarantees the propagation of the countermeasure, until reaching the ASSYST router closest to the attack source, thus allowing to effectively set the limits of the attack.

5.1 The ASSYST Architecture

In Fig. 6 the conceptual model of an ASSYST router is shown. It contains the following modules:

- Packet Classifier Intrusion Detection System (PCIDS): detects attack attempts and provides its characteristics; it is also in charge of identifying packets belonging to an ongoing attack session;
- Security Reference Monitor (SRM): provides the other components with storage capabilities for their useful information (e.g. attack sessions description data, attack paths, ...);
- Security-Aware Traffic Control (SATC): dynamically allocates queues for packets belonging to attack sessions and enables scheduling capabilities according to suitable disciplines; thanks to this module the effects of attack traffic sessions can be controlled;

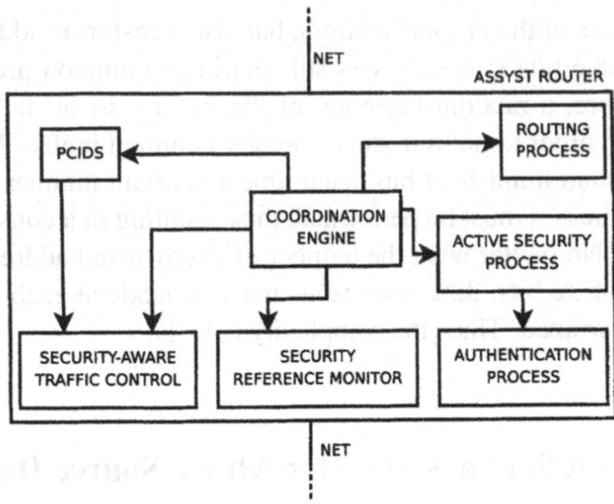

Fig. 6 The ASSYST router architecture

Coordination Engine (CE): coordinates the activity carried out by all the other modules;
Authentication Process (AP): manages authentication among nodes in order to avoid unauthorized access to the whole distributed system;
Routing Process (RP): the local routing module;
Active Security Process: manages communication among routers by means of a suitably designed protocol: Active Security Protocol (ASP).

5.2 Attack Sessions

An attack session is defined by the pair `(IDSession, TrafficDescriptor)`, where `IDSession` is a unique identifier for the session and `TrafficDescriptor` represents the minimum set of information required in order to describe the attack characteristics. More precisely, this last data structure hosts information related to:

- the attack source;
- the attack target;
- the characteristics of an attack.

It enables the PCIDS module to recognize each known attack pattern. It is extensible, so to let the system adapt to new kinds of attacks in a flexible way. The presented approach to model `TrafficDescriptor` is inspired by the IETF Intrusion Detection Message Exchange Format (IDMEF) [56] proposed standard.

5.3 The ASP Protocol

The ASP protocol represents a fundamental component of the architecture, since it enables cooperation among routers involved in an attack session. It works by starting exchanging messages at attack detection time, with the aim of spreading information about traffic characteristics, thus allowing routers to adopt suitable countermeasures. The main protocol messages are reported in Table 10.

#	Name	Description
1	ALERT	Sent, by a router presumably involved in an attack session, to its neighbors.
2	REQUESTSESSION	Sent by a router which receives an ALERT and realizes to be on the path to the attack. This message asks for details on the defense strategy to adopt.
3	CONFIRMSESSION	Sent by a router which receives a REQUESTSESSION message. This message specifies how to treat the attacking traffic.
4	NOPATH	Sent by a router which receives an ALERT message, but does not recognize to be on the path to the attack.
5	ATTACKEND	Sent by a router which detects the end of an attack.
6	ATTACKRESUME	Sent by a router which detects the resumption of a previously ended attack.
7	PATHCONFIGURATION	Detects the presence of a non-ASSYST router on the path to the attack and suitably adapts its defense strategy.
8	AUTHENTICATIONMSG	Contains information useful to router authentication.

Table 10 Main ASP protocol messages

5.4 ASSYST: case studies

This section presents the protocol behavior under different hypothesis, starting from the simplest possible case, and gradually removing the simplifying assumptions.

We start making the following assumptions:

- each DDoS attack is initiated by a single source and targeted to a single host;
- the attacker does not implement any address spoofing mechanisms;
- each router along the path supports the ASP protocol.

In the following paragraphs, we will consider the IP-spoofing assumption and will describe the system behavior in the case of non-ASSYST routers along the attack path.

5.4.1 A simple case: no-spoofing in a fully ASSYST-compliant network

Once the PCIDS detects a suspicious session, it raises an alert event and sends the associated `TrafficDescriptor` to the Coordination Engine (CE). The CE creates an Active Session which triggers the traceback process. Then, it asks the Security Aware Traffic Control (SATC) to allocate a queue for storing packets belonging to the suspicious session and instantiate the most appropriate filter for handling them. In the following, we will call *source router* the router which detects and notifies an attack session and *destination router* the one which receives this notification. Communication among routers is subordinated to the authentication. The source router sends an `Alert` message to all its neighboring nodes. This message also contains an identifier for the created session and the associated `TrafficDescriptor`. Furthermore, being the router the first one detecting the attack, it temporarily designates itself as the last router along the path, sending this information to all of its neighbors. Upon reception of the `Alert` message, routers execute a monitor process aiming at verifying whether the session matches both the detected pattern and the received `TrafficDescriptor`. To the purpose, the CE instantiates a waiting session using the information received with the `Alert` message. The monitor process lasts for a predefined time interval (Alert Interval), after which, if the router did not detect any packet belonging to the attack session, a `NoPath` message is sent to the source router. This happens when the involved router does not reside along the attack path; such a router, anyhow, keeps on monitoring the session in order to detect (and prevent) potential attack path variations. Those routers that are on the attack path, on the other hand, send a `RequestSession` message to the source router, registering themselves to the announced session. By doing this, each router will be aware of which nodes are involved in the attack. Upon reception of a `RequestSession` message, the router performs the following tasks:

- labels the received session as entrusted;
- sends a `ConfirmSession` message to the source router, requiring the `TrafficShapeSpec` structure needed for activating the most appropriate defense strategy;
- releases resources allocated by the Monitor process, since monitoring will be performed by the upstream router along the path.

In order to better understand how ASSYST implements the traceback process, we show an example in Fig. 7. We assume that router R1 is the first one which detects the attack session and triggers the signaling phase by sending the messages 1a, 2a, 1b, and 2b. The message exchanging process ends up with R7 receiving an `Alert` message. R7 fails to contact any upstream node, thus it recognizes itself as the first node along the attack path. It can now detect the attacker's identity by analyzing the source IP address of the packets it receives. As it can be noticed, ASP is a pure networking protocol, in the sense that it does implement a router-level communication paradigm, not involving the end-systems at all.

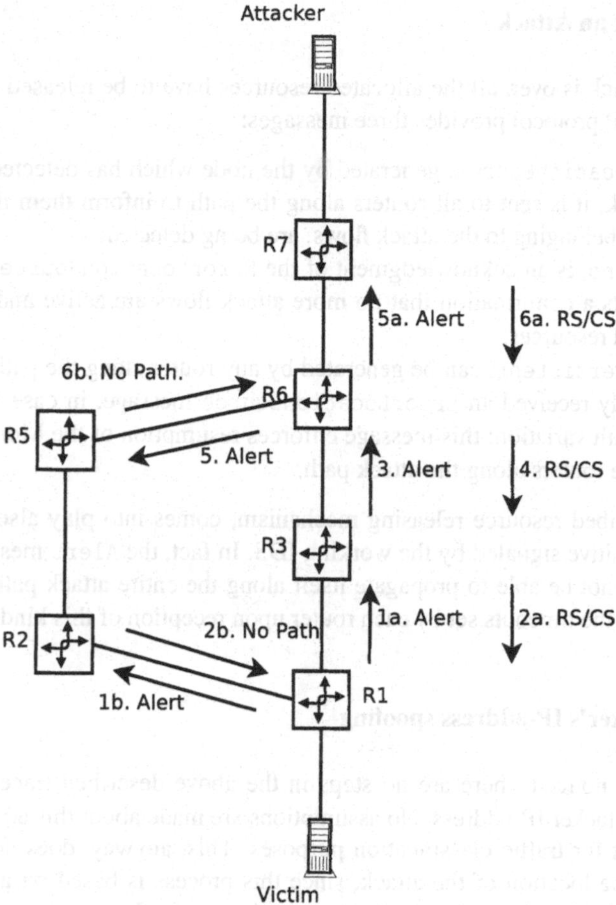

Fig. 7 An example of attack

5.4.2 Attack path variation

When an attacker recognizes that the security system detected the attack, it can try to modify the attack path in order to evade the defense strategy adopted by the system. In this case the new attack path happens to involve routers which have been previously alerted. In fact, routers not involved in the attack, anyhow received an `Alert` message. Hence, thanks to the creation of a *waiting session* associated with the attack, they are able to detect the same attack session. The new alerted router sends a `RequestSession` to its sources, thus registering itself as the new previous node. This causes the current waiting session to switch to a new active session. From now on, the same process recursively applies: the source node sends a `ConfirmSession` containing all the information needed to activate the most appropriate defense strategy.

5.4.3 End of an Attack

When an attack is over, all the allocated resources have to be released. To the purpose, the ASP protocol provides three messages:

1. `ErrorLocationSource`, generated by the node which has detected the end of the attack; it is sent to all routers along the path to inform them that no more packets, belonging to the attack flows, are being detected;
2. `AttackEnd`, is an acknowledgment of the `ErrorLocationSource` message; it represents a confirmation that no more attack flows are active and it frees the allocated resources;
3. `AttackPersistent`, can be generated by any router along the path, which has previously received an `ErrorLocationSource` message, in case it detects an attack path variation; this message enforces resumption of the Monitor process on all the routers along the attack path.

The described resource releasing mechanism, comes into play also in the case of a false positive signaled by the working IDS. In fact, the `Alert` message sent by a router will not be able to propagate itself along the entire attack path, due to the expiration of the timeouts set by each router upon reception of this kind of message.

5.4.4 Attacker's IP-address spoofing

As it can be noticed, there are no steps in the above described traceback, which rely on the attacker IP-address. No assumptions are made about this address, except from using it for traffic classification purposes. This, anyway, does not contribute to identify the location of the attack, since this process is based on a hop-by-hop traceback algorithm driven by the downstreaming traffic flow.

5.4.5 Non-ASSYST router along the attack path

In the absence of a suitable solution, the traceback process might interrupt in the presence of a non-ASSYST router along an attack path. This prevents to approach the attack source close enough, and undermines the overall system usefulness. It is necessary for ASSYST routers to have knowledge at least about their neighbors in the context of the ASSYST overlay network. Once this information is available, an ASSYST router can send an IP-encapsulated message directed to its neighbor, thus skipping the non-ASSYST cloud.

The needed information is obtained through a periodic signaling, aimed at discovering neighbors, establishing a soft-state inside each ASSYST router. This process relies on the `PathConfiguration` message and exploits a similar approach as the one used by the Resource reSerVation Protocol (RSVP) for the same purpose [57]. Both the encapsulated ASP packet and the enveloping IP-packet have a Time-To-Live (TTL) field in their respective header. Its value is decreased of a unit for each traversed node. In case of non-ASSYST routers, only the external IP header is processed and the corresponding TTL value decreased. The internal ASP packet is leaved unchanged, representing an opaque structure in this context. Upon reception of an encapsulated packet by an ASSYST-compliant router, the difference between the TTL values provides information on the existence of a non-ASSYST cloud and the number of non-ASSYST routers crossed. Furthermore, the ASP message contains also the IP address of the "neighboring" ASSYST router (which put it there as well).

5.4.6 Multiple attack sources

In case of multiple attack sources, the protocol has been designed in such a way to split the traceback process into different instances, one independent of each other, which go along all the paths involved in the attack. This process goes forward until approaching as close as possible all the attack sources.

The case in which two different instances reach the same router along the path, has been explicitly addressed, and is called *path merging*. The joining router is able to recognize the attacks as belonging to a single session, and update its internal structures according to the new discovered information.

5.5 Intrusion detection subsystem

In order to properly work, ASSYST has to be fed by the output data coming from an Intrusion Detection System. Alert signals trigger the described processes, according to the picture shown in Fig. 1. Stated the extremely modular structure of this system, IDS integration inside ASSYST architecture, relies on an ad-hoc communication interface. Such an interface allows transfer of the anomalous traffic characteristics toward the ASSYST kernel modules.

Fig. 8 represents the functional principles of the communication interface between the IDS and the CE components. In particular, our contribution is in the design and implementation of the following pieces:

- the driver for bridging the kernel and user addressing spaces;
- the IDS output-plugin, which sends to the PCIDS the detected traffic characteristics through the aforementioned driver;
- the mechanisms enabling asynchronous inter-communication between the PCIDS and the CE components.

In the following, the different phases that characterize the inter-communication process will be described. These are numbered in Fig. 8. Upon generic anomalous traffic detection, the output-plugin notifies its characteristics through the PCIDS driver (1). By means of a shared memory area, the PCIDS collects all the alert

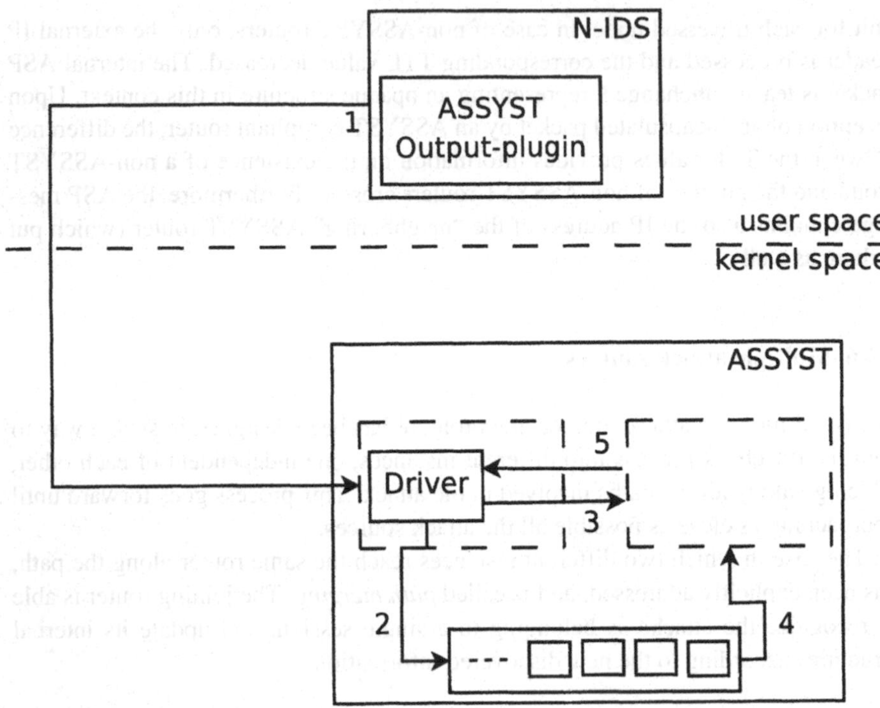

Fig. 8 The ASSYST/IDS interface specification

requests (2) and notifies them to the CE (3). Notification processes have an asynchronous nature, thanks to the tasklet kernel technology [58]. When the CE becomes available, it extracts from the events queue the next alert notification to be managed (4), and tells the PCIDS to be available to accept new requests (5).

5.6 Traffic classification and intrusion reaction

Fig. 9 shows the ASSYST router infrastructure that has been used for traffic classification and intrusion reaction.

This infrastructure consists of a kernel module which performs two main functionalities:

- associates anomalous IP flows with the attack session they belong to (Packet Classifier);
- mitigates attack effects by adopting appropriate traffic scheduling algorithms and, simultaneously, allows traceback process propagation toward the attack sources (Security-Aware Traffic Control).

To this purpose, the Linux Traffic Control module has been integrated in ASSYST; it consists of a collection of tools that enable more complex packet forwarding pro-

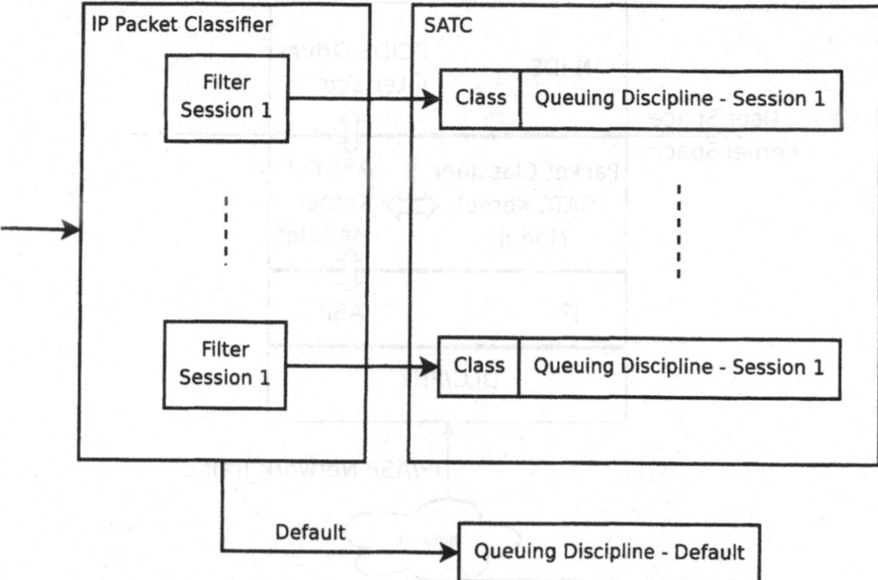

Fig. 9 The PC/SATC internal structure

cesses, replacing the default FIFO management [59]. The most interesting feature consists in the possibility of dynamically creating IP-packets queuing structures and using customizable scheduling algorithms, which can be adapted to the attack session an ASSYST router might be involved in. Fig. 9 helps to clarify this aspect. It is straightforward that this mechanisms tailors the defense strategy on the single attack session characteristics, according to the protection requests (Traffic Shaping Descriptor) shared with the neighbors routers. In order to achieve this objective, the following components have been designed: (i) the kernel interfaces for the dynamical allocation of queuing structures and scheduling policies; (ii) the kernel modules in charge of translating Traffic Shaping descriptors into the activation of the corresponding traffic control modules.

5.7 *ASSYST implementation details*

The ASSYST components and the ASP protocol have been implemented in C programming language and integrated in the 2.4.20 version of the GNU/Linux operating system kernel [60]. The implementation is released under the General Public License [61].

In Fig. 10, the implementation details of the ASSYST modules are presented:

N-IDS: represents a generic Network-based Intrusion Detection System, such as the one presented in the above sections;

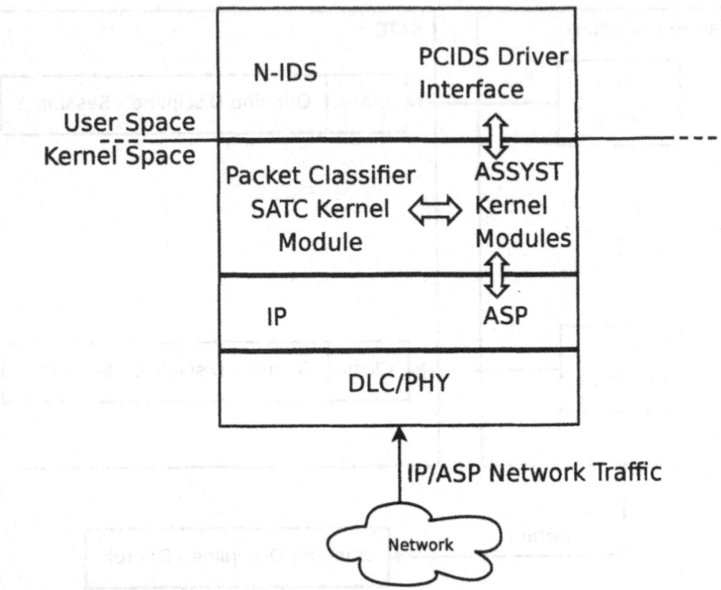

Fig. 10 The ASSYST router architecture inside Linux kernel

- PCIDS Driver Interface: represents the interface between kernel and user addressing spaces; it allows inter-process communication between the chosen IDS (which runs in user space) with the ASSYST kernel modules;
- ASSYST Kernel Modules: the kernel modules which implement the ASSYST components such as the Coordination Engine (CE), the Authentication Process (AP), and the Security Reference Monitor (SRM);
- Packet Classifier/SATC Kernel Modules: these modules implement IP traffic classification functionalities, useful to identify anomalous traffic patterns and to adopt the proper defense strategy;
- ASP: this is the network level module which implements both data structures and communication logic for the ASP protocol.

5.8 ASP protocol implementation details

The implementation of the ASP protocol consisted in the definition of the data structures, protocol message headers, and communication functionalities. The ASP protocol has been realized inside the TCP/IP stack of the Linux kernel, at the network layer. The extension has been plugged-in by adding a new handler in the protocol demultiplexing section of the Linux kernel. The callback function connected to the handler, is invoked upon reception of each ASP packet [58].

5.9 Testing the Approach

In Fig. 11, the testbed used to validate our implementation is shown. It consists of two ASSYST-enabled routers (say `ASSYST_1` and `ASSYST_2`) and two hosts which embody the roles of attacker and victim. The IDS module on the routers has been configured in such a way to consider any ICMP packet as belonging to an attack session. Hence, a DoS attack was emulated by generating ICMP traffic from the attacker toward the victim. Fig. 12 shows some obtained results.

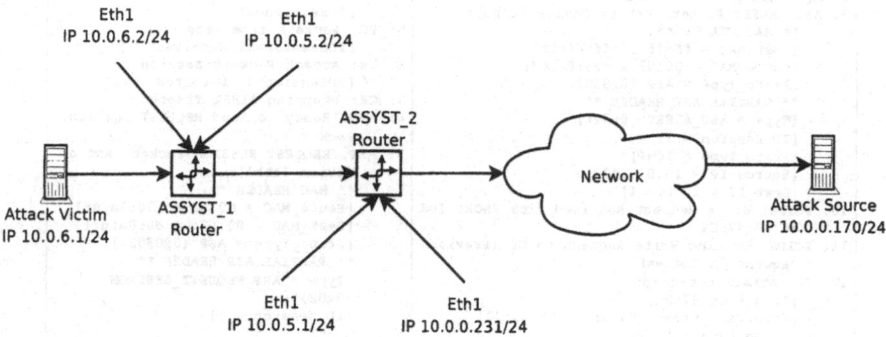

Fig. 11 The ASSYST test-bed

6 Conclusions and Future Work

The experimental results allowed to validate our approach to network security; the overall system provides good performance results in terms of capability in detecting and reacting to distributed malicious activity.

In particular, the IDS framework showed the possibility of combining real-time intrusion detection with pattern recognition techniques, keeping the system overhead under reasonable thresholds and containing the packet loss ratio within certain boundaries. It has been also experimentally demonstrated on real traffic data that the proposed detection methodology allows us to obtain a very low false alarm rate, which is the most important requirement for an effective IDS. Furthermore, the developed anonymization techniques definitely represent a very interesting tool to use for collecting network traffic data without violating users' privacy.

On the side of reaction techniques, contrarily to preventive approaches, ASSYST provides a reactive and resilient mechanism aimed at isolating attackers and limiting their range of action as much as possible.

Next steps will consist in both realizing the distributed IDS adopting new detection techniques, and operating the ASSYST architecture over more complex net-

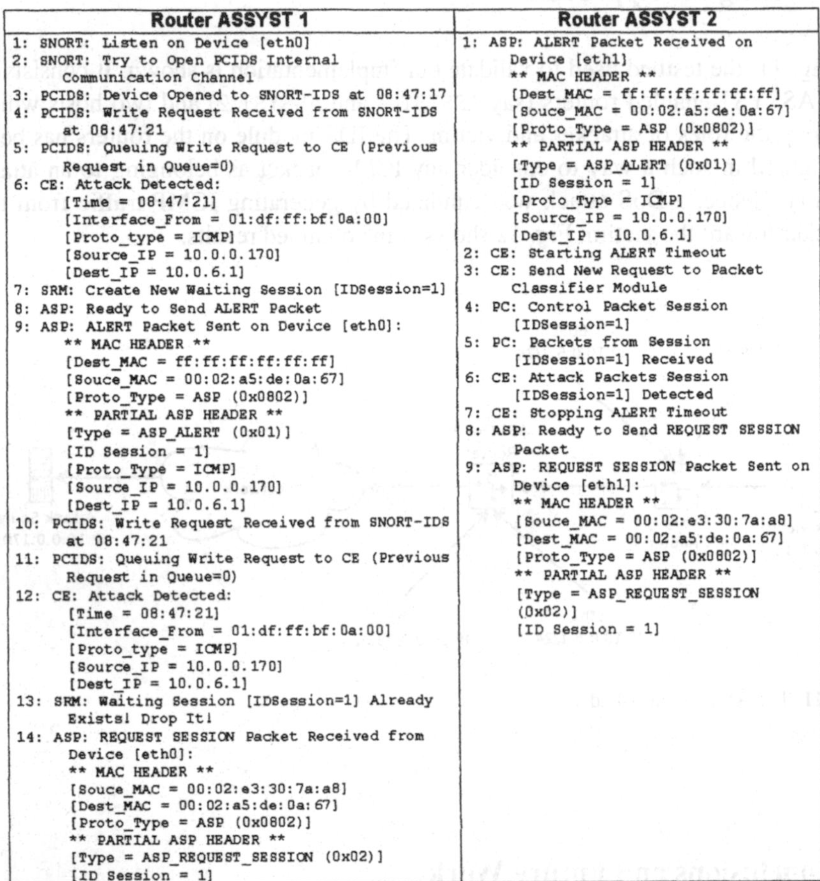

Router ASSYST 1	Router ASSYST 2
1: SNORT: Listen on Device [eth0] 2: SNORT: Try to Open PCIDS Internal Communication Channel 3: PCIDS: Device Opened to SNORT-IDS at 08:47:17 4: PCIDS: Write Request Received from SNORT-IDS at 08:47:21 5: PCIDS: Queuing Write Request to CE (Previous Request in Queue=0) 6: CE: Attack Detected: [Time = 08:47:21] [Interface_From = 01:df:ff:bf:0a:00] [Proto_type = ICMP] [Source_IP = 10.0.0.170] [Dest_IP = 10.0.6.1] 7: SRM: Create New Waiting Session [IDSession=1] 8: ASP: Ready to Send ALERT Packet 9: ASP: ALERT Packet Sent on Device [eth0]: ** MAC HEADER ** [Dest_MAC = ff:ff:ff:ff:ff:ff] [Souce_MAC = 00:02:a5:de:0a:67] [Proto_Type = ASP (0x0802)] ** PARTIAL ASP HEADER ** [Type = ASP_ALERT (0x01)] [ID Session = 1] [Proto_Type = ICMP] [Source_IP = 10.0.0.170] [Dest_IP = 10.0.6.1] 10: PCIDS: Write Request Received from SNORT-IDS at 08:47:21 11: PCIDS: Queuing Write Request to CE (Previous Request in Queue=0) 12: CE: Attack Detected: [Time = 08:47:21] [Interface_From = 01:df:ff:bf:0a:00] [Proto_type = ICMP] [Source_IP = 10.0.0.170] [Dest_IP = 10.0.6.1] 13: SRM: Waiting Session [IDSession=1] Already Exists! Drop It! 14: ASP: REQUEST SESSION Packet Received from Device [eth0]: ** MAC HEADER ** [Souce_MAC = 00:02:e3:30:7a:a8] [Dest_MAC = 00:02:a5:de:0a:67] [Proto_Type = ASP (0x0802)] ** PARTIAL ASP HEADER ** [Type = ASP_REQUEST_SESSION (0x02)] [ID Session = 1]	1: ASP: ALERT Packet Received on Device [eth1] ** MAC HEADER ** [Dest_MAC = ff:ff:ff:ff:ff:ff] [Souce_MAC = 00:02:a5:de:0a:67] [Proto_Type = ASP (0x0802)] ** PARTIAL ASP HEADER ** [Type = ASP_ALERT (0x01)] [ID Session = 1] [Proto_Type = ICMP] [Source_IP = 10.0.0.170] [Dest_IP = 10.0.6.1] 2: CE: Starting ALERT Timeout 3: CE: Send New Request to Packet Classifier Module 4: PC: Control Packet Session [IDSession=1] 5: PC: Packets from Session [IDSession=1] Received 6: CE: Attack Packets Session [IDSession=1] Detected 7: CE: Stopping ALERT Timeout 8: ASP: Ready to Send REQUEST SESSION Packet 9: ASP: REQUEST SESSION Packet Sent on Device [eth1]: ** MAC HEADER ** [Souce_MAC = 00:02:e3:30:7a:a8] [Dest_MAC = 00:02:a5:de:0a:67] [Proto_Type = ASP (0x0802)] ** PARTIAL ASP HEADER ** [Type = ASP_REQUEST_SESSION (0x02)] [ID Session = 1]

Fig. 12 Results obtained by using two ASSYST-enabled routers

work topologies. In this context, an analysis of the system scalability will also be carried out.

As for the anonimyzer, it has to be noted that one of the main purpose of such a tool was developed for, is the distribution of traffic traces aimed at the training of intrusion detection techniques. If there were any attack signatures in the payload, when its content is substituted by random symbols, such signatures would be lost. A further functionality we have planned to implement is hence related to this issue.

Acknowledgment

This work has been partially funded by the Ministero dell'Università e della Ricerca (MiUR) in the framework of the *RECIPE* Project, and by the EU as part of the IST Programme – within the Sixth Framework Programme – in the framework of the *NETQOS* project (details can be seen at `http://www.netqos.eu/`).

References

1. J. D. Howard and T. A. Longstaff. A common language for computer security incidents. Sandia National Laboratories, Albuquerque, USA, October 1998.
2. J. D. Howard. An analysis of security incidents on the internet 1989-1995. Pittsburgh, Pennsylvania, USA. `http://www.cert.org/research/JHThesis/Start.html`, April 1997.
3. G. Vigna and R. Kemmerer. Netstat: a network based intrusion detection system. *Journal of Computer Security*, 7(1), 1999.
4. D. Andersson. Detecting usual program behavior using the statistical component of the next-generation intrusion detection expert system (nides). Technical report, Computer Science Laboratory, 1995.
5. V. Broucek and P. Turner. Bridging the divide: Rising awareness of forensic issues amongst systems administrators. In *Proceedings of the 3rd International System Administration and Network Engineering Conference*, volume 1, Maastricht, The Netherlands, May 27-31 2002. ACM.
6. S. Axelsson. Research in intrusion detection systems: A survey. Technical report, Chalmers University of Technology, 1999.
7. R. Kumar and E. H. Spafford. A software architecture to support misuse intrusion detection. In *Proceedings of the 3rd International System Administration and Network Engineering Conference*, pages 194–204, 1995.
8. M. Meier, S. Schmerl, and H. Koenig. Improving the efficiency of misuse detection. In K. Julisch and C. Kruegel, editors, *Proceedings of the Second International Conference on Detection of Intrusions and Malware, and Vulnerability Assessment*, volume 3548 of *Lecture Notes in Computer Science*, pages 188–205. Springer-Verlag, 2005.
9. B. K. Sy. Signature-based approach for intrusion detection. In P. Perner and A. Imiya, editors, *Proceedings of the 4th International Conference on Machine Learning and Data Mining in Pattern Recognition*, volume 3587 of *Lecture Notes in Artificial Intelligence*. Springer-Verlag, 2005.
10. C. Zhang, J. Jiang, and M. Kamel. Intrusion detection using hierarchical neural networks. *Pattern Recognition Letters*, 26(6):779–791, 2005.
11. A. K. Ghosh and A. Schwartzbard. A study in using neural networks for anomaly and misuse detection. In *Proceedings of the 8th USENIX Security Symposium*, Washington DC (USA), August 26-29 1999.
12. C. E. Brodley T. Lane. Temporal sequence learning and data reduction for anomaly detection. *ACM Transactions on Information and System Security*, 2(3):295–261, 1999.
13. E. Eskin, A. Arnold, M. Prerau, L. Portnoy, and S. J. Stolfo. A geometric framework for unsupervised anomaly detection: Detecting intrusions in unlabeled data. In D. Barbara and S. Jajodia, editors, *Applications of Data Mining in Computer Security*. Kluwer, 2002.
14. S. Singh and M. Markou. Novelty detection: a review - part 2: neural network based approaches. *Signal Processing*, 83(12):2499–2521, 2003.
15. M. Mahoney and P. Chan. An analysis of the 1999 darpa/lincoln laboratory evaluation data for network anomaly detection. In G Vigna, E Jonsson, and C Gel, editors, *Proceeding of Recent Advances in Intrusion Detection (RAID)-2003*, volume 2820 of *Lecture Notes in Computer Science*, pages 220–237. Springer Verlag, September 8-10 2003.

16. M. Ramadas, S. Ostermann, and B. Tjaden. Detecting anomalous network traffic with self-organizing maps. In G. Vigna, E. Jonsson, and C. Kruegel, editors, *Proceeding of Recent Advances in Intrusion Detection (RAID)-2003*, volume 2820 of *Lecture Notes in Computer Science*, pages 36–54. Springer-Verlag, September 8-10 2003.
17. K. Wang and S. J. Stolfo. Anomalous payload-based network intrusion detection. In E. Jonsson, A. Valdes, and M. Almgren, editors, *Proceeding of Recent Advances in Intrusion Detection (RAID)-2004*, volume 3224 of *Lecture Notes in Computer Science*, pages 203–222. Springer-Verlag, 2004.
18. S. Zanero and S. M. Savaresi. Unsupervised learning techniques for an intrusion detection system. In *Proceedings of the 2004 ACM Symposium on Applied Computing*, pages 412–419. ACM, 2004.
19. F. Cuppens and A. Miege. Alert correlation in a cooperative intrusion detection framework. In *Proceedings of the IEEE Symposium on Security and Privacy*, pages 202–215, 2002.
20. F. Valeur, G. Vigna, C. Kruegel, and R. Kemmerer. A comprehensive approach to intrusion detection alert correlation. *IEEE Transactions on Dependable and Secure Computing*, 1(3):146–169, 2004.
21. K. Kendall. A database of computer attacks for the evaluation of intrusion detection systems. Master's thesis, Massachussets Institute of Technology, June 1999.
22. G. Giacinto, F. Roli, and L. Didaci. Fusion of multiple classifiers for intrusion detection in computer networks. *Pattern Recognition Letters*, 24:1759–1803, 2003.
23. W. Lee and S. J. Stolfo. A framework for constructing features and models for intrusion detection systems. *ACM Transactions on Information and System Security (TISSEC)*, 3(4):227–261, November 2000.
24. S. C. Lee and D. V. Heinbuch. Training a neural network based intrusion detector to recognize novel attack. *IEEE Transactions on System, Man, and Cybernetics, Part-A*, 31:294–299, 2001.
25. M. Fugate and J. R. Gattiker. Computer intrusion detection with classification and anomaly detection, using svms. *International Journal of Pattern Recognition and artificial Intelligence*, 17(3):441–458, 2003.
26. L. P. Cordella and C. Sansone. A multi-stage classification system for detecting intrusions in computer networks. *Pattern Analysis and Applications*, 10(2):83–100, 2007.
27. S. Savage, D. Wetherall, A. Karlin, and T. Anderson. Practical network support for ip traceback. Technical report, Dept. of Computer Science and Engineering, University of Washington, Seattle, USA, January 2000.
28. D. X. Song and A. Perrig. Advanced and authenticated marking schemes for ip traceback. Technical report, Dept. of Computer Science and Engineering, University of California, Berkeley, USA, June 2000.
29. U. K. Tupakula and V. Varadharajan. A practical method to counteract denial of service attacks. In *Proceedings of the twenty-sixth Australasian Computer Science Conference*, pages 275–284, Adelaide (Australia), February 2003.
30. U. K. Tupakula and V. Varadharajan. Analysis of automated model against ddos attacks. In *Proceedings of the Australian Telecommunications, Networks and Applications Conference*, Melbourne (Australia), December 2003.
31. J. Mirkovic, M. Robinson, P. Reiher, and G. Kuenning. Alliance formation for ddos defense. In *New Security Paradigms Workshop*. ACM SIGSAC, August 2003.
32. A. R. Baker, B. Caswell, and M. Poor. *Snort 2.1 Intrusion Detection –Second Edition*. Syngress, 2004.
33. S. Singh and M. Markou. Novelty detection: a review - part 1: statistical approaches. *Signal Processing*, 83(12):2499–2521, 2003.
34. W. Lee and S. J. Stolfo. *A Data Mining Framework for Constructing Features and Models for Intrusion Detection Systems*. PhD thesis, Columbia Unversity, 1999.
35. ACM. *Operation Experience with High-Volume Network Intrusion Detection*, October 2004.
36. D. D. Sleator and R. E. Tarjan. Self-adjusting binary search trees. *J. ACM*, 32(3):652–686, 1985.

37. J. McHugh. Testing intrusion detection systems: A critique of the 1998 and 1999 darpa intrusion detection system evaluations as performed by lincoln laboratory. *ACM Transactions on Information and System Security*, 3(4):262–294, November 2000.
38. V. Paxson and S. Floyd. Difficulties in simulating the internet. *IEEE/ACM Transactions on Networking*, 9(4):392–403, 2001.
39. M. Mahoney. *A Machine Learning Approach to Detecting Attacks by Identifying Anomalies in Network Traffic*. PhD thesis, Florida Istitute of Technology, 2003.
40. H. J. George, R. Kohavi, and K. Pfleger. Irrilevant features and subset selection problem. In William W. Cohen & Haym Hirish, editor, *Machine Learning: Proceedings of the Eleventh International Conference*, pages 121–129. Morgan Kaufmann Publishers, 1994.
41. W. W. Cohen and Y. Singer. Simple, fast, and effective rule learner. In *Proceedings of the Sixteenth National Conferance an Artificial Intelligence*, pages 335–342. AAAI Press / The MIT Press, 1999.
42. R. Meir and G. Ratsch. An introduction to boosting and leveraging. In S. Mendelson and A. Smola, editors, *Advanced Lectures an Machine Learning*, pages 119–184. Springer Verlag, 2003.
43. S. Axelsson. *The base-rate fallacy and the difficulty of intrusion detection*, volume 3 of *ACM transaction on information and system security*, pages 186–205. ACM, August 2000.
44. R. Gopalakrishna and E. Spafford. A framework for intrusion detection using interest-driven cooperating agents. In *Proceedings of 4th International Symposium on Recent Advances in Intrusion Detection (RAID)*, October 2001.
45. E. Spafford and D. Zamboni. Intrusion detection using autonomous agents. *Computer Networks*, 34(4):547–570, October 2000.
46. P. A. Porras and P. G. Neumann. EMERALD: Event monitoring enabling responses to anomalous live disturbances. In *Proceedings of 20th NIST-NCSC National Information Systems Security Conference*, October 1997.
47. M. Esposito, C. Mazzariello, F. Oliviero, S. P. Romano, and C. Sansone. Real time detection of novel attack by means of data mining. In C.-S. Chen, J. Felipe, I. Seruca, and J. Cordero, editors, *Enterprise Information Systems VII*, pages 197–204. Springer-Verlag, 2007.
48. M. Smirnov. Autonomic communication – research agenda for a new communication paradigm. Technical report, FOKUS – Fraunhofer Institute for Open Communication System, November 2004.
49. S. D'Antonio, M. Esposito, F. Oliviero, S. P. Romano, and D. Salvi. Behavioral network engineering: making intrusion detection become autonomic. *Annales des Telecommunications*, 61(9-10):1139–1151, 2006.
50. S. D'Antonio, C. Mazzariello, F. Oliviero, and D. Salvi. A distributed multi purpose ip flow monitor. In *Proceedings of the 3rd International Workshop on Internet Performance, Simulation, Monitoring and Measurement, IPS-MoMe*, Warsav, Poland, March 2005.
51. J. Kittler, M. Hatef, R. P. W. Duin, and J. Matas. On combining classifiers. *IEEE Transactions on Pattern Anal. Mach. Intell.*, 20(3):226–239, 1998.
52. L. I. Kuncheva. Switching between selection and fusion in combining classifiers: An experiment. *IEEE Transactions on SMC*, 2(32):146–156, 2002.
53. L. P. Cordella, I. Finizio, C. Mazzariello, and C. Sansone. Using behavior knowledge space and temporal information for detecting intrusions in computer networks. In S. Singh, M. Singh, C. Apt'e, and P. Perner, editors, *Pattern Recognition and Image Analysis, Part II*, volume 3687 of *Lecture Notes in Computer Science*, pages 94–102. Springer, 2005.
54. M. Esposito, C. Mazzariello, and C. Sansone. A network traffic anonymizer. In *Proceedings of the Second Italian Workshop on PRIvacy and SEcurity (PRISE 2007)*, pages 4–7, Rome (Italy), 6th June 2007.
55. University of Napoli *Federico II*. The anonymizer project. `http://sourceforge.net/projects/anonymizer`.
56. H. Debar, M. Huang, and D. Donahoo. Intrusion detection exchange format data model. Technical report, IETF, June 2005.
57. R. Braden, L. Zhang, S. Berson, S. Herzog, and S. Jamin. Resource reservation protocol (rsvp) - version 1 functional specification. Technical report, IETF, September 1997.

58. J. Rubini, A. Corbet. *Linux Device Drivers, 2nd Edition*. O'Relly Edition, June 2001.
59. Traffic control howto. http://www.tldp.org/HOWTO/Traffic-Control-HOWTO/intro.html.
60. Kernel.Org Organization Inc. The kernel archive. http://www.kernel.org.
61. University of Napoli *Federico II* & CRIAI. The assyst project. http://sourceforge.net/projects/assyst.

Glossary of Terms Used in Security and Intrusion Detection

3-way handshake Machine A sends a packet with a SYN flag set to Machine B. B acknowledges A's SYN with a SYN/ACK. A acknowledges B's SYN/ACK with an ACK.

Access Control Access Control ensures that resources are only granted to those users who are entitled to them.

Access Control List (ACL) A mechanism that implements access control for a system resource by listing the identities of the system entities that are permitted to access the resource.

Access Control Service A security service that provides protection of system resources against unauthorized access. The two basic mechanisms for implementing this service are ACLs and tickets.

Access Management Access Management is the maintenance of access information which consists of four tasks: account administration, maintenance, monitoring, and revocation.

Access Matrix An Access Matrix uses rows to represent subjects and columns to represent objects with privileges listed in each cell.

Account Harvesting Account Harvesting is the process of collecting all the legitimate account names on a system.

ACK Piggybacking ACK piggybacking is the practice of sending an ACK inside another packet going to the same destination.

Active Content Program code embedded in the contents of a web page. When the page is accessed by a web browser, the embedded code is automatically downloaded and executed on the user's workstation. Ex. Java, ActiveX (MS)

Activity Monitors Activity monitors aim to prevent virus infection by monitoring for malicious activity on a system, and blocking that activity when possible.

Address Resolution Protocol (ARP) Address Resolution Protocol (ARP) is a protocol for mapping an Internet Protocol address to a physical machine address that is recognized in the local network. A table, usually called the ARP cache, is used to maintain a correlation between each MAC address and its corresponding IP address. ARP provides the protocol rules for making this correlation and providing address conversion in both directions.

Advanced Encryption Standard (AES) An encryption standard being developed by NIST. Intended to specify an unclassified, publicly-disclosed, symmetric encryption algorithm.

Algorithm A finite set of step-by-step instructions for a problem-solving or computation procedure, especially one that can be implemented by a computer.

Applet Java programs; an application program that uses the client's web browser to provide a user interface.

ARPANET Advanced Research Projects Agency Network, a pioneer packet-switched network that was built in the early 1970s under contract to the US Government, led to the development of today's Internet, and was decommissioned in June 1990.

Asymmetric Cryptography Public-key cryptography; A modern branch of cryptography in which the algorithms employ a pair of keys (a public key and a private key) and use a different component of the pair for different steps of the algorithm.

Asymmetric Warfare Asymmetric warfare is the fact that a small investment, properly leveraged, can yield incredible results.

Auditing Auditing is the information gathering and analysis of assets to ensure such things as policy compliance and security from vulnerabilities.

Authentication Authentication is the process of confirming the correctness of the claimed identity.

Authenticity Authenticity is the validity and conformance of the original information.

Authorization Authorization is the approval, permission, or empowerment for someone or something to do something.

Autonomous System One network or series of networks that are all under one administrative control. An autonomous system is also sometimes referred to as a routing domain. An autonomous system is assigned a globally unique number, sometimes called an Autonomous System Number (ASN).

Availability Availability is the need to ensure that the business purpose of the system can be met and that it is accessible to those who need to use it.

Backdoor A backdoor is a tool installed after a compromise to give an attacker easier access to the compromised system around any security mechanisms that are in place.

Bandwidth Commonly used to mean the capacity of a communication channel to pass data through the channel in a given amount of time. Usually expressed in bits per second.

Banner A banner is the information that is displayed to a remote user trying to connect to a service. This may include version information, system information, or a warning about authorized use.

Basic Authentication Basic Authentication is the simplest web-based authentication scheme that works by sending the username and password with each request.

Bastion Host A bastion host has been hardened in anticipation of vulnerabilities that have not been discovered yet.

BIND BIND stands for Berkeley Internet Name Domain and is an implementation of DNS. DNS is used for domain name to IP address resolution.

Biometrics Biometrics use physical characteristics of the users to determine access.

Bit The smallest unit of information storage; a contraction of the term "binary digit;" one of two symbols"0" (zero) and "1" (one) - that are used to represent binary numbers.

Block Cipher A block cipher encrypts one block of data at a time.

Boot Record Infector A boot record infector is a piece of malware that inserts malicious code into the boot sector of a disk.

Border Gateway Protocol (BGP) An inter-autonomous system routing protocol. BGP is used to exchange routing information for the Internet and is the protocol used between Internet service providers (ISP).

Bridge A product that connects a local area network (LAN) to another local area network that uses the same protocol (for example, Ethernet or token ring).

British Standard 7799 A standard code of practice and provides guidance on how to secure an information system. It includes the management framework, objectives, and control requirements for information security management systems.

Broadcast To simultaneously send the same message to multiple recipients. One host to all hosts on network.

Broadcast Address An address used to broadcast a datagram to all hosts on a given network using UDP or ICMP protocol.

Browser A client computer program that can retrieve and display information from servers on the World Wide Web.

Brute Force A cryptanalysis technique or other kind of attack method involving an exhaustive procedure that tries all possibilities, one-by-one.

Buffer Overflow A buffer overflow occurs when a program or process tries to store more data in a buffer (temporary data storage area) than it was intended to hold. Since buffers are created to contain a finite amount of data, the extra information - which has to go somewhere - can overflow into adjacent buffers, corrupting or overwriting the valid data held in them.

Business Continuity Plan (BCP) A Business Continuity Plan is the plan for emergency response, backup operations, and post-disaster recovery steps that will ensure the availability of critical resources and facilitate the continuity of operations in an emergency situation.

Business Impact Analysis (BIA) A Business Impact Analysis determines what levels of impact to a system are tolerable.

Byte A fundamental unit of computer storage; the smallest addressable unit in a computer's architecture. Usually holds one character of information and usually means eight bits.

Cache Pronounced cash, a special high-speed storage mechanism. It can be either a reserved section of main memory or an independent high-speed storage device. Two types of caching are commonly used in personal computers: memory caching and disk caching.

Cache Cramming Cache Cramming is the technique of tricking a browser to run cached Java code from the local disk, instead of the internet zone, so it runs with less restrictive permissions.

Cache Poisoning Malicious or misleading data from a remote name server is saved [cached] by another name server. Typically used with DNS cache poisoning attacks.

Cell A cell is a unit of data transmitted over an ATM network. Certificate-Based Authentication Certificate-Based Authentication is the use of SSL and certificates to authenticate and encrypt HTTP traffic.

CGI Common Gateway Interface. This mechanism is used by HTTP servers (web servers) to pass parameters to executable scripts in order to generate responses dynamically.

Chain of Custody Chain of Custody is the important application of the Federal rules of evidence and its handling.

Challenge-Handshake Authentication Protocol (CHAP) The Challenge-Handshake Authentication Protocol uses a challenge/response authentication mechanism where the response varies every challenge to prevent replay attacks.

Checksum A value that is computed by a function that is dependent on the contents of a data object and is stored or transmitted together with the object, for the purpose of detecting changes in the data.

Cipher A cryptographic algorithm for encryption and decryption.

Ciphertext Ciphertext is the encrypted form of the message being sent.

Circuit Switched Network A circuit switched network is where a single continuous physical circuit connected two endpoints where the route was immutable once set up.

Client A system entity that requests and uses a service provided by another system entity, called a "server." In some cases, the server may itself be a client of some other server.

Collision A collision occurs when multiple systems transmit simultaneously on the same wire.

Competitive Intelligence Competitive Intelligence is espionage using legal, or at least not obviously illegal, means.

Computer Emergency Response Team (CERT) An organization that studies computer and network INFOSEC in order to provide incident response services to victims of attacks, publish alerts concerning vulnerabilities and threats, and offer other information to help improve computer and network security.

Computer Network A collection of host computers together with the sub-network or inter-network through which they can exchange data.

Confidentiality Confidentiality is the need to ensure that information is disclosed only to those who are authorized to view it.

Configuration Management Establish a known baseline condition and manage it.

Cookie Data exchanged between an HTTP server and a browser (a client of the server) to store state information on the client side and retrieve it later for server use. An HTTP server, when sending data to a client, may send along a cookie, which the client retains after the HTTP connection closes. A server can use this mechanism to maintain persistent client-side state information for HTTP-based applications, retrieving the state information in later connections.

Corruption A threat action that undesirably alters system operation by adversely modifying system functions or data.

Cost Benefit Analysis A cost benefit analysis compares the cost of implementing countermeasures with the value of the reduced risk.

Countermeasure Reactive methods used to prevent an exploit from successfully occurring once a threat has been detected. Intrusion Prevention Systems (IPS) commonly employ countermeasures to prevent intruders form gaining further access to a computer network. Other counter measures are patches, access control lists and malware filters.

Covert Channels Covert Channels are the means by which information can be communicated between two parties in a covert fashion using normal system operations. For example by changing the amount of hard drive space that is available on a file server can be used to communicate information.

Cron Cron is a Unix application that runs jobs for users and administrators at scheduled times of the day.

Crossover Cable A crossover cable reverses the pairs of cables at the other end and can be used to connect devices directly together.

Cryptanalysis The mathematical science that deals with analysis of a cryptographic system in order to gain knowledge needed to break or circumvent the protection that the system is designed to provide. In other words, convert the cipher text to plaintext without knowing the key.

Cryptographic Algorithm or Hash An algorithm that employs the science of cryptography, including encryption algorithms, cryptographic hash algorithms, digital signature algorithms, and key agreement algorithms.

Cut-Through Cut-Through is a method of switching where only the header of a packet is read before it is forwarded to its destination.

Cyclic Redundancy Check (CRC) Sometimes called "cyclic redundancy code." A type of checksum algorithm that is not a cryptographic hash but is used to implement data integrity service where accidental changes to data are expected.

Daemon A program which is often started at the time the system boots and runs continuously without intervention from any of the users on the system. The daemon program forwards the requests to other programs (or processes) as appropriate. The term daemon is a Unix term, though many other operating systems provide support for daemons, though they're sometimes called other names. Windows, for example, refers to daemons and System Agents and services.

Data Aggregation Data Aggregation is the ability to get a more complete picture of the information by analyzing several different types of records at once.

Data Custodian A Data Custodian is the entity currently using or manipulating the data, and therefore, temporarily taking responsibility for the data.

Data Encryption Standard (DES) A widely-used method of data encryption using a private (secret) key. There are 72,000,000,000,000,000 (72 quadrillion) or more possible encryption keys that can be used. For each given message, the key is chosen at random from among this enormous number of keys. Like other private key cryptographic methods, both the sender and the receiver must know and use the same private key.

Data Mining Data Mining is a technique used to analyze existing information, usually with the intention of pursuing new avenues to pursue business.

Data Owner A Data Owner is the entity having responsibility and authority for the data.

Data Warehousing Data Warehousing is the consolidation of several previously independent databases into one location.

Datagram Request for Comment 1594 says, "a self-contained, independent entity of data carrying sufficient information to be routed from the source to the destination computer without reliance on earlier exchanges between this source and destination computer and the transporting network." The term has been generally replaced by the term packet. Datagrams or packets are the message units that the Internet Protocol deals with and that the Internet transports. A datagram or packet needs to be self-contained without reliance on earlier exchanges because there is no connection of fixed duration between the two communicating points as there is, for example, in most voice telephone conversations. (This kind of protocol is referred to as connectionless.)

Day Zero The "Day Zero" or "Zero Day" is the day a new vulnerability is made known. In some cases, a "zero day" exploit is referred to an exploit for which no patch is available yet. ("day one"-¿ day at which the patch is made available).

Decapsulation Decapsulation is the process of stripping off one layer's headers and passing the rest of the packet up to the next higher layer on the protocol stack.

Decryption Decryption is the process of transforming an encrypted message into its original plaintext.

Defacement Defacement is the method of modifying the content of a website in such a way that it becomes "vandalized" or embarrassing to the website owner.

Defense In-Depth Defense In-Depth is the approach of using multiple layers of security to guard against failure of a single security component.

Demilitarized Zone (DMZ) In computer security, in general a demilitarized zone (DMZ) or perimeter network is a network area (a subnetwork) that sits between an organization's internal network and an external network, usually the Internet. DMZ's help to enable the layered security model in that they provide subnetwork segmentation based on security requirements or policy. DMZ's provide either a transit mechanism from a secure source to an insecure destination or from an insecure source to a more secure destination. In some cases, a screened subnet which is used for servers accessible from the outside is referred to as a DMZ.

Denial of Service The prevention of authorized access to a system resource or the delaying of system operations and functions.

Dictionary Attack An attack that tries all of the phrases or words in a dictionary, trying to crack a password or key. A dictionary attack uses a predefined list of words compared to a brute force attack that tries all possible combinations.

Diffie-Hellman A key agreement algorithm published in 1976 by Whitfield Diffie and Martin Hellman. Diffie-Hellman does key establishment, not encryption. However, the key that it produces may be used for encryption, for further key management operations, or for any other cryptography.

Digest Authentication Digest Authentication allows a web client to compute MD5 hashes of the password to prove it has the password.

Digital Certificate A digital certificate is an electronic "credit card" that establishes your credentials when doing business or other transactions on the Web. It is issued by a certification authority. It contains your name, a serial number, expiration dates, a copy of the certificate holder's public key (used for encrypting messages and digital signatures), and the digital signature of the certificate-issuing authority so that a recipient can verify that the certificate is real.

Digital Envelope A digital envelope is an encrypted message with the encrypted session key.

Digital Signature A digital signature is a hash of a message that uniquely identifies the sender of the message and proves the message hasn't changed since transmission.

Digital Signature Algorithm (DSA) An asymmetric cryptographic algorithm that produces a digital signature in the form of a pair of large numbers. The signature is computed using rules and parameters such that the identity of the signer and the integrity of the signed data can be verified.

Digital Signature Standard (DSS) The US Government standard that specifies the Digital Signature Algorithm (DSA), which involves asymmetric cryptography.

Disassembly The process of taking a binary program and deriving the source code from it.

Disaster Recovery Plan (DRP) A Disaster Recovery Plan is the process of recovery of IT systems in the event of a disruption or disaster.

Discretionary Access Control (DAC) Discretionary Access Control consists of something the user can manage, such as a document password.

Disruption A circumstance or event that interrupts or prevents the correct operation of system services and functions.

Distance Vector Distance vectors measure the cost of routes to determine the best route to all known networks.

Distributed Scans Distributed Scans are scans that use multiple source addresses to gather information.

Domain A sphere of knowledge, or a collection of facts about some program entities or a number of network points or addresses, identified by a name. On the Internet, a domain consists of a set of network addresses. In the Internet's domain name system, a domain is a name with which name server records are associated that describe sub-domains or host. In Windows NT and Windows 2000, a domain is a set of network resources (applications, printers, and so forth) for a group of users. The user need only to log in to the domain to gain access to the resources, which may be located on a number of different servers in the network.

Domain Hijacking Domain hijacking is an attack by which an attacker takes over a domain by first blocking access to the domain's DNS server and then putting his own server up in its place.

Domain Name A domain name locates an organization or other entity on the Internet. For example, the domain name "www.sans.org" locates an Internet address for "sans.org" at Internet point 199.0.0.2 and a particular host server named "www". The "org" part of the domain name reflects the purpose of the organization or entity (in this example, "organization") and is called the top-level domain name. The "sans" part of the domain name defines the organization or entity and together with the top-level is called the second-level domain name.

Domain Name System (DNS) The domain name system (DNS) is the way that Internet domain names are located and translated into Internet Protocol addresses. A domain name is a meaningful and easy-to-remember "handle" for an Internet address.

Due Care Due care ensures that a minimal level of protection is in place in accordance with the best practice in the industry.

Due Diligence Due diligence is the requirement that organizations must develop and deploy a protection plan to prevent fraud, abuse, and additional deploy a means to detect them if they occur.

DumpSec DumpSec is a security tool that dumps a variety of information about a system's users, file system, registry, permissions, password policy, and services.

Dumpster Diving Dumpster Diving is obtaining passwords and corporate directories by searching through discarded media.

Dynamic Link Library - DLL A collection of small programs, any of which can be called when needed by a larger program that is running in the computer. The small program that lets the larger program communicate with a specific device such as a printer or scanner is often packaged as a DLL program (usually referred to as a DLL file).

Dynamic Routing Protocol Allows network devices to learn routes. Ex. RIP, EIGRP Dynamic routing occurs when routers talk to adjacent routers, informing each other of what networks each router is currently connected to. The routers must communicate using a routing protocol, of which there are many to choose from. The process on the router that is running the routing protocol, communicating with its neighbor routers, is usually called a routing daemon. The routing daemon updates the kernel's routing table with information it receives from neighbor routers.

Eavesdropping Eavesdropping is simply listening to a private conversation which may reveal information which can provide access to a facility or network.

Echo Reply An echo reply is the response a machine that has received an echo request sends over ICMP.

Echo Request An echo request is an ICMP message sent to a machine to determine if it is online and how long traffic takes to get to it.

Egress Filtering Filtering outbound traffic.

Emanations Analysis Gaining direct knowledge of communicated data by monitoring and resolving a signal that is emitted by a system and that contains the data but is not intended to communicate the data.

Encapsulation The inclusion of one data structure within another structure so that the first data structure is hidden for the time being.

Encryption Cryptographic transformation of data (called "plaintext") into a form (called "cipher text") that conceals the data's original meaning to prevent it from being known or used.

Ephemeral Port Also called a transient port or a temporary port. Usually is on the client side. It is set up when a client application wants to connect to a server and is destroyed when the client application terminates. It has a number chosen at random that is greater than 1023.

Escrow Passwords Escrow Passwords are passwords that are written down and stored in a secure location (like a safe) that are used by emergency personnel when privileged personnel are unavailable.

Ethernet The most widely-installed LAN technology. Specified in a standard, IEEE 802.3, an Ethernet LAN typically uses coaxial cable or special grades of twisted pair wires. Devices are connected to the cable and compete for access using a CSMA/CD protocol.

Event An event is an observable occurrence in a system or network.

Exponential Backoff Algorithm An exponential backoff algorithm is used to adjust TCP timeout values on the fly so that network devices don't continue to timeout sending data over saturated links.

Exposure A threat action whereby sensitive data is directly released to an unauthorized entity.

Extended ACLs (Cisco) Extended ACLs are a more powerful form of Standard ACLs on Cisco routers. They can make filtering decisions based on IP addresses (source or destination), Ports (source or destination), protocols, and whether a session is established.

Extensible Authentication Protocol (EAP) A framework that supports multiple, optional authentication mechanisms for PPP, including clear-text passwords, challenge-response, and arbitrary dialog sequences.

Exterior Gateway Protocol (EGP) A protocol which distributes routing information to the routers which connect autonomous systems.

False Rejects False Rejects are when an authentication system fails to recognize a valid user.

Fast File System The first major revision to the Unix file system, providing faster read access and faster (delayed, asynchronous) write access through a disk cache and better file system layout on disk. It uses inodes (pointers) and data blocks.

Fault Line Attacks Fault Line Attacks use weaknesses between interfaces of systems to exploit gaps in coverage.

File Transfer Protocol (FTP) A TCP/IP protocol specifying the transfer of text or binary files across the network.

Filter A filter is used to specify which packets will or will not be used. It can be used in sniffers to determine which packets get displayed, or by firewalls to determine which packets get blocked.

Filtering Router An inter-network router that selectively prevents the passage of data packets according to a security policy. A filtering router may be used as a firewall or part of a firewall. A router usually receives a packet from a network and decides where to forward it on a second network. A filtering router does the same, but first decides whether the packet should be forwarded at all, according to some security policy. The policy is implemented by rules (packet filters) loaded into the router.

Finger A protocol to lookup user information on a given host. A Unix program that takes an e-mail address as input and returns information about the user who owns that e-mail address. On some systems, finger only reports whether the user is currently logged on. Other systems return additional information, such as the user's full name, address, and telephone number. Of course, the user must first enter this information into the system. Many e-mail programs now have a finger utility built into them.

Fingerprinting Sending strange packets to a system in order to gauge how it responds to determine the operating system.

Firewall A logical or physical discontinuity in a network to prevent unauthorized access to data or resources.

Flooding An attack that attempts to cause a failure in (especially, in the security of) a computer system or other data processing entity by providing more input than the entity can process properly.

Forest A forest is a set of Active Directory domains that replicate their databases with each other.

Fork Bomb A Fork Bomb works by using the fork() call to create a new process which is a copy of the original. By doing this repeatedly, all available processes on the machine can be taken up.

Form-Based Authentication Form-Based Authentication uses forms on a webpage to ask a user to input username and password information.

Forward Lookup Forward lookup uses an Internet domain name to find an IP address

Forward Proxy Forward Proxies are designed to be the server through which all requests are made.

Fragment Offset The fragment offset field tells the sender where a particular fragment falls in relation to other fragments in the original larger packet.

Fragment Overlap Attack A TCP/IP Fragmentation Attack that is possible because IP allows packets to be broken down into fragments for more efficient transport across various media. The TCP packet (and its header) are carried in the IP packet. In this attack the second fragment contains incorrect offset. When packet is reconstructed, the port number will be overwritten.

Fragmentation The process of storing a data file in several "chunks" or fragments rather than in a single contiguous sequence of bits in one place on the storage medium.

Frames Data that is transmitted between network points as a unit complete with addressing and necessary protocol control information. A frame is usually transmitted serial bit by bit and contains a header field and a trailer field that "frame" the data. (Some control frames contain no data.)

Full Duplex A type of duplex communications channel which carries data in both directions at once. Refers to the transmission of data in two directions simultaneously. Communications in which both sender and receiver can send at the same time.

Fully-Qualified Domain Name A Fully-Qualified Domain Name is a server name with a hostname followed by the full domain name.

Fuzzing The use of special regression testing tools to generate out-of-spec input for an application in order to find security vulnerabilities. Also see "regression testing".

Gateway A network point that acts as an entrance to another network.

Gethostbyaddr The gethostbyaddr DNS query is when the address of a machine is known and the name is needed.

Gethostbyname The gethostbyname DNS quest is when the name of a machine is known and the address is needed.

GNU GNU is a Unix-like operating system that comes with source code that can be copied, modified, and redistributed. The GNU project was started in 1983 by Richard Stallman and others, who formed the Free Software Foundation.

Gnutella An Internet file sharing utility. Gnutella acts as a server for sharing files while simultaneously acting as a client that searches for and downloads files from other users.

Hardening Hardening is the process of identifying and fixing vulnerabilities on a system.

Hash Function An algorithm that computes a value based on a data object thereby mapping the data object to a smaller data object.

Cryptographic Hash Functions hash functions are used to generate a one way "check sum" for a larger text, which is not trivially reversed. The result of this hash function can be used to validate if a larger file has been altered, without having to compare the larger files to each other. Frequently used hash functions are MD5 and SHA1.

Header A header is the extra information in a packet that is needed for the protocol stack to process the packet.

Hijack Attack A form of active wiretapping in which the attacker seizes control of a previously established communication association.

Honey Client see Honeymonkey.

Honey pot Programs that simulate one or more network services that you designate on your computer's ports. An attacker assumes you're running vulnerable services that can be used to break into the machine. A honey pot can be used to log access attempts to those ports including the attacker's keystrokes. This could give you advanced warning of a more concerted attack.

Honeymonkey Automated system simulating a user browsing websites. The system is typically configured to detect web sites which exploit vulnerabilities in the browser. Also known as Honey Client.

Hops A hop is each exchange with a gateway a packet takes on its way to the destination.

Host Any computer that has full two-way access to other computers on the Internet. Or a computer with a web server that serves the pages for one or more Web sites.

Host-Based ID Host-based intrusion detection systems use information from the operating system audit records to watch all operations occurring on the host that the intrusion detection software has been installed upon. These operations are then compared with a pre-defined security policy. This analysis of the audit trail imposes potentially significant overhead requirements on the system because of the increased amount of processing power which must be utilized by the intrusion detection system. Depending on the size of the audit trail and the processing ability of the system, the review of audit data could result in the loss of a real-time analysis capability.

HTTP Proxy An HTTP Proxy is a server that acts as a middleman in the communication between HTTP clients and servers.

HTTPS When used in the first part of a URL (the part that precedes the colon and specifies an access scheme or protocol), this term specifies the use of HTTP enhanced by a security mechanism, which is usually SSL.

Hub A hub is a network device that operates by repeating data that it receives on one port to all the other ports. As a result, data transmitted by one host is retransmitted to all other hosts on the hub.

Hybrid Attack A Hybrid Attack builds on the dictionary attack method by adding numerals and symbols to dictionary words.

Hybrid Encryption An application of cryptography that combines two or more encryption algorithms, particularly a combination of symmetric and asymmetric encryption.

Hyperlink In hypertext or hypermedia, an information object (such as a word, a phrase, or an image; usually highlighted by color or underscoring) that points (indicates how to connect) to related information that is located elsewhere and can be retrieved by activating the link.

Hypertext Markup Language (HTML) The set of markup symbols or codes inserted in a file intended for display on a World Wide Web browser page.

Hypertext Transfer Protocol (HTTP) The protocol in the Internet Protocol (IP) family used to transport hypertext documents across an internet.

Identity Identity is whom someone or what something is, for example, the name by which something is known.

Incident An incident as an adverse network event in an information system or network or the threat of the occurrence of such an event.

Incident Handling Incident Handling is an action plan for dealing with intrusions, cyber-theft, denial of service, fire, floods, and other security-related events. It is comprised of a six step process: Preparation, Identification, Containment, Eradication, Recovery, and Lessons Learned.

Incremental Backups Incremental backups only backup the files that have been modified since the last backup. If dump levels are used, incremental backups only backup files changed since last backup of a lower dump level.

Inetd (xinetd) Inetd (or Internet Daemon) is an application that controls smaller internet services like telnet, ftp, and POP.

Inference Attack Inference Attacks rely on the user to make logical connections between seemingly unrelated pieces of information.

Information Warfare Information Warfare is the competition between offensive and defensive players over information resources.

Ingress Filtering Ingress Filtering is filtering inbound traffic.

Input Validation Attacks Input Validations Attacks are where an attacker intentionally sends unusual input in the hopes of confusing an application.

Integrity Integrity is the need to ensure that information has not been changed accidentally or deliberately, and that it is accurate and complete.

Integrity Star Property In Integrity Star Property a user cannot read data of a lower integrity level then their own.

Internet A term to describe connecting multiple separate networks together.

Internet Control Message Protocol (ICMP) An Internet Standard protocol that is used to report error conditions during IP datagram processing and to exchange other information concerning the state of the IP network.

Internet Engineering Task Force (IETF) The body that defines standard Internet operating protocols such as TCP/IP. The IETF is supervised by the Internet Society Internet Architecture Board (IAB). IETF members are drawn from the Internet Society's individual and organization membership.

Internet Message Access Protocol (IMAP) A protocol that defines how a client should fetch mail from and return mail to a mail server. IMAP is intended as a replacement for or extension to the Post Office Protocol (POP). It is defined in RFC 1203 (v3) and RFC 2060 (v4).

Internet Protocol (IP) The method or protocol by which data is sent from one computer to another on the Internet.

Internet Protocol Security (IPsec) A developing standard for security at the network or packet processing layer of network communication.

Internet Standard A specification, approved by the IESG and published as an RFC, that is stable and well-understood, is technically competent, has multiple, independent, and interoperable implementations with substantial operational experience, enjoys significant public support, and is recognizably useful in some or all parts of the Internet.

Interrupt An Interrupt is a signal that informs the OS that something has occurred.

Intranet A computer network, especially one based on Internet technology, that an organization uses for its own internal, and usually private, purposes and that is closed to outsiders.

Intrusion Detection A security management system for computers and networks. An IDS gathers and analyzes information from various areas within a computer or a network to identify possible security breaches, which include both intrusions (attacks from outside the organization) and misuse (attacks from within the organization).

IP Address A computer's inter-network address that is assigned for use by the Internet Protocol and other protocols. An IP version 4 address is written as a series of four 8-bit numbers separated by periods.

IP Flood A denial of service attack that sends a host more echo request ("ping") packets than the protocol implementation can handle.

IP Forwarding IP forwarding is an Operating System option that allows a host to act as a router. A system that has more than 1 network interface card must have IP forwarding turned on in order for the system to be able to act as a router.

IP Spoofing The technique of supplying a false IP address.

ISO International Organization for Standardization, a voluntary, non-treaty, non-government organization, established in 1947, with voting members that are designated standards bodies of participating nations and non-voting observer organizations.

Issue-Specific Policy An Issue-Specific Policy is intended to address specific needs within an organization, such as a password policy.

ITU-T International Telecommunications Union, Telecommunication Standardization Sector (formerly "CCITT"), a United Nations treaty organization that is composed mainly of postal, telephone, and telegraph authorities of the member countries and that publishes standards called "Recommendations."

Jitter Jitter or Noise is the modification of fields in a database while preserving the aggregate characteristics of that make the database useful in the first place.

Jump Bag A Jump Bag is a container that has all the items necessary to respond to an incident inside to help mitigate the effects of delayed reactions.

Kerberos A system developed at the Massachusetts Institute of Technology that depends on passwords and symmetric cryptography (DES) to implement ticket-based, peer entity authentication service and access control service distributed in a client-server network environment.

Kernel The essential center of a computer operating system, the core that provides basic services for all other parts of the operating system. A synonym is nucleus. A kernel can be contrasted with a shell, the outermost part of an operating system that interacts with user commands. Kernel and shell are terms used more frequently in Unix and some other operating systems than in IBM mainframe systems.

Lattice Techniques Lattice Techniques use security designations to determine access to information.

Layer 2 Forwarding Protocol (L2F) An Internet protocol (originally developed by Cisco Corporation) that uses tunneling of PPP over IP to create a virtual extension of a dial-up link across a network, initiated by the dial-up server and transparent to the dial-up user.

Layer 2 Tunneling Protocol (L2TP) An extension of the Point-to-Point Tunneling Protocol used by an Internet service provider to enable the operation of a virtual private network over the Internet.

Least Privilege Least Privilege is the principle of allowing users or applications the least amount of permissions necessary to perform their intended function.

Legion Software to detect unprotected shares.

Lightweight Directory Access Protocol (LDAP) A software protocol for enabling anyone to locate organizations, individuals, and other resources such as files and devices in a network, whether on the public Internet or on a corporate Intranet.

Link State With link state, routes maintain information about all routers and router-to-router links within a geographic area, and creates a table of best routes with that information.

List Based Access Control List Based Access Control associates a list of users and their privileges with each object.

Loadable Kernel Modules (LKM) Loadable Kernel Modules allow for the adding of additional functionality directly into the kernel while the system is running.

Log Clipping Log clipping is the selective removal of log entries from a system log to hide a compromise.

Logic Gate A logic gate is an elementary building block of a digital circuit. Most logic gates have two inputs and one output. As digital circuits can only understand binary, inputs and outputs can assume only one of two states, 0 or 1.

Loopback Address The loopback address (127.0.0.1) is a pseudo IP address that always refer back to the local host and are never sent out onto a network.

MAC Address A physical address; a numeric value that uniquely identifies that network device from every other device on the planet.

Malicious Code Software (e.g., Trojan horse) that appears to perform a useful or desirable function, but actually gains unauthorized access to system resources or tricks a user into executing other malicious logic.

Malware A generic term for a number of different types of malicious code.

Mandatory Access Control (MAC) Mandatory Access Control controls is where the system controls access to resources based on classification levels assigned to both the objects and the users. These controls cannot be changed by anyone.

Masquerade Attack A type of attack in which one system entity illegitimately poses as (assumes the identity of) another entity.

Md5 A one way cryptographic hash function. Also see "hash functions" and "sha1"

Measures of Effectiveness (MOE) Measures of Effectiveness is a probability model based on engineering concepts that allows one to approximate the impact a give action will have on an environment. In Information warfare it is the ability to attack or defend within an Internet environment.

Monoculture Monoculture is the case where a large number of users run the same software, and are vulnerable to the same attacks.

Morris Worm A worm program written by Robert T. Morris, Jr. that flooded the ARPANET in November, 1988, causing problems for thousands of hosts.

Multi-Cast Broadcasting from one host to a given set of hosts.

Multi-Homed You are "multi-homed" if your network is directly connected to two or more ISP's.

Multiplexing To combine multiple signals from possibly disparate sources, in order to transmit them over a single path.

NAT Network Address Translation. It is used to share one or a small number of publically routable IP addresses among a larger number of hosts. The hosts are assigned private IP addresses, which are then "translated" into one of the publicaly routed IP addresses. Typically home or small business networks use NAT to share a single DLS or Cable modem IP address. However, in some cases NAT is used for servers as an additional layer of protection.

National Institute of Standards and Technology (NIST) National Institute of Standards and Technology, a unit of the US Commerce Department. Formerly known as the National Bureau of Standards, NIST promotes and maintains measurement standards. It also has active programs for encouraging and assisting industry and science to develop and use these standards.

Natural Disaster Any "act of God" (e.g., fire, flood, earthquake, lightning, or wind) that disables a system component.

Netmask 32-bit number indicating the range of IP addresses residing on a single IP network/subnet/supernet. This specification displays network masks as hexadecimal numbers. For example, the network mask for a class C IP network is displayed as 0xffffff00. Such a mask is often displayed elsewhere in the literature as 255.255.255.0.

Network Address Translation The translation of an Internet Protocol address used within one network to a different IP address known within another network. One network is designated the inside network and the other is the outside.

Network Mapping To compile an electronic inventory of the systems and the services on your network.

Network Taps Network taps are hardware devices that hook directly onto the network cable and send a copy of the traffic that passes through it to one or more other networked devices.

Network-Based IDS A network-based IDS system monitors the traffic on its network segment as a data source. This is generally accomplished by placing the network interface card in promiscuous mode to capture all network traffic that crosses its network segment. Network traffic on other segments, and traffic on other means of communication (like phone lines) can't be monitored. Network-based IDS involves looking at the packets on the network as they pass by some sensor. The sensor can only see the packets that happen to be carried on the network segment it's attached to. Packets are considered to be of interest if they match a signature.Network-based intrusion detection passively monitors network activity for indications of attacks. Network monitoring offers several advantages over traditional host-based intrusion detection systems. Because many intrusions occur over networks at some point, and because networks are increasingly becoming the targets of attack, these techniques are an excellent method of detecting many attacks which may be missed by host-based intrusion detection mechanisms.

Non-Printable Character A character that doesn't have a corresponding character letter to its corresponding ASCII code. Examples would be the Linefeed, which is ASCII character code 10 decimal, the Carriage Return, which is 13 decimal, or the bell sound, which is decimal 7. On a PC, you can often add non-printable characters by holding down the Alt key, and typing in the decimal value (i.e., Alt-007 gets you a bell). There are other character encoding schemes, but ASCII is the most prevalent.

Non-Repudiation Non-repudiation is the ability for a system to prove that a specific user and only that specific user sent a message and that it hasn't been modified.

Null Session Known as Anonymous Logon, it is a way of letting an anonymous user retrieve information such as user names and shares over the network or connect without authentication. It is used by applications such as explorer.exe to enumerate shares on remote servers.

Octet A sequence of eight bits. An octet is an eight-bit byte.

One-Way Encryption Irreversible transformation of plaintext to cipher text, such that the plaintext cannot be recovered from the cipher text by other than exhaustive procedures even if the cryptographic key is known.

One-Way Function A (mathematical) function, f, which is easy to compute the output based on a given input. However given only the output value it is impossible (except for a brute force attack) to figure out what the input value is.

Open Shortest Path First (OSPF) Open Shortest Path First is a link state routing algorithm used in interior gateway routing. Routers maintain a database of all routers in the autonomous system with links between the routers, link costs, and link states (up and down).

OSI OSI (Open Systems Interconnection) is a standard description or "reference model" for how messages should be transmitted between any two points in a telecommunication network. Its purpose is to guide product implementers so that their products will consistently work with other products. The reference model defines seven layers of functions that take place at each end of a communication. Although OSI is not always strictly adhered to in terms of keeping related functions together in a well-defined layer, many if not most products involved in telecommunication make an attempt to describe themselves in relation to the OSI model. It is also valuable as a single reference view of communication that furnishes everyone a common ground for education and discussion.

OSI layers The main idea in OSI is that the process of communication between two end points in a telecommunication network can be divided into layers, with each layer adding its own set of special, related functions. Each communicating user or program is at a computer equipped with these seven layers of function. So, in a given message between users, there will be a flow of data through each layer at one end down through the layers in that computer and, at the other end, when the message arrives, another flow of data up through the layers in the receiving computer and ultimately to the end user or program. The actual programming and hardware that furnishes these seven layers of function is usually a combination of the computer operating system, applications (such as your Web browser), TCP/IP or alternative transport and network protocols, and the software and hardware that enable you to put a signal on one of the lines attached to your computer. OSI divides telecommunication into seven layers. The layers are in two groups. The upper four layers are used whenever a message passes from or to a user. The lower three layers (up to the network layer) are used when any message passes through the host computer or router. Messages intended for this computer pass to the upper layers. Messages destined for some other host are not passed up to the upper layers but are forwarded to another host. The seven layers are: Layer 7: The application layer...This is the layer at which communication partners are identified, quality of service is identified, user authentication and privacy are considered, and any constraints on data syntax are identified. (This layer is not the application itself, although some applications may perform application layer functions.) Layer 6: The presentation layer...This is a layer, usually part of an operating system, that converts incoming and outgoing data from one presentation format to another (for example, from a text stream into a popup window with the newly arrived text). Sometimes called the syntax layer. Layer 5: The session layer...This layer sets up, coordinates, and terminates conversations, exchanges, and dialogs between the applications at each end. It deals with session and connection coordination. Layer 4: The transport layer...This layer manages the end-to-end control (for example, determining whether all packets have arrived) and error-checking. It ensures complete data transfer. Layer 3: The network layer...This layer handles the routing of the data (sending it in the right direction to the right destination on outgoing transmissions and receiving incoming transmissions at the packet level). The network layer does routing and forwarding. Layer 2: The data-link layer...This layer provides synchronization for the physical level and does bit-stuffing for strings of 1's in excess of 5. It furnishes transmission protocol knowledge and management. Layer 1: The physical layer...This layer conveys the bit stream through the network at the electrical and mechanical level. It provides the hardware means of sending and receiving data on a carrier.

Overload Hindrance of system operation by placing excess burden on the performance capabilities of a system component.

Packet A piece of a message transmitted over a packet-switching network. One of the key features of a packet is that it contains the destination address in addition to the data. In IP networks, packets are often called datagrams.

Packet Switched Network A packet switched network is where individual packets each follow their own paths through the network from one endpoint to another.

Partitions Major divisions of the total physical hard disk space.

Password Authentication Protocol (PAP) Password Authentication Protocol is a simple, weak authentication mechanism where a user enters the password and it is then sent across the network, usually in the clear.

Password Cracking Password cracking is the process of attempting to guess passwords, given the password file information.

Password Sniffing Passive wiretapping, usually on a local area network, to gain knowledge of passwords.

Patch A patch is a small update released by a software manufacturer to fix bugs in existing programs.

Patching Patching is the process of updating software to a different version.

Payload Payload is the actual application data a packet contains.

Penetration Gaining unauthorized logical access to sensitive data by circumventing a system's protections.

Penetration Testing Penetration testing is used to test the external perimeter security of a network or facility.

Permutation Permutation keeps the same letters but changes the position within a text to scramble the message.

Personal Firewalls Personal firewalls are those firewalls that are installed and run on individual PCs.

Pharming This is a more sophisticated form of MITM attack. A users session is redirected to a masquerading website. This can be achieved by corrupting a DNS server on the Internet and pointing a URL to the masquerading websites IP. Almost all users use a URL like www.worldbank.com instead of the real IP (192.86.99.140) of the website. Changing the pointers on a DNS server, the URL can be redirected to send traffic to the IP of the pseudo website. At the pseudo website, transactions can be mimicked and information like login credentials can be gathered. With this the attacker can access the real www.worldbank.com site and conduct transactions using the credentials of a valid user on that website.

Phishing The use of e-mails that appear to originate from a trusted source to trick a user into entering valid credentials at a fake website. Typically the e-mail and the web site looks like they are part of a bank the user is doing business with.

Ping of Death An attack that sends an improperly large ICMP echo request packet (a "ping") with the intent of overflowing the input buffers of the destination machine and causing it to crash.

Ping Scan A ping scan looks for machines that are responding to ICMP Echo Requests.

Ping Sweep An attack that sends ICMP echo requests ("pings") to a range of IP addresses, with the goal of finding hosts that can be probed for vulnerabilities.

Plaintext Ordinary readable text before being encrypted into ciphertext or after being decrypted.

Point-to-Point Protocol (PPP) A protocol for communication between two computers using a serial interface, typically a personal computer connected by phone line to a server. It packages your computer's TCP/IP packets and forwards them to the server where they can actually be put on the Internet.

Point-to-Point Tunneling Protocol (PPTP) A protocol (set of communication rules) that allows corporations to extend their own corporate network through private "tunnels" over the public Internet.

Poison Reverse Split horizon with poisoned reverse (more simply, poison reverse) does include such routes in updates, but sets their metrics to infinity. In effect, advertising the fact that there routes are not reachable.

Polyinstantiation Polyinstantiation is the ability of a database to maintain multiple records with the same key. It is used to prevent inference attacks.

Polymorphism Polymorphism is the process by which malicious software changes its underlying code to avoid detection.

Port A port is nothing more than an integer that uniquely identifies an endpoint of a communication stream. Only one process per machine can listen on the same port number.

Port Scan A port scan is a series of messages sent by someone attempting to break into a computer to learn which computer network services, each associated with a "well-known" port number, the computer provides. Port scanning, a favorite approach of computer cracker, gives the assailant an idea where to probe for weaknesses. Essentially, a port scan consists of sending a message to each port, one at a time. The kind of response received indicates whether the port is used and can therefore be probed for weakness.

Possession Possession is the holding, control, and ability to use information.

Post Office Protocol, Version 3 (POP3) An Internet Standard protocol by which a client workstation can dynamically access a mailbox on a server host to retrieve mail messages that the server has received and is holding for the client. Practical Extraction and Reporting Language (Perl) A script programming language that is similar in syntax to the C language and that includes a number of popular Unix facilities such as sed, awk, and tr.

Preamble A preamble is a signal used in network communications to synchronize the transmission timing between two or more systems. Proper timing ensures that all systems are interpreting the start of the information transfer correctly. A preamble defines a specific series of transmission pulses that is understood by communicating systems to mean "someone is about to transmit data". This ensures that systems receiving the information correctly interpret when the data transmission starts. The actual pulses used as a preamble vary depending on the network communication technology in use.

Pretty Good Privacy (PGP) Trademark of Network Associates, Inc., referring to a computer program (and related protocols) that uses cryptography to provide data security for electronic mail and other applications on the Internet.

Private Addressing IANA has set aside three address ranges for use by private or non-Internet connected networks. This is referred to as Private Address Space and is defined in RFC 1918. The reserved address blocks are: 10.0.0.0 to 10.255.255.255 (10/8 prefix) 172.16.0.0 to 172.31.255.255 (172.16/12 prefix) 192.168.0.0 to 192.168.255.255 (192.168/16 prefix)

Program Infector A program infector is a piece of malware that attaches itself to existing program files.

Program Policy A program policy is a high-level policy that sets the overall tone of an organization's security approach.

Promiscuous Mode When a machine reads all packets off the network, regardless of who they are addressed to. This is used by network administrators to diagnose network problems, but also by unsavory characters who are trying to eavesdrop on network traffic (which might contain passwords or other information).

Proprietary Information Proprietary information is that information unique to a company and its ability to compete, such as customer lists, technical data, product costs, and trade secrets.

Protocol A formal specification for communicating; an IP address the special set of rules that end points in a telecommunication connection use when they communicate. Protocols exist at several levels in a telecommunication connection.

Protocol Stacks (OSI) A set of network protocol layers that work together.

Proxy Server A server that acts as an intermediary between a workstation user and the Internet so that the enterprise can ensure security, administrative control, and caching service. A proxy server is associated with or part of a gateway server that separates the enterprise network from the outside network and a firewall server that protects the enterprise network from outside intrusion.

Public Key The publicly-disclosed component of a pair of cryptographic keys used for asymmetric cryptography.

Public Key Encryption The popular synonym for "asymmetric cryptography".

Public Key Infrastructure (PKI) A PKI (public key infrastructure) enables users of a basically unsecured public network such as the Internet to securely and privately exchange data and money through the use of a public and a private cryptographic key pair that is obtained and shared through a trusted authority. The public key infrastructure provides for a digital certificate that can identify an individual or an organization and directory services that can store and, when necessary, revoke the certificates.

Public-Key Forward Secrecy (PFS) For a key agreement protocol based on asymmetric cryptography, the property that ensures that a session key derived from a set of long-term public and private keys will not be compromised if one of the private keys is compromised in the future.

Race Condition A race condition exploits the small window of time between a security control being applied and when the service is used.

Radiation Monitoring Radiation monitoring is the process of receiving images, data, or audio from an unprotected source by listening to radiation signals.

Reconnaissance Reconnaissance is the phase of an attack where an attackers finds new systems, maps out networks, and probes for specific, exploitable vulnerabilities.

Reflexive ACLs (Cisco) Reflexive ACLs for Cisco routers are a step towards making the router act like a stateful firewall. The router will make filtering decisions based on whether connections are a part of established traffic or not.

Registry The Registry in Windows operating systems in the central set of settings and information required to run the Windows computer.

Regression analysis The use of scripted tests which are used to test software for all possible input is should expect. Typically developers will create a set of regression tests that are executed before a new version of a software is released. Also see "fuzzing".

Request for Comment (RFC) A series of notes about the Internet, started in 1969 (when the Internet was the ARPANET). An Internet Document can be submitted to the IETF by anyone, but the IETF decides if the document becomes an RFC. Eventually, if it gains enough interest, it may evolve into an Internet standard.

Resource Exhaustion Resource exhaustion attacks involve tying up finite resources on a system, making them unavailable to others.

Response A response is information sent that is responding to some stimulus. Reverse Address Resolution Protocol (RARP)

RARP Reverse Address Resolution Protocol is a protocol by which a physical machine in a local area network can request to learn its IP address from a gateway server's Address Resolution Protocol table or cache. A network administrator creates a table in a local area network's gateway router that maps the physical machine (or Media Access Control - MAC address) addresses to corresponding Internet Protocol addresses. When a new machine is set up, its RARP client program requests from the RARP server on the router to be sent its IP address. Assuming that an entry has been set up in the router table, the RARP server will return the IP address to the machine which can store it for future use.

Reverse Engineering Acquiring sensitive data by disassembling and analyzing the design of a system component.

Reverse Lookup Find out the hostname that corresponds to a particular IP address. Reverse lookup uses an IP (Internet Protocol) address to find a domain name.

Reverse Proxy Reverse proxies take public HTTP requests and pass them to back-end webservers to send the content to it, so the proxy can then send the content to the end-user.

Risk Risk is the product of the level of threat with the level of vulnerability. It establishes the likelihood of a successful attack.

Risk Assessment A Risk Assessment is the process by which risks are identified and the impact of those risks determined.

Risk Averse Avoiding risk even if this leads to the loss of oportunity. For example, using a (more expensive) phone call vs. sending an e-mail in order to avoid risks associated with e-mail may be considered "Risk Averse"

Rivest-Shamir-Adleman (RSA) An algorithm for asymmetric cryptography, invented in 1977 by Ron Rivest, Adi Shamir, and Leonard Adleman.

Role Based Access Control Role based access control assigns users to roles based on their organizational functions and determines authorization based on those roles.

Root Root is the name of the administrator account in Unix systems.

Rootkit A collection of tools (programs) that a hacker uses to mask intrusion and obtain administrator-level access to a computer or computer network.

Router Routers interconnect logical networks by forwarding information to other networks based upon IP addresses.

Routing Information Protocol (RIP) Routing Information Protocol is a distance vector protocol used for interior gateway routing which uses hop count as the sole metric of a path's cost.

Routing Loop A routing loop is where two or more poorly configured routers repeatedly exchange the same packet over and over.

RPC Scans RPC scans determine which RPC services are running on a machine.

Rule Set Based Access Control (RSBAC) Rule Set Based Access Control targets actions based on rules for entities operating on objects.

S/Key A security mechanism that uses a cryptographic hash function to generate a sequence of 64-bit, one-time passwords for remote user login. The client generates a one-time password by applying the MD4 cryptographic hash function multiple times to the user's secret key. For each successive authentication of the user, the number of hash applications is reduced by one.

Safety Safety is the need to ensure that the people involved with the company, including employees, customers, and visitors, are protected from harm.

Scavenging Searching through data residue in a system to gain unauthorized knowledge of sensitive data.

Secure Electronic Transactions (SET) Secure Electronic Transactions is a protocol developed for credit card transactions in which all parties (customers, merchant, and bank) are authenticated using digital signatures, encryption protects the message and provides integrity, and provides end-to-end security for credit card transactions online.

Secure Shell (SSH) A program to log into another computer over a network, to execute commands in a remote machine, and to move files from one machine to another.

Secure Sockets Layer (SSL) A protocol developed by Netscape for transmitting private documents via the Internet. SSL works by using a public key to encrypt data that's transferred over the SSL connection.

Security Policy A set of rules and practices that specify or regulate how a system or organization provides security services to protect sensitive and critical system resources.

Segment Segment is another name for TCP packets.

Sensitive Information Sensitive information, as defined by the federal government, is any unclassified information that, if compromised, could adversely affect the national interest or conduct of federal initiatives.

Separation of Duties Separation of duties is the principle of splitting privileges among multiple individuals or systems.

Server A system entity that provides a service in response to requests from other system entities called clients.

Session A session is a virtual connection between two hosts by which network traffic is passed.

Session Hijacking Take over a session that someone else has established.

Session Key In the context of symmetric encryption, a key that is temporary or is used for a relatively short period of time. Usually, a session key is used for a defined period of communication between two computers, such as for the duration of a single connection or transaction set, or the key is used in an application that protects relatively large amounts of data and, therefore, needs to be re-keyed frequently.

SHA1 A one way cryptographic hash function. Also see "MD5"

Shadow Password Files A system file in which encryption user password are stored so that they aren't available to people who try to break into the system.

Share A share is a resource made public on a machine, such as a directory (file share) or printer (printer share).

Shell A Unix term for the interactive user interface with an operating system. The shell is the layer of programming that understands and executes the commands a user enters. In some systems, the shell is called a command interpreter. A shell usually implies an interface with a command syntax (think of the DOS operating system and its "C:¿" prompts and user commands such as "dir" and "edit").

Signals Analysis Gaining indirect knowledge of communicated data by monitoring and analyzing a signal that is emitted by a system and that contains the data but is not intended to communicate the data.

Signature A Signature is a distinct pattern in network traffic that can be identified to a specific tool or exploit.

Simple Integrity Property In Simple Integrity Property a user cannot write data to a higher integrity level than their own.

Simple Network Management Protocol (SNMP) The protocol governing network management and the monitoring of network devices and their functions. A set of protocols for managing complex networks.

Simple Security Property In Simple Security Property a user cannot read data of a higher classification than their own.

Smartcard A smartcard is an electronic badge that includes a magnetic strip or chip that can record and replay a set key.

Smurf The Smurf attack works by spoofing the target address and sending a ping to the broadcast address for a remote network, which results in a large amount of ping replies being sent to the target.

Sniffer A sniffer is a tool that monitors network traffic as it received in a network interface.

Sniffing A synonym for "passive wiretapping."

Social Engineering A euphemism for non-technical or low-technology means - such as lies, impersonation, tricks, bribes, blackmail, and threats - used to attack information systems.

Socket The socket tells a host's IP stack where to plug in a data stream so that it connects to the right application.

Socket Pair A way to uniquely specify a connection, i.e., source IP address, source port, destination IP address, destination port.

SOCKS A protocol that a proxy server can use to accept requests from client users in a company's network so that it can forward them across the Internet. SOCKS uses sockets to represent and keep track of individual connections. The client side of SOCKS is built into certain Web browsers and the server side can be added to a proxy server.

Software Computer programs (which are stored in and executed by computer hardware) and associated data (which also is stored in the hardware) that may be dynamically written or modified during execution.

Source Port The port that a host uses to connect to a server. It is usually a number greater than or equal to 1024. It is randomly generated and is different each time a connection is made.

Spam Electronic junk mail or junk newsgroup postings.

Spanning Port Configures the switch to behave like a hub for a specific port.

Split Horizon Split horizon is a algorithm for avoiding problems caused by including routes in updates sent to the gateway from which they were learned.

Split Key A cryptographic key that is divided into two or more separate data items that individually convey no knowledge of the whole key that results from combining the items.

Spoof Attempt by an unauthorized entity to gain access to a system by posing as an authorized user.

SQL Injection SQL injection is a type of input validation attack specific to database-driven applications where SQL code is inserted into application queries to manipulate the database.

Stack Mashing Stack mashing is the technique of using a buffer overflow to trick a computer into executing arbitrary code.

Standard ACLs (Cisco) Standard ACLs on Cisco routers make packet filtering decisions based on Source IP address only.

Star Property In Star Property, a user cannot write data to a lower classification level without logging in at that lower classification level.

State Machine A system that moves through a series of progressive conditions.

Stateful Inspection Also referred to as dynamic packet filtering. Stateful inspection is a firewall architecture that works at the network layer. Unlike static packet filtering, which examines a packet based on the information in its header, stateful inspection examines not just the header information but also the contents of the packet up through the application layer in order to determine more about the packet than just information about its source and destination.

Static Host Tables Static host tables are text files that contain hostname and address mapping.

Static Routing Static routing means that routing table entries contain information that does not change.

Stealthing Stealthing is a term that refers to approaches used by malicious code to conceal its presence on the infected system.

Steganalysis Steganalysis is the process of detecting and defeating the use of steganography.

Steganography Methods of hiding the existence of a message or other data. This is different than cryptography, which hides the meaning of a message but does not hide the message itself. An example of a steganographic method is "invisible" ink.

Stimulus Stimulus is network traffic that initiates a connection or solicits a response.

Store-and-Forward Store-and-Forward is a method of switching where the entire packet is read by a switch to determine if it is intact before forwarding it.

Straight-Through Cable A straight-through cable is where the pins on one side of the connector are wired to the same pins on the other end. It is used for interconnecting nodes on the network.

Stream Cipher A stream cipher works by encryption a message a single bit, byte, or computer word at a time.

Strong Star Property In Strong Star Property, a user cannot write data to higher or lower classifications levels than their own.

Sub Network A separately identifiable part of a larger network that typically represents a certain limited number of host computers, the hosts in a building or geographic area, or the hosts on an individual local area network.

Subnet Mask A subnet mask (or number) is used to determine the number of bits used for the subnet and host portions of the address. The mask is a 32-bit value that uses one-bits for the network and subnet portions and zero-bits for the host portion.

Switch A switch is a networking device that keeps track of MAC addresses attached to each of its ports so that data is only transmitted on the ports that are the intended recipient of the data.

Switched Network A communications network, such as the public switched telephone network, in which any user may be connected to any other user through the use of message, circuit, or packet switching and control devices. Any network providing switched communications service.

Symbolic Links Special files which point at another file.

Symmetric Cryptography A branch of cryptography involving algorithms that use the same key for two different steps of the algorithm (such as encryption and decryption, or signature creation and signature verification). Symmetric cryptography is sometimes called "secret-key cryptography" (versus public-key cryptography) because the entities that share the key. Symmetric Key A cryptographic key that is used in a symmetric cryptographic algorithm.

SYN Flood A denial of service attack that sends a host more TCP SYN packets (request to synchronize sequence numbers, used when opening a connection) than the protocol implementation can handle.

Synchronization Synchronization is the signal made up of a distinctive pattern of bits that network hardware looks for to signal that start of a frame.

Syslog Syslog is the system logging facility for Unix systems.

System Security Officer (SSO) A person responsible for enforcement or administration of the security policy that applies to the system.

System-Specific Policy A System-specific policy is a policy written for a specific system or device.

T1, T3 A digital circuit using TDM (Time-Division Multiplexing).

Tamper To deliberately alter a system's logic, data, or control information to cause the system to perform unauthorized functions or services.

TCP Fingerprinting TCP fingerprinting is the user of odd packet header combinations to determine a remote operating system.

TCP Full Open Scan TCP Full Open scans check each port by performing a full three-way handshake on each port to determine if it was open.

TCP Half Open Scan TCP Half Open scans work by performing the first half of a three-way handshake to determine if a port is open.

TCP Wrapper A software package which can be used to restrict access to certain network services based on the source of the connection; a simple tool to monitor and control incoming network traffic.

TCP/IP A synonym for "Internet Protocol Suite;" in which the Transmission Control Protocol and the Internet Protocol are important parts. TCP/IP is the basic communication language or protocol of the Internet. It can also be used as a communications protocol in a private network (either an Intranet or an Extranet).

TCPDump TCPDump is a freeware protocol analyzer for Unix that can monitor network traffic on a wire.

TELNET A TCP-based, application-layer, Internet Standard protocol for remote login from one host to another.

Threat A potential for violation of security, which exists when there is a circumstance, capability, action, or event that could breach security and cause harm.

Threat Assessment A threat assessment is the identification of types of threats that an organization might be exposed to.

Threat Model A threat model is used to describe a given threat and the harm it could to do a system if it has a vulnerability.

Threat Vector The method a threat uses to get to the target.

Time to Live A value in an Internet Protocol packet that tells a network router whether or not the packet has been in the network too long and should be discarded.

Tiny Fragment Attack With many IP implementations it is possible to impose an unusually small fragment size on outgoing packets. If the fragment size is made small enough to force some of a TCP packet's TCP header fields into the second fragment, filter rules that specify patterns for those fields will not match. If the filtering implementation does not enforce a minimum fragment size, a disallowed packet might be passed because it didn't hit a match in the filter. STD 5, RFC 791 states: Every Internet module must be able to forward a datagram of 68 octets without further fragmentation. This is because an Internet header may be up to 60 octets, and the minimum fragment is 8 octets.

Token Ring A token ring network is a local area network in which all computers are connected in a ring or star topology and a binary digit or token-passing scheme is used in order to prevent the collision of data between two computers that want to send messages at the same time.

Token-Based Access Control Token based access control associates a list of objects and their privileges with each user. (The opposite of list based.)

Token-Based Devices A token-based device is triggered by the time of day, so every minute the password changes, requiring the user to have the token with them when they log in.

Topology The geometric arrangement of a computer system. Common topologies include a bus, star, and ring. The specific physical, i.e., real, or logical, i.e., virtual, arrangement of the elements of a network. Note 1: Two networks have the same topology if the connection configuration is the same, although the networks may differ in physical interconnections, distances between nodes, transmission rates, and/or signal types. Note 2: The common types of network topology are illustrated

Traceroute Traceroute is a tool the maps the route a packet takes from the local machine to a remote destination.

Transmission Control Protocol (TCP) A set of rules (protocol) used along with the Internet Protocol to send data in the form of message units between computers over the Internet. While IP takes care of handling the actual delivery of the data, TCP takes care of keeping track of the individual units of data (called packets) that a message is divided into for efficient routing through the Internet. Whereas the IP protocol deals only with packets, TCP enables two hosts to establish a connection and exchange streams of data. TCP guarantees delivery of data and also guarantees that packets will be delivered in the same order in which they were sent.

Transport Layer Security (TLS) A protocol that ensures privacy between communicating applications and their users on the Internet. When a server and client communicate, TLS ensures that no third party may eavesdrop or tamper with any message. TLS is the successor to the Secure Sockets Layer.

Triple DES A block cipher, based on DES, that transforms each 64-bit plaintext block by applying the Data Encryption Algorithm three successive times, using either two or three different keys, for an effective key length of 112 or 168 bits.

Triple-Wrapped S/MIME usage: data that has been signed with a digital signature, and then encrypted, and then signed again.

Trojan Horse A computer program that appears to have a useful function, but also has a hidden and potentially malicious function that evades security mechanisms, sometimes by exploiting legitimate authorizations of a system entity that invokes the program.

Trunking Trunking is connecting switched together so that they can share VLAN information between them.

Trust Trust determine which permissions and what actions other systems or users can perform on remote machines.

Trusted Ports Trusted ports are ports below number 1024 usually allowed to be opened by the root user.

Tunnel A communication channel created in a computer network by encapsulating a communication protocol's data packets in (on top of) a second protocol that normally would be carried above, or at the same layer as, the first one. Most often, a tunnel is a logical point-to-point link - i.e., an OSI layer 2 connection - created by encapsulating the layer 2 protocol in a transport protocol (such as TCP), in a network or inter-network layer protocol (such as IP), or in another link layer protocol. Tunneling can move data between computers that use a protocol not supported by the network connecting them.

UDP Scan UDP scans perform scans to determine which UDP ports are open.

Unicast Broadcasting from host to host.

Uniform Resource Identifier (URI) The generic term for all types of names and addresses that refer to objects on the World Wide Web.

Uniform Resource Locator (URL) The global address of documents and other resources on the World Wide Web. The first part of the address indicates what protocol to use, and the second part specifies the IP address or the domain name where the resource is located. For example, http://www.pcwebopedia.com/index.html .

Unix A popular multi-user, multitasking operating system developed at Bell Labs in the early 1970s. Created by just a handful of programmers, Unix was designed to be a small, flexible system used exclusively by programmers.

Unprotected Share In Windows terminology, a "share" is a mechanism that allows a user to connect to file systems and printers on other systems. An "unprotected share" is one that allows anyone to connect to it.

User A person, organization entity, or automated process that accesses a system, whether authorized to do so or not.

User Contingency Plan User contingency plan is the alternative methods of continuing business operations if IT systems are unavailable.

User Datagram Protocol (UDP) A communications protocol that, like TCP, runs on top of IP networks. Unlike TCP/IP, UDP/IP provides very few error recovery services, offering instead a direct way to send and receive datagrams over an IP network. It's used primarily for broadcasting messages over a network. UDP uses the Internet Protocol to get a datagram from one computer to another but does not divide a message into packets (datagrams) and reassemble it at the other end. Specifically, UDP doesn't provide sequencing of the packets that the data arrives in.

Virtual Private Network (VPN) A restricted-use, logical (i.e., artificial or simulated) computer network that is constructed from the system resources of a relatively public, physical (i.e., real) network (such as the Internet), often by using encryption (located at hosts or gateways), and often by tunneling links of the virtual network across the real network. For example, if a corporation has LANs at several different sites, each connected to the Internet by a firewall, the corporation could create a VPN by (a) using encrypted tunnels to connect from firewall to firewall across the Internet and (b) not allowing any other traffic through the firewalls. A VPN is generally less expensive to build and operate than a dedicated real network, because the virtual network shares the cost of system resources with other users of the real network.

Virus A hidden, self-replicating section of computer software, usually malicious logic, that propagates by infecting - i.e., inserting a copy of itself into and becoming part of - another program. A virus cannot run by itself; it requires that its host program be run to make the virus active.

Vulnerability A flaw or weakness in a system's design, implementation, or operation and management that could be exploited to violate the system's security policy.

War Chalking War chalking is marking areas, usually on sidewalks with chalk, that receive wireless signals that can be accessed.

War Dialer A computer program that automatically dials a series of telephone numbers to find lines connected to computer systems, and catalogs those numbers so that a cracker can try to break into the systems.

War Dialing War dialing is a simple means of trying to identify modems in a telephone exchange that may be susceptible to compromise in an attempt to circumvent perimeter security.

War Driving War driving is the process of traveling around looking for wireless access point signals that can be used to get network access.

Web of Trust A web of trust is the trust that naturally evolves as a user starts to trust other's signatures, and the signatures that they trust.

Web Server A software process that runs on a host computer connected to the Internet to respond to HTTP requests for documents from client web browsers.

WHOIS An IP for finding information about resources on networks.

Windowing A windowing system is a system for sharing a computer's graphical display presentation resources among multiple applications at the same time. In a computer that has a graphical user interface (GUI), you may want to use a number of applications at the same time (this is called task). Using a separate window for each application, you can interact with each application and go from one application to another without having to reinitiate it. Having different information or activities in multiple windows may also make it easier for you to do your work. A windowing system uses a window manager to keep track of where each window is located on the display screen and its size and status. A windowing system doesn't just manage the windows but also other forms of graphical user interface entities.

Windump Windump is a freeware tool for Windows that is a protocol analyzer that can monitor network traffic on a wire.

Wired Equivalent Privacy (WEP) A security protocol for wireless local area networks defined in the standard IEEE 802.11b.

Wireless Application Protocol A specification for a set of communication protocols to standardize the way that wireless devices, such as cellular telephones and radio transceivers, can be used for Internet access, including e-mail, the World Wide Web, newsgroups, and Internet Relay Chat.

Wiretapping Monitoring and recording data that is flowing between two points in a communication system.

World Wide Web ("the Web", WWW, W3) The global, hypermedia-based collection of information and services that is available on Internet servers and is accessed by browsers using Hypertext Transfer Protocol and other information retrieval mechanisms.

Worm A computer program that can run independently, can propagate a complete working version of itself onto other hosts on a network, and may consume computer resources destructively.

Wrap To use cryptography to provide data confidentiality service for a data object.

Index